Secrets of Tennessee Gardening

by Karen Angelucci

A 12-month road map to gardening success

Foreword by Jon Carloftis

ACCLAIM PRESS

MORLEY, MISSOURI

Acclaim Press
— Your Next Great Book —

P.O. Box 238
Morley, Missouri 63767
(573) 262-2121
www.acclaimpress.com

Publishing Consultant:
Keith Steele

Cover Photo of the Author by Mark Landis

Publishing Rights:
Acclaim Press, Inc.

Library of Congress Control Number:
2007923783

ISBN-13: 978-0-9790025-6-4
ISBN-10: 0-9790025-6-7

First Printing 2007
Printed in the United States of America
10 9 8 7 6 5 4 3 2 1

Acknowledgements

This book is dedicated to Mike,

Thanks for the love, the journey, the kids, and the free time to write my journal.

Without his confidence this project would have never began or finished.

I would like to acknowledge Dortha Smith Oatts for her inspiration and guidance. A huge thanks goes to Dr. Mary Hotze Witt, whose extreme knowledge and generosity contributed to this journal. Thanks to my friends Candace Harker, Ray Dueltgen, Mary D. Corkern and Abe Fosson.

Thanks to my parents, Nelson and Carolyn Williams, for all the love that allows for freedom of thought and creativity. I thank my grandmothers, Emma Lou Wade and Grace Elnora Williams, who past too soon, but not before they passed their love of gardening and the desire to write.

CONTENTS

INTRODUCTION

My journal has become a guide to provide practical and easy to follow chores for the Volunteer State of Tennessee. I have included chores for each month to help maintain a great landscape all year long. My compilation is directed toward those of us who are too busy with everyday life to research garden books.

If you live in East, Middle or West Tennessee you may need to shift the months as needed to provide the same timely chores. Gardening is dependent on Mother Nature so exact time of each chore will vary.

This journal is a collection of the past decade of my garden ventures and the tips I have acquired long the way as well as trial and error garden experiences. I have reviewed many books for my data as well as gardening experience that started at the age of five.

I am not responsible for anyone who tries some of my helpful tips. Sorry, gardening can be a gamble. Many of these entries have stood the test of time as far as "hear say" and are only intended to be fun and entertaining.

This journal will remind you when and how to perform garden chores throughout the year. It will entertain you with many quotes, lore, and poetry from various people throughout history. This journal should be read any time of the year to guide you toward a successful garden.

Do not follow where the path may lead
Go instead where there is no path and leave a trail.
-Ralph Waldo Emerson (1803-1882)

FOREWORD

Jon Carloftis

When I first met Karen several years ago at a book fair, we shared a table together and spoke with attendees for hours upon hours about gardening, our respective books, and whatever subjects came up. Although her enthusiasm impressed me initially, it was her down-to-earth approach and knowledge that made me realize that she was a gardener after my own heart.

Instead of using terms that might have made a beginner feel intimidated, she spoke with each person as if their failed petunias or prize roses were the most important things in the news. And you know what? Despite all of the wars and politics and daily problems that come our way, to a gardener of any level, this simple hobby of planting, nurturing, and watching a plant grow brings a lot of happiness not only to the person who does the work, but to the many people who are lucky enough to enjoy the sweet smell of garden phlox as they walk by the garden on a hot summer day.

Think of the smiles that are invoked by the climbing rose in full glory as drivers race along their regular commute. Think of the

children that are able to explore a vegetable garden, watch a moon flower slowly open, or intently follow a hummingbird moth as it flutters from bee balm to bee balm. These are important things in life! Gardening touches all of our senses and creates memories that stay with us forever.

Karen's books give us the knowledge we really want and need. What should we be doing in the month of May? What is the history behind the funny common names of the flowers? How do we take care of the pests that can quickly overtake our beloved gardens? The most important part of Karen's message is on the same wavelength as mine: we are all busy with family, careers, pets, friends . . . the list goes on in today's hectic lives. The more effort put in to our gardens will reap more benefits . . . but it is also OK to not feel like a failure if everything doesn't go as well as planned. Mother Nature can be tough, but she always gives another chance next year and hopefully, we will do better. Isn't that comforting to know?

Enjoy this book as much as I do. It would be impressive to say that Tolstoy is on my nightstand, but that would be a lie. What I really want to know is how to keep my cabbages and peas looking good and ready for eating this next year.

Jon Carloftis
Author of *First a Garden* and *Beyond the Window Sill*

Secrets of Tennessee Gardening

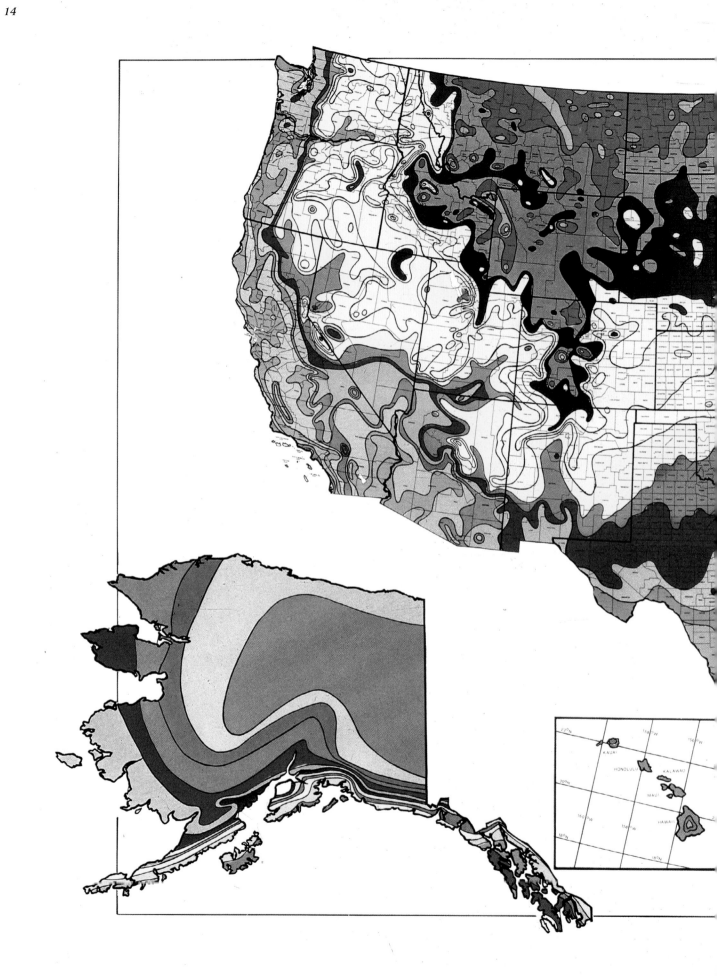

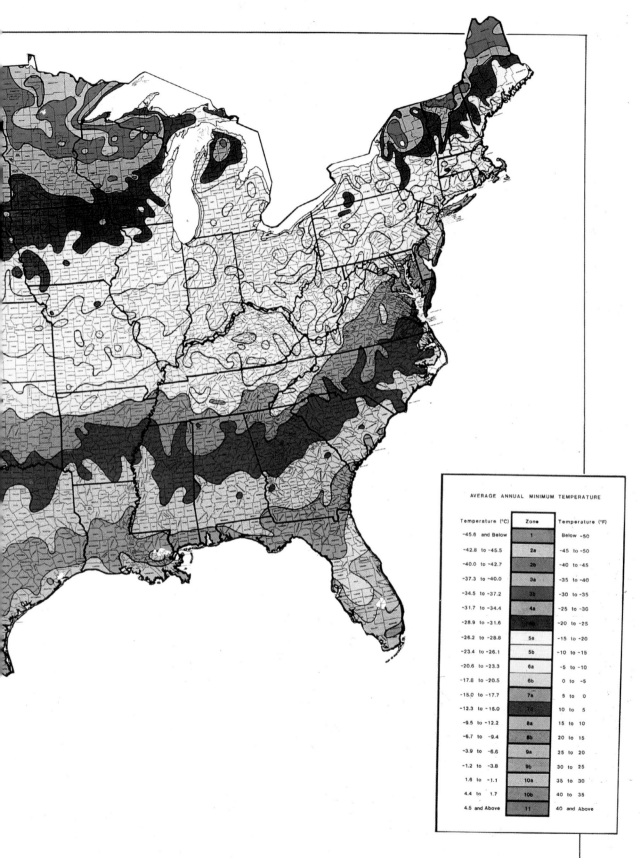

AVERAGE ANNUAL MINIMUM TEMPERATURE

Temperature (°C)	Zone	Temperature (°F)
-45.6 and Below	1	Below -50
-42.8 to -45.5	2a	-45 to -50
-40.0 to -42.7	2b	-40 to -45
-37.3 to -40.0	3a	-35 to -40
-34.5 to -37.2	3b	-30 to -35
-31.7 to -34.4	4a	-25 to -30
-28.9 to -31.6	4b	-20 to -25
-26.2 to -28.8	5a	-15 to -20
-23.4 to -26.1	5b	-10 to -15
-20.6 to -23.3	6a	-5 to -10
-17.8 to -20.5	6b	0 to -5
-15.0 to -17.7	7a	5 to 0
-12.3 to -15.0	7b	10 to 5
-9.5 to -12.2	8a	15 to 10
-6.7 to -9.4	8b	20 to 15
-3.9 to -6.6	9a	25 to 20
-1.2 to -3.8	9b	30 to 25
1.6 to -1.1	10a	35 to 30
4.4 to 1.7	10b	40 to 35
4.5 and Above	11	40 and Above

Map courtesy of ARS/USDA

March Garden Chore List

In the Garden:

- ❑ Prepare soil for planting.
- ❑ Add soil amendments to adjust pH, according to most recent soil test.
- ❑ Hold-off mulching until the soil warms to 55 to 60 degrees.
- ❑ Near the end of March, remove mulch from plants and clean gardens.
- ❑ Add 10-10-10 to gardens and compost piles.

Flowers and Herbs:

- ❑ Plan for containers and window boxes.
- ❑ Cut remaining spent perennials.
- ❑ Cut ornamental and native grasses to 3 inches.
- ❑ Plant, transplant, and divide over-crowed late-blooming perennials.
- ❑ Plant cool-weather annual transplants outdoors.
- ❑ Plant tender summer bulbs in a shallow tray of moist peat moss to get an early start on the season.
- ❑ Plant bare-root roses.

Seeds:

- ❑ Buy seeds and equipment before the good supplies are gone.
- ❑ Sow warm-weather seeds indoors.
- ❑ Sow cool-weather annual seeds directly into the garden.

Vegetables and Fruits:

- ❑ Turn cover crops when soil is dry enough.
- ❑ Sow cool-weather vegetables directly to the garden.
- ❑ Plant cool-weather transplants.
- ❑ Fertilize established fruit trees.
- ❑ Cut grapevine heavily.
- ❑ Plant fruit trees and strawberries.

Trees and Shrubs:

- ❑ Finish pruning trees and shrubs.
- ❑ Plant or transplant trees and shrubs.
- ❑ Fertilizer trees with a light application of 10-10-10.
- ❑ Apply an acid-type fertilizer (aluminum sulfate) to all acid-loving plants.

Lawn Care:

- ❑ Fill low spots with soil and reseed.
- ❑ Aerate and dethatch the lawn if needed.
- ❑ Apply pre-emergent crabgrass and annual bluegrass herbicide.

Composting:

- ❑ Turn compost pile.
- ❑ Add manure to pile to generate heat.

Water Ponds:

- ❑ Remove netting from ponds and remove any accumulated leaves.
- ❑ Start the season by feeding fish lightly.
- ❑ Divide bog plants if needed.
- ❑ Plant hardy water lilies.

Indoors Plants:

- ❑ Repot houseplants that have become root-bound.
- ❑ Thicken houseplants by removing leggy growth.
- ❑ Fertilize houseplants with a liquid plant food such as 20-20-20.

Chapter 1

March Garden

It is early spring: frost melts down
The furrow in the west wind,
Plowshares glisten in the sun,
The sleek, black land shines open.

-Virgil (c. 70 –19 B.C.)

March is a crazy month; who knows what Mother Nature has in store. You can count on a dusting or two of snow before this month is over. Although the weather does not cooperate, we still have growing foliage to refresh and revive our soul. True patience is required this month. Blue skies and warm air bring us bursting buds, growing plants and flowers. Spring arrives and warms our spirits, finally the earth is reborn. The rain gives life to all that is living and we can open our hearts and windows to the coming season. Bulbs come alive and brighten our landscape while the base of the forest glows green as moss covers downed trees. Near the end of this month the sweet scents of hyacinth and winter honeysuckle fill the air. The forsythia reigns, along with the flowering almond, bringing vibrant beauty to the landscape.

Winter, once drab, gives in to spring.

While some gardeners have already cleared the debris from their gardens some are waiting for the last snowfall. Uncovering plants in the garden is a gamble this month. If you do uncover plants be prepared to protect them if the temperature drops.

If you neglected to pot bulbs for forcing last fall, the florist and garden centers have bulbs to purchase that are ready to bloom. This is a great way to bring the outdoors in and beautify your home.

General Maintenance

Gardening is a labour of tranquility and satisfaction; natural and instructive, and as such contributes to the most serious contemplation, experience, health and longevity.

-John Evelyn (1620-1706)

My hoe as it bites the ground revenges my wrongs, and I have less lust to bite my enemies. In smoothing the rough hillocks, I smooth my temper.

- Ralph Waldo Emerson (1803-1882)

Like the musician,
The painter, the poet,
And the rest,
The true lover of flowers
Is born, not made.

-Celia Thaxter (1835-1894)

Garden Lore

Thunder in spring,
Cold will bring.

As the days begin to lengthen
So the cold begins to strengthen.

Soil

* When soil crumbles between your fingers it is ready to be worked. Continue to prepare soil for planting by double digging or tilling the soil. If you choose to till the soil do not over-till and produce flour. This will decrease its draining ability. If you have trouble with clay soil, amend it with sharp sand or granite meal, peat moss, and topsoil.
* Add soil amendments to adjust pH, according to current soil test. Prepare gardens for annuals by working the soil, adding compost, peat moss, well-rotted cow manure, humus, and a fertilizer that is all-purpose and slow-release such as 10-10-10; apply every 6 to 8 weeks throughout the growing season.
* Whether it's providing oxygen through cultivation, applying moisture or amending soil with organic matter, you are encouraging soil organisms and they will aid in supplying plenty of nutrients for your soil.
* Amend used potting soil with perlite or vermiculite and a fertilizer such as 10-10-10.

Time to Fertilize

The earth neither grows old or wears out if it is dunged.

-Lucius Junius Moderatus Columella (c. 45 A.D., 1st century)

* As the days grow longer plants need more fertilization. The secret to any great garden is Nitrogen, Phosphorus, and Potassium. These three ingredients are the building blocks for healthy plants. All living plants actually need 17 elements to grow and bloom. Carbon, hydrogen, and oxygen are free of charge because they exist in air. The other elements will have to be supplied by you. The big three, which are N-P-K, are the main elements you need to worry about. The remaining elements are calcium, magnesium, sulfur, iron, manganese, copper, zinc, boron, molybdenum, chlorine, and trace elements. Don't apply nitrogen too close to bloom time or when roots are developing as with newly planted trees and shrubs. This close application will only encourage leafy growth when you want root and flower growth.
* For optimum results, have your soil tested. This soil test will provide a profile of your soil fertility. You can use this information to amend your garden and spring is the best time to apply. In Tennessee the growing season is about 190 days long. Knowing this you can schedule fertilization applications,
* Tennesseans are blessed because the land has plenty of Phosphorus and Potassium, leaving nitrogen to be replenished. That's why an all-purpose fertilizer such as 10-10-10 will meet most of Tennessee's soil needs.

Tennessee soil is so rich in limestone the soil produces good plant growth. Grasses like timothy and alfalfa utilize the mineral elements and the animals grazing on them enjoy the benefits, the primary one being strong bone development. This is a must for the State Horse the Tennessee Walking Horse.

In-The-Garden Maintenance

"Just living is not enough," said the butterfly.
"One must have sunshine, freedom, and a little flower."
-Hans Christian Anderson
(1805-1875)

I want each plant to be given the amount of air & food necessary for its development. Robust health is ever inspiring to look upon…. I would rather have a healthful, flourishing specimen of a common thing than an unhappy, merely existing, example of the rarest plant known.
- Ernest Wilson (1876-1930)

* Hold-off mulching until the soil warms to 55 to 60 degrees. Mulching now will only confuse your plants. Mulch will keep the soil cool and delay it's warming, giving plants a slower start on the season. It will be better to mulch when the soil temperature is warm and the plants have recognized that spring is here to stay.
* Choose an overcast day near the end of March to remove mulch from plants and clean gardens. Be extra careful not to damage newly emerging shoots. Keep mulch handy in case of a late freeze. It is better to leave mulch on too long than to remove it too early.
* Replace plants that have been lifted from the soil as a result of the soil freezing and thawing.
* Take time to organize your garden tools and supplies.
* Try to avoid digging and stepping in wet flowerbeds; this will only compact the soil, which is not beneficial to plants.
* Remove weeds before they flower and set seed.
* Add 10-10-10 to all garden beds and compost piles every 6 to 8 weeks throughout the growing season.
* Some plants do not require fertilizing; they thrive on poor soil.
>   Artemisia
>   Bee balm *(Monarda didyma)*
>   Canna
>   Coreopsis
>   Daylily *(Hemerocallis)*
>   Hosta, plaintain lily, funkia
>   Iris
>   Nasturtium *(Tropaeolum)*
>   Poppy *(Papaver)*
>   Sage *(Salvia)*
>   Thrift *(Armeria maritima)*
>   Yarrow *(Achillea)*

* If you have a southern Magnolia (*M. grandiflora*) tree, its leaf clean-up speaks for itself. The leaves of the magnolia are slow to break down. It is best to remove them immediately from the lawn before they suffocate the grass.
* Take this time to repair arbors, trellises, and yard art.
* Open cold frame, if weather permits, to ventilate plants; be sure to close before the sun sets to trap warm air in for the evening. Keep soil moist inside cold frame.

N-P-K defined:
(N) = Nitrogen: increase leaf and stem growth, increase green color, quick energy, quick results. Spring is the best season for nitrogen application. Nitrogen is very soluble and leaches from the soil quickly.
(P) = Phosphorus: increase root development, fruit production and seeds. Phosphorus is essential for good plant health and has a major role in setting of flower and fruit. Phosphorus moves through the soil slowly.
(K) = Potassium, also called potash: increases flowers & fruit, aids in cold-and disease-resistance. Potassium is soluble in water, but in clay soil it doesn't move quickly. Note: (K) is from Kalium, the Latin word for potassium.

Garden Lore

• *St. Patrick used the hop clover (Trifolium dubium), or white clover (Trifolium repens) or shamrock to explain the Godhead or Trinity; Father, Son and Holy Spirit.*
• *Finding a four leaf clover will bring double the luck!*
• *Charms were made from the white clover to ward-off evil.*
• *When March blows it's horn, your barn will be filled with hay and corn.*
• *Seeing the first blossom in spring on any particular day can determine your fate.*

• *Monday's flower brings good fortune.*
• *Tuesday's flower brings success.*
• *Wednesday's flower brings marriage.*
• *Thursday's flower brings small profits.*
• *Friday's flower brings wealth.*
• *Saturday's flower brings misfortune.*
• *Sunday's flower brings good luck.*

• *March damp and warm doth the farmer much harm*
But a March without water dowers the farmer's daughter.

The air is like a butterfly
With frail blue wings.
The happy earth looks at the sky
And sings.
        Joyce Kilmer (1886-1918)

Containers

* Clean last seasons flower pots with a solution of 10% bleach and water (1 ½ cups bleach per gallon of water) to remove residual disease from last season.
* If you have time this month, when you are not in the yard, plan for containers and window boxes. You will be ready when the many flats of annuals arrive at the garden centers.

Perennials and Biennials

All my life through, the sights of Nature made me rejoice like a child.
        -Marie Curie (1867-1934)

God Almighty first planted a garden; and indeed, it is the purest of human pleasures. It is the greatest refreshment to the spirits of man, without which buildings and palaces are but gross handiworks.
        -Sir Frances Bacon (1561-1626)

* Cut remaining spent perennials and remove dead foliage from biennials.
* Wait to prune semi-woody perennials such as lavender and artemisia until chance of frost has past.
* Cut spent foliage from liriope to 2 inches before new growth emerges. A sharp-blade mower works fine on large plantings.
* Cut winter-damaged ground covers to 6 inches to allow for new growth.
* Cut ornamental and native grasses to 3 inches before new growth appears. If clumps of grass are large, wrap with string about waist high and cut with hedge trimmers or chain saw. If it's time to dig and divide you may find it easier to chop with an axe.
* Buy dormant plants from local nurseries and garden centers.
* As soon as plants are available, plant transplants of cool-weather biennials.

Canterbury bells *(Campanula medium)*
English daisy *(Bellis perennis)*
Foxglove *(Digitalis purpurea)*
Honesty *(Lunaria annua)*
Sweet William *(Dianthus barbatus)*
Wallflower *(Cheiranthus)*

* Plant, transplant, and divide over-crowded late-blooming perennials when new shoots are 2 to 4 inches tall. Protect plants if freezing occurs. Pay special attention to sun/shade requirements, soil, and proper spacing of perennials.

Division guide for perennials:
Divide fall bloomers in spring.
Divide spring-bloomers after they bloom.
Divide summer-bloomers in early fall.

* Trim and begin to train vigorous climbers such as:
    Climbing hydrangea *(Hydrangea anomala)*
    Ivy *(Hedera)*
    Wisteria – prune side shoots growing from main cane to 6 buds each, remove weak growth.
* Before cutting clematis determine what group it falls in.
    Group 1) Blooms early to mid-spring -- requires no pruning; except to keep in bounds after blooming. (Includes early-bloomers: *C. montana, C. armandii,C. macropetala, C. alpina, C. paniculata)*
    Group 2) Blooms on last year's growth from spring to early summer. Prune after flowering and it may re-bloom in the fall. (Includes early, large-flowering cultivars: *C. 'Lincon's Star', C. 'Williams Kennett', C. 'Nelly Moser', C. 'Will Goodwin', C. 'Duchess of Edinburgh')*
    Group 3) Blooms summer to fall on new growth. Prune above a new bud every spring, to 6 to 12 inches. (Includes late flowering cultivars: *C. 'Jackmanii', C. 'Ernest Markham', C. 'Comtesse de Bouchard')*
* Prune dead, weak, and excess canes and clip a few roots on wisteria if it hasn't bloomed. Push a shovel blade through the soil about 12 inches away from the plant. Prune one third to one half of the rooting area. Hopefully root pruning will stress-out the plant and cause it to bloom.
* Divide ferns when the foliage shows signs of unfurling.
* Think about using variegated plant material to create the illusion of light in a shade area. Choose from variegated hostas, ivys, and liriope.
* Some vines are becoming more and more a nuisance. Be cautious when choosing from this list:
    English Ivy *(Hedera helix)*
    Five-leaf akebia, chocolate vine *(Akebia quinata)*
    Japanese honeysuckle *(Lonicera japonica)*
    Kudzu, *(Puearia lobata)*
    Oriental bittersweet, staff vine *(Celastrus orbiculatus)*
    Porcelain-berry vine *(Ampelopsis brevipedunculata)*
    Silver-fleece vine, Russian vine *(Polygonum aubertii)*
    Trumpet vine, trumpet creeper, cow-itch-vine,
        devil's shoelaces, hell vine *(Campsis radicans)*
    Wintercreeper *(Euonymus fortunei)*
    Wisteria

 *Annuals*   *I perhaps owe having become a painter to flowers.*
        -Claude Monet (1840-1926)

Annuals are divided into three categories:

1. Tender annuals are destroyed by the first touch of frost.
2. Half-hardy annuals can survive light frost in fall.
3. Hardy annuals will tolerate and survive in winter. They may even self-sow.

Garden Lore

* *So many mists in March we see, so many frosts in May will be.*
* *Better to be bitten by a snake than to feel the sun in March.*
* *The March sun lets snow stand on a stone.*
* *A peck of March dust is worth a king's ransom.*
* *March wind brings April showers.*

Garden Phenology

* *Plant perennials when maple leaves are beginning to unfurl.*
* *The same amount of rain that falls in March will fall also in June.*

Garden Phenology

• *When chokeberry and aspen trees leaf-out plant pansies, snapdragons, and other hardy cool-weather annuals.*

* Plant cool-weather annual transplants outdoors. These annuals can be planted in gardens or containers and need little protection from frost.

* Tennessee will often have a freeze or two in March so you may want to be prepared to cover these cool-weather annuals to be safe. If rain is scarce you will need to water plants regularly.

> Ornamental kale /cabbage (*Brassica oleracea*)
> Pansy (*Viola x wittrockiana*)
> Snapdragon (*Antirrhinum majus*)

* Pansies that were planted last fall will need leggy growth and spent blooms removed; feed with 10-10-10. Pansies have a long blooming season and make an incredible show in the spring if planted in the fall. They will tolerate the weather and develop strong root systems over winter. By spring there will be instant color.

* Bring geraniums into the light if you stored them in the dark. Repot and water lightly if the plants are shriveled. Cut straggly growth on geraniums that you have overwintered indoors. Take cuttings from new growth and plant in moist sand; cover with plastic bag. Cuttings will also root in a glass of water. Feed with a diluted liquid fertilizer every 10 days.

* If you overwintered fuchsia, lantana, coleus, or begonias, move them to a sunny window. When new growth emerges, re-pot and shape. Take cuttings for extra plants.

Bulbs, Corms, Rhizomes, and Tubers

Garden Lore

• *Never bring just one daffodil into the house; brings bad luck.*
• *A handful of daffodils bring happiness.*
• *Spring has arrived when you can step on seven daisies with one foot.*

* If you forced bulbs for indoor blooms this winter, after the foliage has died, plant the bulbs in the garden. Supply bulbs with a water-soluble fertilizer such as 20-20-20. If you forced bulbs in water or tulips, they are usually spent and ready for the compost pile.

* Wait until bulb foliage has turned yellow before cutting. Bulbs need to replenish energy lost from the blooming stage.

* Divide clumps of late-winter blooming bulbs such as snowdrops and winter aconites.

* Don't mix cut daffodils with other cut flowers; bad chemistry.

* Remove and relocate bulbs in the landscape that are the wrong color and height. Don't be afraid to relocate plants.

* Divide and repot canna rhizomes if you stored them for the winter, this will give them a head start on the season. Lay rhizomes horizontal in moist peat moss about 1 inch deep. Transplant them to the garden when danger of frost has past. In USDA Zone 7 cannas are hardy and do not need to be stored for the winter.

* Plant begonia, dahlias, gloxinia, and tuberoses (*Polianthes*) in a shallow tray of moist peat moss to encourage root growth. Tops of tubers should

Garden Lore

• *Lore reminds us not to pick pansies while the dew is upon it, for that will bring death to a loved one. If picked on a beautiful day; a storm will come.*
• *Sow sweet peas before sunrise on St. Patrick's Day for more fragrant and larger flowers.*

be planted just below the soil. Move to a 70-degree area that has bright light and keep soil moist. Transplant to pots and move outdoors when the last spring frost has passed. Remember to plant begonias with the concave or hollow side of the tuber up and tipped to avoid holding water; round side down. In southern Tennessee (Zone 7) these tender bulbs can be planted near the end of March.

* Pot caladiums and elephant ears (*Caladium esculenta* or *Colocasia esculenta*) by planting knobby side up or on their sides if you cannot decide. Plant 2 inches deep in moist peat moss and place in a sunny window. Move caladiums to the garden or into containers when night temperatures are above 60 degrees.

* After spring bulbs bloom feed with a granular fertilizer such as 10-10-10.

Roses

Spring unlocks the flowers to paint the laughing soil.   Reginald Heber (1783-1826)

* Don't damage or expose new shoots to direct sun. On an overcast day, uncover mulch gradually keeping mulch handy in case of a late frost.

* When shopping for new roses only buy #1 grade.

* Plant bare-root roses in March before they break dormancy; protect from freezing. New bare-root roses need to be soaked in water over night prior to planting to re-hydrate. Plant roses to receive at least 6 hours of sunlight a day. Apply 2 cups of bone meal in the hole while planting. Set the graft union at or slightly below soil level; water well.

* Do not use granular fertilizer on new roses in the first growing season, although it may be beneficial to use a liquid fertilizer such as 20-20-20.

* Spring application for established rose bushes: Apply when shoots are 2 to 3 inches tall; apply 3 inches around and away from plant. Water well with 1 to 2 gallons of water. Repeat these applications every 6 weeks until September 1.

     -1 cup of bone meal

     -All-purpose fertilizer such as 10-10-10; ½ cup per plant.

* Prune established modern roses at the end of the month when buds begin to swell. Prune at a 45-degree angle, ¼ inches above a strong outward facing bud of new growth. Cut to creamy white wood. If the pith is brown, cut lower. Protect new cuts from rose cane borer damage by smearing with white glue or clear nail polish. Trim dead, damaged, and diseased canes; remove weak growth that is less than pencil size. More pruning results in a more compact bush with larger flowers. Modern roses do well pruned in a vase shape allowing more air circulation and sunlight penetration through center of the shrub.

* Do not prune climbers unless you want to remove dead, diseased, and thin tangled growth or decrease size; prune after it blooms.

* Start a fungicide spray program when new shoots appear to control powdery mildew, rust, and black spot. These applications should be applied weekly, or after heavy rain. It is best applied in the early morning or evening to avoid sunburn. Continue spray program until mid-October.

* Check new growth for aphids, which can suck the life out of the precious new growth! If the infestation is light, blast them with a spray of water.

Garden Phenology

• *Prune roses when forsythia blooms.*

*I wandered lonely as a cloud
That floats on high o'er vales
   and hills,
When all at once I saw a crowd,
A host, of golden daffodils;
Beside the lake, beneath the
   trees,
Fluttering and dancing in the
   breeze.*

*Continuous as the stars that
   shine
And twinkle on the Milky Way,
They stretched in never-ending
   line
Along the margin of a bay:
Ten thousand saw I at a glance,
Tossing their heads in sprightly
   dance.*

*The waves beside them danced,
   but they
Out-did the sparkling waves in
   glee:
A Poet could not but be gay,
In such a jocund company:
I gazed--and gazed--but little
   thought
What wealth the show to me
   had brought:*

*For oft, when on my couch I lie
In vacant or in pensive mood,
They flash upon that inward
   eye
Which is the bliss of solitude;
And then my heart with
   pleasure fills,
And dances with the daffodils.*
   William Wordsworth (1770-1850)

Herbs

Those herbs which perfume the air most delightfully, not passed by as the rest, but, being trodden upon and crushed, are three; that is, burnet, wild thyme and watermints. Therefore, you are to set whole alleys of them, to have the pleasure when you walk or tread.
    -Sir Frances Bacon (1561-1626)

* Sow annual herb seeds indoor 6 to 10 weeks before transplanting after the last frost:

    Basil, sweet *(Ocimum basilicum)*
    Chives *(Allium schoenoprasum)*
    Feverfew *(Chrysanthemum parthenium)*
    Marjoram *(Origanum majorana)*
    Parsley *(Peroselinum)* soak seed overnight in warm water to
        speed germination.
    Rosemary *(Rosmarinus officinalis)*

* Direct sow herb seeds such as:

    Cilantro *(Coriandrum sativum)*
    Dill *(Anethum graveolens)*
    Nasturtium *(Tropaeolum majus)*
    Parsley *(Petroselinum)*

* For more flavorful plants, thyme, oregano, mint and French tarragon should be started from divisions.
* Dig and divide herbs if needed, now through May.

    Agrimony *(Agrimonia eupatoria)*
    Arnica *(Arnica montana)*
    Chamomile, Roman *(Chamaemelum nobile)*
    Chives *(Allium schoenoprasum)*
    Clary sage *(Salvia sclarea)*
    Comfrey *(Symphytum officinale)*
    Costmary *(Chrysanthemum balsamita)*
    Feverfew *(Tanacetum parthenium)*
    Goldenrod *(Solidago spp.)*
    Horehound *(Marrubium vulgare)*
    Hyssop *(Hyssopus officinalis)*
    Lady's bedstraw *(Galium verum)*
    Lemon balm *(Melissa officinalis)*
    Mint *(Mentha spp.)*
    Mugwort *(Artemisia vulgaris)*
    Oregano *(Origanum vulgare)*
    Pennyroyal, English *(Mentha pulegium)*
    Perilla, beefsteak plant *(Perilla frutescens)*
    Savory, winter *(Satureja montana)*
    Sorrel *(Rumex spp.)*
    Southernwood *(Artemisia abrotanum)*
    Sweet cicely *(Myrrhis odorata)*
    Sweet woodruff *(Galium odoratum)*
    Tansy *(Tanacetum vulgare)*
    Tarragon, French *(Artemisia dracunculus)*
    Thyme *(Thymus vulgaris)*
    Valarian *(Valerian officinalis)*
    Yarrow *(Achillea millefolium)*

Garden Lore

• *To deter the devil, pour boiling water where you will sow parsley.*
• *Disrespect for Perilla or beefsteak plant means death; anyone caught stepping on the plant would himself be trampled to death!*

Seeds

As long as the earth endures, seedtime and harvest, cold and heat, and summer and winter, day and night will never cease.
  -Genesis 8:22

* Buy seeds and equipment before the good supplies are gone. Use clean tools and sterile potting mix when sowing seeds indoors.
* When calculating dates for sowing seeds, remember seedlings need a week to ten days outdoors to harden before planting in the garden.
*Sow seeds indoors 6 to 10 weeks before your zones last frost date for annuals, biennials and perennial herbs and flowers. This early indoor sowing will allow you to have larger plants to transplant after the last frost. Check seed packets for recommended time to sow. Use a meat-basting syringe for gentle watering.
* Moisten peat moss and peat pots with warm water for quick absorption.
* If you started seeds indoors in February and the seedlings have their first set of true leaves, it's time to thin. Snip weak seedlings at soil level and do not disturb the soil.
* Transplant seedlings by lifting them from the soil with a pencil, small stick, or a table fork. Do not pull tender stems. Pot seedlings into a container or peat pot that is a little bigger than the original container. Use potting mix and sterile containers or clean used containers with water and 10% bleach solution (1 ½ cups per one gallon of water). Fertilize with a diluted liquid fertilizer such as 20-20-20.
* Before sowing plants that climb or vine, it is wise to erect a support. If you wait, you may damage roots installing a trellis.
* Sow cool-weather annual seeds directly into the garden this month and next.

> Baby's-breath *(Gypsophila elegans)*
> Calliopsis *(Coreopsis tinctoria)*
> Candytuft *(Iberis umbellata)*
> Common stock, gilliflower *(Matthiola incana)*
> Cornflower, bachelor's button *(Centaurea cyanus)*
> Forget-me-nots *(Myosotis sylvatica)*
> Iceland poppy *(Papaver nudicaule)*
> Johnny-jump-up *(Viola tricolor)*
> Larkspur *(Consolida ambiqua)*
> Love-in-a-mist *(Nigella damascena)*
> Pansy *(Viola x wittrockiana)*
> Poppy, (corn, Flanders, or Shirley) *(Papaver rhoeas)*
> Poppy, California *(Eschschozia californica)*
> Pot marigold *(Calendula officinalis)*
> Sweet alyssum *(Lobularia maritima)*
> Sweet pea *(Lathyrus odoratus)*
> Virginia stock *(Malcomia maritima)*

* To direct-sow: dig a shallow trench in moist soil, sow seeds and keep area moist until germination occurs. Refer to seed packet on how deep to sow.
* Sow grass seed in containers early in the month for Easter decorations.
* Fertilize emerging seedlings with a dilute liquid fertilizer such as 20-20-20.

Moon Lore

From the new moon until full sheen
Sow afternoon, and it will be clean;
From the full into the new light,
Sow mornings, and it will not blight.

Sow peas on and beanes in the wane
of the moone,
Who soweth them sooner, he soweth
too soon.
That they with the planet may rest
and arise,
And flourish with bearing most
plentiful wise.
    Thomas Tusser (1515-1580)

Gardening by the Moon

Light of the moon (Waxing to Full)

Waxing Moon: Time to sow seeds and plant flowers, transplant and plant trees. If the soil is too dry wait until the full moon when soil is more moist. Planting close to the full moon brings larger harvest and larger blooms.

Best time to plant above ground vegetables such as: asparagus, barley, beans, broccoli, Brussels sprouts, cauliflower, celery, cereals, corn, endive, kohlrabi, leek, lettuce, melons, oats, parsnips, radishes, rutabaga, spinach,

Full Moon: Best time to harvest due to increased moisture content. (example, grapes, tomatoes, strawberries) Transplanting flowers during a new moon will bloom double. Plant during the full moon:
    artichoke, cabbage,
    chicory, cucumbers,
    eggplant, lentils, pepper,
    pumpkin, squash, tomatoes,
    watermelon

Dark of the moon (Waning to New)

Waning Moon: Best time to kill weeds, plant bulbs, biennials, and perennials, harvest root vegetables, prune plant material, dry herb, and flowers.
    Best time to plow, cultivate, weed and reap.
    Best time to plant below ground crops:
        beets, carrots, onions, potatoes, turnips

New Moon or Dark of the moon:
        * "Below the ground" or root crops should be harvested such as carrots and potatoes.
        * Harvest apples to avoid rotting.
        * Nothing should be planted in the last quarter.
        * Begin compost heaps.

Vegetables

Shine! Shine! Shine!
Pour down your warmth,
great sun!
    Walt Whitman (1819-1892)

* March, April, and May are peak planting months, be prepared.
* Prepare garden soil for planting by cultivating.
* Turn cover crops when soil is dry enough. Do not plant until "green manure" has fully decomposed.
* Plan your garden plot or try growing vegetables in containers on your porch.

* Run crops north to south to take advantage of the sun's rays.
* Empty the cold frame and make room to harden-off seedlings for April transplanting. Open cold frame a few inches when day temperatures are above 40 degrees and open completely at 60 degrees and above. Close cold frame during late afternoons to trap heat for the night.
* When calculating dates for seed sowing, remember seedlings need up to 2 weeks in a protected area outdoors to harden off.
* Prepare supports for peas out of deciduous twigs.
* Plan ahead for fall and buy seeds for pumpkins, squash and gourds now.
* Garden space for carrots should be finely dug to 12 inches deep with no rocks or debris for straight carrots.
* Sow seeds indoors for slow-growing summer crops. Start seeds indoors 10 to 12 weeks before last expected frost. Grow seedlings in a warm southern window or greenhouse until spring transplanting. Soil temperature should be 55 degrees before transplanting.

> Cabbage
> Cucumbers
> Eggplant
> Okra
> Peppers
> Squash
> Tomatoes

* Sow cool-weather crops directly to the garden for spring harvest.

> Beets
> Carrots
> Kale
> Lettuce
> Onion sets
> Parsnips
> Peas- snow or Chinese, snap, and shelling or English, dust with
> inoculate (a nitrogen fixing bacteria that increases yield)
> My friend Ray says, "Peas like cold, wet feet."
> Potatoes, Irish
> Radish
> Spinach
> Swiss chard

* Plant cool-weather transplants as they become available.

> Broccoli
> Brussels sprouts
> Cabbage
> Cauliflower
> Chard
> Endive
> Kale
> Leeks
> Lettuce, bibb
> Onion sets, plants
> Shallot sets, plants

* Stagger harvest times by planting transplants weekly.
* Give cole crops (broccoli, cabbage, cauliflower) plenty of space when planting. They grow to potential if they are not crowded.
* Check garlic that you planted last fall and fertilize with 10-10-10.

If you do not sow in the spring you will not reap in the autumn.
> Irish Proverb

Garden Phenology

• *Plant peas, when daffodils begin to bloom.*
• *Plant cool-weather crops when the lilac has leafed-out.*

Garden Lore

• *A wet march makes a sad harvest.*
• *Thunder in March, corn to parch.*
• *March dry, good rye.*
• *Plant peas when you can sit bare-bottomed upon the soil.*
• *On St. Patrick's night sow cabbage seeds in your pajamas for good growth.*
• *In honor of St. David, patron Saint of Wales, plant leeks on March 1st. He claimed the leek protected him and his countrymen at war.*

* Thin lettuce and radish seedlings in cold frame, if you sowed in February.
* If you are limited on garden space, sow spinach and lettuce among bulb foliage. Not only will it add an interesting look to your flowering bulbs but you can eat it.
* Use floating row cover to protect crops from birds and insects.
* Apply fertilizer according to last autumn's soil test.
* Add manure to asparagus and rhubarb beds.
* Do not harvest rhubarb in the first year of planting. The leaves are poisonous so when you do harvest only eat the stalks.
* Fertilize asparagus with 10-10-10 before the spears begin to emerge from the ground.
* Fertilize seedlings with a diluted liquid fertilizer such as 20-20-20.
* Scatter wood ashes around potatoes, carrots, radishes, and onions to improve the flavor.

Fruit

And the fruits will outdo what the flowers have promised.

Francois de Malherbe (1555-1628)

* If you are interested in an orchard it would be wise to educate yourself on the chemicals involved. Contact your local county extension office for details.
* The most important defense against insects and disease, besides buying resistant varieties, is good sanitation. In the fall remove downed leaves and fruit, even dried shriveled apples on the tree can overwinter disease.
* Fertilize established fruit trees with 10-10-10 before mid-month.
* Apply 10-10-10 around berry-producing plants.
* Cut grapevine heavily before buds begin to swell. Cut old growth to four buds.
* Thin red raspberries and blackberries, leaving vigorous canes on 8-inch centers; mulch with compost and aged manure.
* Complete pruning chores before buds swell. Remove suckers and water sprouts. Wait to prune cherries, plums, and peaches after they bloom. This will reduce late frost damage and canker diseases.
* Plant fruit trees, strawberries, blueberries, loganberries, boysenberries, and grapes. This month is last call for planting bare-root plant material.
* Remove straw from strawberries when new growth appears.
* Sow melons indoors for May transplanting.
* If a pregnant woman plants a tree it will bear extra fruit.
* Remember apple, pear, sweet cherries, pecans, plum, walnut, and apricot trees need two plants available to cross pollinate. Peaches, tart cherries, strawberries, blackberries and grapes are self-pollinating, so one plant will produce fruit.
* Protect early blossoms of fruit trees from late freezes. Throw light blanket or sheet over small trees.

Trees and Shrubs

It is the first mild day of March:
Each minute sweeter than before,
The redbreast sings from the tall larch
That stands beside our door.
        William Wordsworth (1770-1850)

Ten little leaf buds growing on
  a tree
Curled up as tightly as can be
See them keeping snug and
  warm,
During the winter's cold and
  storm.
Now along comes windy
  March,
With his breath now soft, now
  harsh.
First he swings them roughly so
Then more gently to and fro
'Til the raindrops from the
  skies
Falling pitter, patter-wise
Open wide the leaf bud's eyes.

* Try forcing blooms from the dogwood, beautybush, magnolia, forsythia, apple or crabapple and mock orange. Refer to page 197 for instructions.
* Sprinkle wood ashes or lime around your lilac after the first cut of the lawn. Lilacs love alkaline soil.
* Supply nitrogen to azaleas and rhododendrons by sprinkling cottonseed meal around each plant.
*Finish pruning chores on trees & shrubs. Prune spring-bloomers after they bloom.
* Some trees lose sap or "bleed" profusely when pruned in the spring. Wait to prune these trees in early summer after their leaves have fully developed.

>   Birch *(Betula)*
>   Cottonwood *(Populus deltoides)*
>   Dogwood *(Cornus)*
>   Elm *(Ulmas)*
>   Fir *(Abies)*
>   Locust *(Robina psuedoacacia)*
>   Maple *(Acer)*
>   Pine *(Pinus)*
>   Spruce *(Picea)*
>   Willow *(Salix)*
>   Yellowwood *(Cladrastis lutea)*

* Prune summer-flowering shrubs that bloom on new growth.

>   Abelia
>   Beautyberry *(Callicarpa)*
>   Bluebeard *(Caryopteris x clandonensis)*
>   Butterfly bush *(Buddleia davidii)*
>   Crape myrtle *(Lagerstroemia indica)*
>   Heavenly bamboo *(Nandina domestica)*
>   Hibiscus
>   Hydrangea, "Annabel," snowball *(Hydrangea arborescens)*
>   Hydrangea, "Peegee," "Grandiflora," "Tardiva" *(Hydrangea paniculata)*
>   Rose of Sharon *(Hibiscus syriacus)*
>   Spiraea, summer-blooming
>   Summersweet *(Clethra alnifolia)*

* If your Hydrangea blooms on new wood such as snowball hydrangea *(Hydrangea arborescens)* or "Annabel" hydrangea it can be pruned now. The closer to the ground you prune this shrub the fewer but larger blooms are produced. Pruning to 1 to 2 feet will ensure that the new wood can support the larger blooms.
* If you have a "Pee Gee," "Tardiva," or "Grandiflora" hydrangea *(Hydrangea paniculata)* prune to a pair of buds at the base of each stem. Prune shrub to look like a tree for a great affect. Reduce its size, if you wish, by removing entire stems to ground level.

Garden Phenology

• *When buds break on flowering crabapple and wild plum, expect eastern tent caterpillar eggs to hatch.*

• *Watch for hatching gypsy moth caterpillars when the redbud and shadbush are in bloom. Use a Bt (Bacillus thuringiensis) product to control or take worm out of trees and destroy.*

* If you have a big-leaf hydrangea (*Hydrangea macrophylla*) you will want to prune immediately after it blooms in the summer or leave spent flower heads on for winter appeal. This variety blooms on wood produced in the previous year. After the last freeze prune spent flower heads, as well as winter-damaged foliage, to a healthy bud. If you cut old wood you will be removing this year's bloom.
* Trim hedges this month that are not spring-bloomers; prune so that the base is wider than the top. This will allow the sun to reach the lower branches. You may want to wait to trim or prune sensitive plant material such as boxwoods or hollies after the last frost.
* Transplant evergreen and deciduous trees and shrubs while they are still dormant.
* Plant container-grown, bare-root, and burlapped trees and shrubs.
* Remove all non-biodegradable burlap, protective covers, string, tight plant labels, and wires from plant material.
* Last call for planting bare-root plant material. Soak bare-root plants in water overnight prior to planting. These bare-root trees and shrubs are best planted before they leaf out.
* When planting trees and shrubs, dig the hole twice as deep as the width of the root-ball.
* If you want to transplant spring bloomers, wait until the bloom fades. Pruning and deadheading can be done when transplanting.
* Divide and transplant deciduous clump-forming shrubs.
>Bluebeard (*Caryopteris x clandonensis*)
>Forsythia
>Japanese kerria (*Kerria japonica*)
>Lace shrub (*Stephanandra incisa*)
>Spirea
>Virginia sweetspire (*Itea virginica*)
* Planting past March or April is not advisable due to the hot season ahead. Roots need time to develop to survive the summer heat.
* You should heel-in bare-root plants that cannot be planted right away into a well-drained area until planting time.
* After spring blooming trees and shrubs have bloomed fertilize with a complete all-purpose fertilizer such as 10-10-10.
* Give established deciduous trees, broadleaf and needled evergreens a light application of fertilizer such as 10-10-10 now and again in the fall.
* As trees mature they require less feeding.
* An acid-type fertilizer (sulfur) can be applied to all acid-lovers. Most acid-lovers like a soil pH of 5.5-6.5. Repeat this application bi-monthly until June. Most perennials, flowering shrubs, and roses will also benefit from this application. Follow instructions on all packages of fertilizer. There will be a lighter application in the fall.

Shrubs	**Trees**
Bayberry (*Myrica*)	Cedar (*Cedrus*)
Blueberry (*Vaccinium*)	Fir (*Abies*)
Japanese Pieris (*Pieris japonica*)	Oak (*Quercus*)
Rhododendron and azalea	Holly (*Ilex*)
Serviceberry (*Amelanchier*)	Magnolia
Sourwood (*Oxydendron arboreum*)	Pine (*Pinus*)
Yew (*Taxus*)	Spruce (*Picea*)

Over the land freckled with snow half-thawed
The speculating rooks at their nests cawed
And saw from elm-tops, delicate as flower of grass,
What we below could not see,
Winter pass.
Edward Thomas (1878-1917)

* Avoid applying this acidic supplement to plants that require alkaline soil such as:

Shrubs	*Trees*
Barberry *(Berberis)*	Bur oak *(Quercus macrocarpa)*
Boxwood *(Buxus)*	Catalpa
Cotoneaster	Kentucky coffee tree
Forsythia	*(Gymnocladus dioicus)*
Lace shrub *(Stephanandra incisa)*	Redbud *(Cercis)*
Lilac *(Syringa)*	
Privet *(Ligustrum)*	
Spiraea	

* Young trees develop stronger trunks if not staked; let the tree sway with the wind.

* Try layering deciduous shrubs. Refer to page 47 for instruction.

    Bottlebrush buckeye *(Aesculus parviflora)*

    Flowering quince *(Chaenomeles speciosa)*

    Japanese pieris *(Pieris japonica)*

    Juniper *(Juniperus)*

    Lilac *(Syringa vulgaris)*

    Oak-leaf hydrangea *(Hydrangea quercifolia)*

    Rose-of-Sharon *(Hibiscus syriacus)*

    Tree peony *(Paeonia suffruticosa)*

* If you are lost in the woods in March, remember that moss grows thicker on the north side of trees.

Lawn Care

What a man needs in gardening is a cast-iron back, with a hinge in it.
    Charles Dudley Warner (1829-1900)

Maintenance

* If you are planning a total renovation of your lawn it is best if you postpone until August or September due to the heat stress coming our way.

* Fill low spots with soil and reseed bad areas.

* Rake areas of lawn if needed to remove lawn debris.

* Seeding chores should be finished near the end of the month. After March the heat stress is damaging to new grass. You will need to wait until August to seed your lawn.

* Aerate and dethatch the lawn if needed. Do this prior to fertilization or weed control.

    Dethatching removes dead root and leaf layer that will accumulate and impede water and nutrient flow. Remove thatch layer when it is 1/3-inch thick. Thatch is not often a problem on cool-weather grasses.

    Aeration will help open clay or compacted soil, allowing water and nutrient uptake.

* Laying sod can be performed anytime during the growing season. Spring and fall will provide best weather for laying sod.

When the soil dries, it's time to mow. Cut Kentucky bluegrass at 2 to 2.5 inches. Cut fescue at 2 to 3 inches.

* Raise mower for the first two or three cuts of the season and then lower it. When the hot season arrives raise mower again.

The trees reflected in the
  river –
They are unconscious of a
  spiritual world so near to
  them.
So are we.
Nathaniel Hawthorne
(1804-1864)

Garden Lore

• *In March much snow, to plants and trees much woe.*

• *To ensure good health for a child pass him through the branches of a maple tree.*

Garden Phenology

• *Fertilize the lawn when the forsythia begins to bloom.*
• *Apply pre-emergent crab-grass control when forsythia blooms.*

Fertilization

* If you didn't apply a general fertilizer, such as 10-10-10 on your established cool season lawn (Kentucky bluegrass, tall fescue, perennial ryegrass) in February go ahead and apply this month. This application can be combined with a pre-emergent crabgrass control at the end of this month or first of April.
* On new lawns use a base fertilizer, which is higher in phosphorus and potassium. Apply this prior to seeding to encourage root formation.

Insect and Weed Control

* Apply crabgrass and annual bluegrass preventer when daytime temperatures are between 65 to 70 degrees for 4 to 5 days. This application can be combined with a fertilizer. It may be April before temperatures allow this application. This pre-emergent application should be applied about one month before germination of crabgrass and not after mid-April. Crabgrass requires the soil temperature to be 50 to 55 degrees and warmer to germinate, making this time of year the best for crabgrass control. Once crabgrass has sprouted a post-emergent herbicide will be needed.
* Check local soil temperatures to decide application time for crabgrass control.
* It is recommended to apply a post-emergent herbicide to control dandelions when the basal rosette of leaves appear or during the puffball stage.
* Use post-emergent weed killer on wild garlic and wild onions.
* Avoid applying herbicide to newly seeded areas.

Composting

Well done is better than well said.
    -Benjamin Franklin (1706-1790)

* Turn compost pile first of the month. Sift large debris only. Fine compost tends to pack tight when watered heavily. We use compost to increase pore space. Chunky is good.
* If rain is scarce, water compost pile to keep it active.
* If the rain is heavy, cover pile with plastic to avoid leaching of nutrients.
*Add manure to compost pile to generate heat.

Water Ponds

Laying out grounds may be considered a liberal art, in some sort of poetry and painting.
    -Wordsworth (1770-1850)

* Remove netting from ponds and remove any accumulated leaves.
* As temperatures rise to around 55 degrees, and fish are more active, start the season by feeding fish lightly with a low-protein food. When water temperatures are 70 degrees feed fish high-protein feed. Fish like to be fed frequently but in small amounts.
* Divide bog plants every 2 to 3 years.

* Plant hardy water lilies when temperatures reach 60 degrees. Wait to plant tropical plants when water temperature reaches 70 degrees.
* Fertilize water plants when water temperature rises above 55 degrees. Use special tablets to fertilize water plants.
* Water level needs to be 1 to 4 inches above pot tops on aquatic plants.
* If you are building a new pond or adding to an existing pond, be sure to make the pond depth 18 to 36 inches. At this depth you can plant water lilies and overwinter fish.
* Have your pond's pH tested. The pH should stay around 6.8 to 7.4 from spring to fall.

March Indoors Gardening

With rushing winds and gloomy skies
The dark and stubborn winter dies:
Far-off, unseen, spring faintly cries,
Bidding her earliest child arise:
March!

-Bayard Taylor (1825-1878)

* As the days get longer, repot houseplants that have become root-bound. Move plants up to the next pot size.
* Did you know that cactuses, as well as many plants, bloom better when they are root-bound?
* Thicken houseplants by removing leggy growth.
* Start fertilizing foliage houseplants with a liquid plant food such as 20-20-20; apply more diluted than directed. Apply fertilizer every other watering to those plants that are actively growing and get sufficient light. Plants that do not get sufficient light fertilize once a month until October.
* Store bought houseplants may not need fertilizing for the first 6 months due to the commercial grower adding fertilizer to the soil.
* Continue to turn houseplants each week to keep them straight and balanced.
* Set houseplants outside on a warm day for a few hours in a sheltered area. Leach the soil by saturating the soil with water and flushing salts.

Garden Lore

If March comes in like a lion, it will go out like a lamb.
If March comes in like a lamb, it will go out like a lion.

April Garden Chore List

In the Garden:
- ❑ Clean gardens by removing weeds, winter mulch and debris.
- ❑ Replenish gardens with organic matter and compost.

Flowers and Herbs:
- ❑ Mid-April to May 1 plant summer annuals.
- ❑ Deadhead spent flowers.
- ❑ Provide supports for plants.
- ❑ Plan for summer container gardens.
- ❑ Continue to divide perennials.
- ❑ Fertilize flowerbeds with 10-10-10.
- ❑ Pinch annuals to get fuller plants.
- ❑ Deadhead spring bulbs; don't trim foliage from bulbs until they have turned yellow.
- ❑ Prune dead, diseased, crossing, and damaged canes on roses.
- ❑ Complete rose planting.

Seeds:
- ❑ Sow annual and biennial herb seeds directly to the garden.
- ❑ Continue to sow seeds indoors for annuals, perennials and biennials.
- ❑ As seedlings sprout, keep them thinned to avoid overcrowding.
- ❑ Sow warm-weather fruits and vegetables indoors.

Vegetables and Fruits:
- ❑ Plan for successive plantings to have vegetables all summer and fall.
- ❑ Practice crop rotation to reduce disease and insects.
- ❑ Plant strawberries.
- ❑ Thin, stake, and top-dress brambles with compost.
- ❑ Secure grape vines.
- ❑ Complete pruning of fruit trees.

Trees and Shrubs:
- ❑ Continue to plant trees and shrubs.
- ❑ Prune spring flowering trees and shrubs after blooms fade.
- ❑ Prune conifers when new growth or "candles" are produced.

Lawn Care:
- ❑ Seeding the lawn after mid-April is not advisable.
- ❑ Mow lawns at 2 to 3 inches to resist disease and weed infestation.
- ❑ Edging will define your landscape.
- ❑ Apply a post-emergent broadleaf and grassy weed killer.

Composting:
- ❑ Turn the compost pile.

Water Ponds:
- ❑ Clean pond if needed.
- ❑ Shop for new aquatic plants around late April to early May.

Indoors Plants:
- ❑ Spring clean houseplants by rinsing dust with water; remove spent flowers, dead and yellowing leaves.
- ❑ Take cuttings from houseplants for extra outdoor plants this summer.
- ❑ Pinch leggy houseplants to encourage new growth.

Chapter 2

April Garden

*April cold with dropping rain
willows and lilacs brings again,
the whistle of returning birds
and trumpet-lowing of the herds.*
    -Ralph Waldo Emerson (1803-1882)

As the earth awakes it brings with it a marvelous display of blooming trees and shrubs. After months of winter, bulbs send their foliage proclaiming springs arrival. Spring is nature's finest hour and nothing compares to the warm sun in April. The air is cool and sweetened by lilacs. The sun is close and her rays glisten in our windows. The warming air sweeps away the clouds and all that is left are clear blue skies. The air will carry seeds and pollen allowing plants to grow and people to suffer. There is no season that displays such great transformation as springtime. Violets color our countryside while daffodils naturalize along road banks. Wildflowers will cover the forest floors before deciduous trees leaf out.

Break away from your garden chores long enough to attend some gardening lectures this month. Your local arboretum, garden centers and local county extension office will offer classes and they are always helpful since we continually learn. Even established gardens continue to teach us as spring arrives.

It is important to know your last local frost date. Planting tender crops or flowers before this date can be a gamble due to the chance of frost. It is also wise to buy plants that thrive in your zone. Gardening will be more successful and less maintenance will be required for these plants.

Our nation observes Arbor Day and Earth Day this month. Check out local activities to educate and entertain your family and friends.

General Maintenance

I sing of brooks, of blossoms, birds, and bowers:
Of April, May, or June, and July flowers.
I sing of Maypoles, Hock-carts, wassails, wakes,
Of bridegrooms, brides, and of the bridal cakes.
      Robert Herrick (1591-1674) "Hesperides"

Winter's done, and April's in
*   the skies,*
Earth, look up with laughter in
*   your eyes!*
      Charles G.D. Roberts,
      "An April Adoration," 1896

Water

Water is the driving force of all nature.
      -Leonardo Da Vinci (1452-1519)

* Rain is very important in April and May. Many gardens and crops depend on it for a rich harvest. Plants need 1 inch of water a week for optimum growth. To monitor rainfall place a rain gauge close to a walkway.
* Deep watering to reach roots is more beneficial than just surface or foliage wetting.
* Don't forget about plants under eaves and tall evergreens. These plants may never receive enough water unless you remember to do it by hand.
* Water your gardens early in the day to allow the foliage to dry by day to decrease disease. Watering late in the day will increase disease due to excess moisture in the night. Minimize overhead watering to decrease spread of disease.
* If you have a new area that needs lots of watering you should consider soaker hoses. Besides conserving water, soaker hoses will save you lots of time and worry when a dry spell hits. Moisture is also kept away from leaves decreasing chance of foliage disease.

Garden Lore

• *A wet spring is a sign of dry weather for harvest.*
• *This April, with his stormy showers doth make the earth yield pleasant flowers.*
• *When clouds appear like towers, the earth is refreshed by frequent showers.*
• *Ring around the moon, rain real soon.*
• *The early settlers and Native Americans called the full moon in April Planter's Moon, Seed Moon or Sprouting Grass Moon.*
• *Cobwebs on the grass are a sign of fair weather.*
• *Red sun at dusk or dawn indicates dry weather.*
• *A round-topped cloud and flattened base, carries rainfall in its face.*
• *When mountains and cliffs in the clouds appear, some sudden and violent showers are near.*
• *Moist April, clear June.*
• *A cold April brings us bread and wine.*
• *Expect rain if hens spread and ruffle their tail feathers.*
• *Used by priest to sprinkle holy water, clusters of vervain (Verbena) was a common tool.*

In April's sweet month,
When leaves begin to spring
Little lanks skip like fairies,
And birds build and sing.
      Mother Goose

In-The-Garden Maintenance

Sweet April showers
Do spring May flowers.
Thomas Tusser (1515-1580)

Now every field is clothed with grass, and every tree with leaves; now the woods put forth their blossoms, and the year assumes its gay attire.
-Virgil (c. 70-19 B.C.)

* Don't overdo it! Remember to stretch those muscles and drink plenty of water.
* Continue to clean gardens and borders by removing weeds, winter mulch, and debris.

Rodent Control:
Here are a few deterrents to try.
> * Take a mixture of castor oil, liquid detergent, water and put it in spray bottle.
> * Dust plants with baby powder.
> * Mixture of cayenne pepper and boiled water; use when cool.
> * Hang bars of soap around garden to deter deer. Refer to page 158 for more deer repelling plant material.
> * If you have a problem with raccons stealing your corn, try underplanting with squash. These crafty critters are not fond of the prickly foliage squash has to offer.
> * If you are having trouble with rabbits in your vegetable garden, you may have to build a two-foot fence made of chicken wire. It is important that you let the wire hug the ground to keep the rabbits from crawling under.

* Don't be tempted to plant summer annuals until after your region's last frost date. The last killing frost will stunt and damage heat-loving plants.
* Remember sun/shade requirements when planting perennials, biennials, and annuals.
> **"Full sun"** .... Requires 8 hours of sunlight a day
> **"Partial sun"** ...... Requires 4 to 6 hours of sunlight a day with filtered sun in the afternoon
> **"Partial shade"** .. Requires 4 to 6 hours of morning sun; afternoon sun is too intense
> **"Shade"** .... Requires less than 6 hours of sunlight a day

* Deadhead spent flowers throughout the season to save energy the plant would otherwise spend on seed production.
* Clean sprayers with 4 tablespoons of baking soda per pint of water. Discard in a safe area away from drains and water sources.
* Use a pre-emergent weed preventer in the landscape to reduce the germination of weed seeds. Do not use a pre-emergent weed killer in areas where you would like plants to reseed themselves such as:
> Allium
> Baby's breath (*Gypsophila muralis*)
> Cockscomb (*Celosia*)
> Columbine (*Aquilegia*)
> Coreopsis

May we continue to dance stars into being, re-magick the earth, plant seeds, birth great trees in our midst, and like Aphrodite, coming ashore out of the sea, let flowers and grasses spring up under our dancing feet.
-Unknown

Garden Lore

• The Anglo Saxon Goddess of spring and fertility was Eostre, Ostara or Easter. Believers lit bonfires in her memory in the early mornings to protect their crops. Easter sent a rabbit (another symbol of fertility) to deliver rainbow colored eggs to celebrate the rebirth of spring; sound familiar?

• Rain on Easter Sunday will bring rain for seven Sundays.

• A rainy Easter betokens a good harvest.

Cornflower, bachelor's button (*Centaurea cyanus*)
Cosmos
Feverfew (*Chrysanthemum parthenium*)
Forget-me-nots (*Myosotis sylvatica*)
Foxglove (*Digitalis purpurea*)
Hollyhock (*Alcea*)
Impatiens
Johnny-jump-up (*Viola tricolor*)
Larkspur (*Consolida ambiqua*)
Love-in-a-mist (*Nigella damascena*)
Melampodium
Money plant, honesty (*Lunaria annua*)
Morning glory (*Impomoea*)
Poppies (*Papaver*)
Pot marigold (*Calendula officinalis*)
Queen Anne's lace (*Daucus carota*)
Spider flower (*Cleome hasslerana*)
Sweet rocket (*Hesperis matronalis*)
Sweet William (*Dianthus barbatus*)
Vervain (*Verbena bonariensis*)

* Provide supports for plants that need it before they get too heavy.
* Open cold frame on warm sunny days to ventilate plants; be sure to close before the sun goes down to trap warm air in for the evening. Keep soil moist inside cold frame.
* Use cold frame for hardening plants to prepare them for the garden.
* Take note of what is missing in your spring landscape.
* Visit a local arboretum and botanical garden to see what should be blooming in your yard this month.

Container Gardening

Long as there's a sun that sets, primroses will have their glory; Long as there are violets, they will have a place in story.
　　　-William Wordsworth (1770-1850)

* Plan for summer container gardens.
* Plant hybrid lily bulbs in outdoor containers. Water lightly until new growth appears; then increase water.

Perennials and Biennials

Ah! Sweet primrose you have come,
To tell us of the spring:
The hedgerows bloom, the woods are green,
And now the birdies sing.
　　　　　-Thomas Hood (1799-1845)

* Replenish gardens with organic matter and compost.
* When planting transplants, loosen the roots from the sides and base of the plant if they are root-bound.
* Cut dead foliage on perennials.
* Continue to remove protective mulch and winter debris from perennials.
* Perennials can be divided now if the weather permits. The plants should be 2 to 4 inches tall before division. Discard the inner portion of the perennial clump if it appears to lack vigor or the crown is soft to the touch.
*Most perennials will require division after 3 to 4 years in order to produce maximum blooms.
* Thin bamboo clumps by removing 20 % to 30 % of old canes.
* Poppies have taproots and do not like to be transplanted. They can be moved successfully by taking a large division of the plant and extra soil when transplanting.
* Sprinkle a handful of slow-release fertilizer such as 10-10-10 around each perennial clump or broadcast entire garden.
* Fertilize foxgloves when flower spikes appear with 10-10-10.
* When planting hostas, remember blue varieties are more shade tolerant and green varieties can handle minimal sun. Variegated varieties will show whiter when planted in semi-shade. The blue varieties don't attract slugs as bad as other varieties.
* New growth on hostas can be damaged from late frost or freezes. Large leaf hostas seem to be affected the most. This will not kill the plant; it will only delay its beauty.
* Keep showy stonecrop (*Sedum spectabile*) at 4 to 5 inches tall for a month and you will create a more compact plant.
* Thin self-sown seedlings and transplant, or give to a friend.
* Transplant lily of the valley "pips" or roots.
* Prune ground covers such as ivy, purple wintercreeper, and vinca minor.

Guide for buying perennials, biennials, and annuals
　Avoid:
　Large plants in small containers (root-bound)
　Plants in full bloom (adapt slower, grown too fast for their
　　containers)
　Tall lanky spindly plants (received too little light)
　Yellowish, pale plants (poor nourishment)
　Limp, flaccid (too dry)
　Signs of insects or disease
　Brown roots

Garden Lore
• *If the primrose shows its yellow gown, spring will soon be coming to town.*
• *If you want to see garden fairies you have to drink primrose tea while carrying an emerald.*
• *Till the soil in April Showers, you will have neither fruit nor flowers.*
• *Transplanting wild daisies to a prepared garden is very bad luck.*

Daisies pied, and Violets blue,
And Lady-smocks, all silver
*　white,*
And cuckoo-birds of yellow
*　hue*
Do paint the meadows with
*　delight.*
　-Williams Shakespeare (1564-1616)

Garden Lore

• *April showers bring May flowers.*
• *If the first three days in April are foggy, rain in June will make lanes boggy.*

Look for:
Short/stocky plants
Firm texture
Sturdy, pencil-size thick stems
Compact, bushy growth
Good green color
Few blooms, hopefully unopened
Insect and disease-resistant varieties
Moist, not dry
White roots

My garden is an honest place. Every tree and every vine are incapable of concealment, and tell after two or three months exactly what sort of treatment they have had.
Ralph Waldo Emerson (1803-1882)

* The garden centers are full of annuals. Hold off until mid to late April to plant warm-season annuals. Check your local last frost date before planting.
* Gently loosen roots on transplants from the sides and base of the plant if they are root-bound.
* Pinch annuals to get fuller plants. By removing most of the blooms, you will encourage new growth and better root development. You will create a plant that is compact with many blooms, well worth the wait.
* Deadhead pansies and primroses to encourage more blooms.
* Pinch sweet peas when they are 4 inches tall to encourage bushy plants.
* Practice crop rotation of annual flower gardens to deter insects and disease. After 2 or 3 years, plant annuals in a new garden or plant something different.
* Encourage more blooms on snapdragons by removing flower stalks as soon as they fade. Cut stalk as low as possible to a good leafy side shoot. Hopefully a second set of blooms will extend the flowering season.
* Thin annual seedlings that were sown last month by snipping at soil level rather than pulling and disturbing neighboring plants.
*Thin seedlings from self-sown annuals such as nigella, larkspur, and foxgloves before they become too crowded in the garden. Try transplanting the seedlings to fill voids.
* Take cuttings from overwintered annuals for extra plants this summer. Refer to page 122 for instructions.
Begonia
Coleus
Fuchsia
Geranium *(Pelargonium)*
Impatiens

See! The winter is past; the rains are over and gone. Flowers appear on the Earth; The season of singing has come...
    -Song of Songs 2:11,12

Here are sweet peas, on tiptoe for a flight With wings of gentle flush O'er delicate white.
    -John Keats (1795-1821)

Bulbs, Corms, Rhizomes, and Tubers,

*Clean and round,
heavy & sound,
inside a bulb
a flower is found.*
-Anonymous

Garden Lore

• *It is unlucky to bring daffodils in the house if the goslings have not hatched.*

• *If you find the first daffodil of the season you will have more gold than silver this year.*

* Repot bulbs that are in containers if needed and add compost.
* Deadhead daffodils, tulips, and hyacinths; don't trim foliage from bulbs until they have turned yellow. The leaves nourish the bulbs for next year's bloom. Deadheading decreases energy spent on seed production.
* If you receive an Easter lily you can plant it in the garden after the last frost date. Plant it a little deeper than it was originally in the purchased container. It should bloom next July.
* Tender summer bulbs are grown all over the world, but they are not hardy in Tennessee. We can only enjoy these beauties from late spring to early autumn. With exception of the lily, most summer bulbs, corms, and tubers will need to be removed from the garden in the fall to avoid winter freezing. You will need to decide if you want to dig and store these every fall or treat them as annuals and discard. Knowing these jobs to be necessary in late fall, place them in garden spots where their removal won't create havoc to their neighbors. Many tender bulbs and tubers can be planted into containers and set into the soil in the garden or on top, among other plants. In the fall, all you have to do is move the container to basement with no water. This is a lot less digging, drying, storing, and replanting. In southern Tennessee (Zone 7) tender bulbs can be planted after Mid-April.

> *If of thy mortal goods thou are bereft,
> And from thy slender store two loaves
> Alone to thee are left,
> Sell one, and with the dole
> Buy hyacinths to feed the soul.*
> -Moslih Eddin Saadi (c.1184-1291)

* Caladiums thrive in warm, moist shady areas. Caladiums love bottom heat so place them on a warm driveway in the shade when you harden them.
* Go ahead and stake peonies before flower heads unfold and get too heavy.
* Prune smaller buds on peonies to send more energy to the larger buds for larger flowers.

Garden Lore

•*Plant 1 garlic clove beside each rose bush to deter insects and black spot.*
•*Plant chives among roses to deter insects.*

Roses

The best rose-bush, after all, is not that which has the fewest thorns, but that which bears the finest roses.
-Henry Van Dyke (1852-1933)

* Remove mounded earth or mulch from rose bushes after temperatures rise and new growth appears. Be prepared to re-cover if temperatures fall.
* Protect roses with boxes, tall buckets or burlap in case of freezing weather.
* Prune dead, diseased, crossing, and damaged canes by the first week of April. Prune canes to grow outward instead of inward. This will encourage good air circulation and increase light penetration. Wait to prune climbers and ramblers until after they bloom.
* To encourage new growth apply ¼ cup of Epsom salts every 6 weeks. It is recommended to make first application immediately after the first flowering. The magnesium from Epsom salts help plants produce chlorophyll.
* Fertilize with a liquid fertilizer such as 20-20-20 or a formulated fertilizer specifically for roses. Repeat applications every 2 weeks until September.
* Complete rose planting.
* Weed, weed, weed!
* Do not use insecticides unless you have an insect problem.
* Try layering your favorite rose that has lax canes to create a new shrub. Refer to instructions on page 47.

The rose is red, the violet blue;
Sugar is sweet --- and so are you.
These are the words you bade me say
For a pair of new gloves on Easter day.
-Mother Goose

Herbs

I know a bank whereon the wild thyme blows
Where oxlips and the nodding violet grows...
-William Shakespeare (1564-1616)
A Midsummer's Night Dream

* Sow annual and biennial herb seeds directly to the garden this month.

Annuals	Biennials
Anise *(Pimpinella anisum)*	Burdock *(Arctium lappa)*
Borage *(Borago officinalis)*	Caraway *(Carum carvi)*
Chervil *(Anthriscus cerefolium)*	Parsley, curled *(Petroselinum crispum)*
Dill *(Anethum graveolens)*	
Mustard *(Brassica spp.)*	
Nasturtiums *(Tropaeolum majus)*	
Safflower *(Carthamus tinctorius)*	

Come forth into the light of things, let nature be your teacher.
-William Wordsworth (1770-1850)

* Sow perennial herbs such as thyme and sage.
* Plant or transplant mint into a plastic container before planting in the garden. This will help control its invasive manner.

* Thin seedlings sown last month.
* Plant lemon thyme along paths and around stepping-stones for a fragrant walk.
* Cut one-third of lavender to rejuvenate plant. Cutting old wood may cause plant to die. Side dress with wood ashes.

Herbal Remedies:
Use care. Make sure you check reliable sources on how to prepare these natural remedies.

Basil (*Ocimum basilicum*) to repel insects and sooth sore gums.
Bee balm (*Monarda didyma)* for nasal congestion and cough.
Blackberry and raspberry leaves to calm diarrhea.
Catnip (*Nepeta cataria)*) for colic babies and stress reliever.
Chamomile (*Chamaemelum)* to sooth nerves and sleep aid.
Fennel (*Foeniculum vulgare)* to ease asthma and arthritis.
Marigold (*Calendula officinalis*) to cure cuts, congestion,
    conjunctivitis, and soothes digestive tract.
Parsley (*Petroselinum crispum*) to beat bad breath.
Peppermint (*Mentha x piperita*) for indigestion and nausea.
Thyme (*Thymus vulgaris*) for cough reliever.

* Rule of thumb: It takes three times as many fresh herbs to equal the same amount of dried herbs for flavoring in a recipe.

Till April starts, and calls around
The sleeping fragrance from the ground,
And lightly o've the living scene
Scatters his freshest, tenderest green.
        Thomas Gray (1716-1771)

 Seeds

The love of gardening is a seed that
once sown never dies.
        -Gertrude Jekyll (1843-1932)

* Grow grass in pots or decorative trays for spring decoration.
* Continue to sow seeds indoors for annuals, perennial and biennial herbs, and flowers and vegetables.
* Moisten peat moss and peat pots with warm water for quick absorption.
* As seedlings sprout, keep them thinned to avoid overcrowding.
* Near the end of the month, move annuals seedlings grown indoors to a cold frame to harden. If you do not have a cold frame, gradually move plants outdoors. Supply protection from the elements, especially wind, by day and bring them in at night until they are acclimated to their new home. This process should take 2 weeks.
* Water seedlings from the bottom by using a shallow tray of water. Watering the top will disturb roots and wash away soil media from seedling. Allow seedlings to sit in water until entire potting mix is moist; then remove from shallow tray of water.

Garden Lore
• *Because parsley takes a long time to germinate, it was said it goes down and back to the devil 7 times.*
• *Rosemary only grows where the mistress is master.*
• *Sow fennel, sow trouble.*

One for the blackbird,
one for the crow,
One for the cutworm,
and one to grow.

Garden Lore

• *Under the snow the vegetables
    purr,
Like an old man 'neath a mantle
    of fur.*

• *April wet, good wheat.*
• *If it thunders on All Fool's Day, it
brings good crops of corn and hay.*
• *On the last night of April, wet
a handkerchief and hang it over
a corn stalk. The next morning
(May 1ˢᵗ) sun will dry the handkerchief and leave the initials of your
future husband wrinkled within.*

I want death to find me planting my cabbages.
- Michel de Montainge (1533-1592)

* Continue to cultivate vegetable garden and prepare for planting.
* Harvest lettuce, onions, and radishes. Radishes will get hot and spicy if allowed to grow too large.

It's time to Garden!

Seeds:	*Transplants:*
Asparagus (perennial)	Asparagus crowns (1 year old)
Beets	Broccoli
Carrots	Brussels sprouts
Chard	Cabbage
Endive	Cauliflower
Horseradish (perennial)	
Kale, collards	
Kohlrabi	
Leeks	
Lettuce, leaf & loose (only requires 2 to 4 hours of sunlight a day)	
Mustard	
Onion sets	
Parsnips	
Peas, late	
Potatoes, Irish	
Radish (only requires 2 to 4 hours of sunlight a day)	
Rhubarb (perennial)	
Salsify	
Spinach	
Turnips	

* Rhubarb should be in the ground for a few years before harvest.
* Grow a gourmet mix of mesclun for a tasty salad. Mesclun is a mixture of young salad greens and herbs. Choose from romaine, red or bibb lettuce, mustard, red chard, radicchio, curly endive, arugula, spinach, dandelion, parsley, basil, thyme, nasturtium, and chive blossoms.
* Sprinkle borax lightly around beets to sweeten the taste.
* Plan for successive plantings to have vegetables all summer and fall.
* Plant vegetables with an all-purpose granular fertilizer such as 10-10-10.
* Block light (blanch) from cauliflower when heads are two to three inches in diameter by tying leaves over budding heads. The heads will turn purplish-pink if the sun is not blocked.
* Practice crop rotation of annual vegetables every 2 to 3 years to reduce disease and insects.
* Consider building a sturdy metal trellis to grow small melons, tomatoes, cucumbers, and squash vertically. This practice will deter borers and rabbits.

*O amateurs of gardening, be
amateurs of humanity also.*
*Charles Joseph, Prince de Ligne
(1781)*

* Sidedressing vegetables at certain stages of development will increase productivity. Here are a few to remember:

Beans	After blooms and before pod formation
Broccoli	3 weeks after planting
Cabbage	3 weeks after planting
Cauliflower	3 weeks after planting
Corn	When plant is 12 inches tall
Cucumbers	1 week after blooming begins and then 3 weeks later
Eggplant	After first fruit appears
Kale	When plant is 1/3 its mature size
Muskmelons ..	1 week after blooming begins and then 3 weeks later
Onions...........	2 weeks after bulb forms
Peas..............	After blooms and before pods form
Peppers..........	After first fruit sets
Potatoes........	6 weeks after planting
Spinach	When plant is 1/3 its mature size
Tomatoes.......	2 weeks prior to first picking and then 2 weeks later

* Be aware that over fertilizing these vegetables may create more foliage and less quality produce:

- Beets
- Carrots
- Lettuce
- Parsnips
- Squash
- Sweet potatoes
- Turnips
- Watermelon

* As well as feeding vegetables there is also a best time to give water. Listed are significant stages of vegetable growth that require more water.

Asparagus.....	When ferns develop
Beans	When pods begin to expand
Broccoli	Head enlargement
Cabbage	Head enlargement
Carrot	Root development
Cauliflower ...	Head enlargement
Corn	When silks appear and ear enlargement
Cucumber.....	During flower stage and fruit development
Melon	During flower stage and fruit development
Peas..............	Flowering and pod enlargement
Potato	Tuber enlargement
Radish	Root enlargement
Squash..........	During flower stage and fruit development
Turnips	Root enlargement

> *A calendar, a calendar! Look in the moonshine.*
> -William Shakespeare (1564-1616)

Garden Phenology

- *Plant crops such as rhubarb, asparagus, and horseradish when peach and plum trees bloom.*
- *Sow beets, lettuce, and peas when leaves first appear on the lilac.*

Oats, peas, beans, and barley grow,
Oats, peas, beans, and barley grow,
Can you or I or anyone know?
Why oats, peas, beans, and barley grow?

First the farmer sows the seed,
Stands erect and take his ease,
Stamps his foot and claps his hands
And turns him round to view his land.

Traditional folk song

April hath put a spirit of youth
in everything.
         -William Shakespeare
              (1564-1616)

For glad spring has sprung,
And to the ardent sun
The earth, long time so bleak,
Turns a frost-bitten cheek.
       -Celia Thaxter (1835-1894)

Fruit

If frost do continue, take this for a law,
The strawberries look to be covered with straw,
Laid overly trim upon crotches and bows,
And after uncovered as weather allows.
    S. W. Fletcher, Strawberry-Growing (1917)

* Be aware of honeybees, the official agricultural insect for Tennessee, avoid using pesticides while they pollinate.
* After petal drop spray cherry, peach, and plum trees to protect against disease.
* Plant and transplant strawberries and protect from late freezes.
* Remove mulch from strawberry patch as the growing season begins.
* Fertilizing strawberries now will only create lots of leaves; fertilize lightly when blossoms appear.
* Control weeds around fruit planting with a pre-emergent herbicide.
* Thin, stake, and top-dress brambles (any prickly plant) with compost.
* Secure grape vines with heavy string.
* Complete pruning of fruit trees.

* Toast St. Urban of Langres on April 2, he is the patron saint of wine lovers and vineyards.

Trees and Shrubs

Just now the lilac is in bloom
All before my little room;
And in my flowerbeds I think
Smile the carnation and the pink;
And from the borders, well I know,
The poppy and the pansy blow.
      - Rupert Brooke (1887-1915)

* The landscape is filled with color from spring bloomers such as forsythia, dogwoods, mountain laurel, ornamental pear, purple leaf plum, redbud, flowering cherries, saucer and star magnolias.
* If you were given a hydrangea as a gift, transplant it into the garden after the bloom fades. Plant in full sun to part-shade. The color next season will depend on the pH of the soil at the new site. If you prefer pink blooms create alkaline soil (5 to 5.5) by increasing pH with lime. If you prefer blue flowers create acid soil (6 to 6.5) by decreasing pH with sulfur.
* Continue to plant container-grown and burlapped trees and shrubs. Do not amend soil when planting because the root system will adapt better to homogeneous soil. Transplant using un-amended original soil.
* When planting azaleas, rhododendrons, mountain laurel (*Kalmia*), and camellias use ½ soil, ½ pine bark, and ½ cup of acid-type fertilizer (aluminum sulfate).
* Winter-flowering trees and shrubs should be going on sale soon; take your wish list.
* Remove protection from big leaf hydrangea (*Hydrangea macrophylla*) as weather improves. Prepare to cover if freezing weather is forecasted.

Garden Lore

• *If apple trees bloom in April the crop will be plentiful; if they bloom in May the crop will be poor.*

• *A warm March brings a cold April.*

• *If you hang onions from the tree, the birds will not come.*

* Prune conifers such as pines, firs, red cedar, junipers, and spruces when new growth or "candles" are produced. Cut one-third of new growth to keep shrubs compact; do not prune old growth.
* Cut pyracantha to create a more compact shrub.
* Try propagating by layering shrubs this month. Make a few ½ inch cuts in a branch that is the diameter of a pencil; bend it to touch the ground. Apply a small amount of rooting hormone on wounded area. Lay the wounded branch on the ground and cover branch with soil; secure it with a rock, brick or lawn staple. The wounds will produce roots and this fall or next spring you will have a new plant to transplant. Snip the branch to separate the new from the old. Transplant new plant to desired location.

> Azalea *(Rhododendron)*
> Bottlebrush buckeye *(Aesculus parviflora)*
> Flowering quince *(Chaenomeles speciosa)*
> Japanese pieris *(Pieris japonica)*
> Juniper *(Juniperus)*
> Lilac *(Syringa)*
> Oak-leaf hydrangea *(Hydrangea quercifolia)*
> Rose-of-Sharon *(Hibiscus syriacus)*
> Tree peony *(Paeonia suffruticosa)*
> Witch hazel *(Hamamelis)*

* Watch for leaf miners on holly and boxwoods. Use appropriate insecticide control.
* Check trees for tent caterpillars; prune, rake or scrape webs with hands and destroy.
* Remove bagworm cases from trees and shrubs and destroy.
* Did you know that the dogwood bloom is the very small yellow area inside of the "flower" and the white and pink you see are part of the leaf called bracts?
* Listen for the melodious tunes of the Mocking-bird. This Tennessee state bird can be found near thick briar patches or nested between the rails of a fence.

> *Go forwarde in the name of God, graffe set, plant, and*
> *nourish up trees in every corner of your grounde.*
> *-Father John Gerard (1564-1637)*

> *One generation plants the trees;*
> *Another gets the shade.*
> *Chinese Proverb*

April is the cruelest month,
  breeding
Lilacs out of the dead land,
  mixing
Memory and desire, stirring
Dull roots with spring rain.
  T.S. Eliot (1888-1965)
  The Waste Land, 1922

Garden Phenology

• *When the lilac blooms expect grasshopper eggs to hatch.*

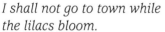

I shall not go to town while the lilacs bloom.
  -Henry Wadsworth Longfellow
       (1807-1882)

Garden Lore

• *When silver maples show the under side of their leaves, a storm will soon appear.*

• *When oak is out before ash,*
'twill be a summer of wet and splash,
But if ash before oak
'twill be a summer of fire and smoke.

• *Burn Ash-wood green,*
'Tis fire for a queen;
Burn Ash-wood sear,
'Twill make a man swear.

• *Plant an ash tree to keep away snakes. This belief led women to hang their baby's cradle from an ash tree while they tended to the fields.*

• *The seeds of an ash tree are considered an aphrodisiac.*

• *Grass grows slower if cut during a waning moon.*

• *It was once thought that honeysuckle next to the door of your house or barn would protect livestock and deter evil. Maybe this explains why Tennessee is covered with this introduced invasive exotic plant that is now on the* **do-not-plant** *list.*

• *"Dogwood winter" or "locust winter" is a cold spell that arrives mid-April and spoils our spring fever.*

• *The dogwood, once very large and strong, was chosen as the timber for the cross. While Jesus suffered, he saved future dogwoods from being cut and used for crosses by stunting their growth. The four leaf bracts resemble the cross and the center resembles the crown of thorns. There are even nail prints on this cross of foliage.*

• *Pluck a white dogwood blossom and place in on your bosom and the first man you meet wearing a white hat has the name of your future husband.*

• *The red bud tree originally had white blooms until Judas Iscariot was hung from one. The blooms turn red after that due to shame.*

• *The serviceberry gets its name from the nomadic preachers who traveled in the spring. This tree is also called the shadbush because it blooms with the seasonal run of the Shad fish.*

Lawn Care

The warm, moist kiss of April on the grass;
The stooping sun, the wet and fragrant plain;
The voice of life, low-whispered as I pass;
The vision of the summer through the rain.
                    -Philip Henry Savage (1868-1899)

Maintenance

* Seeding the lawn after mid-April is not advisable due to weed competition, heat of the season, and stress due to reduction of rainfall.
* Remember lawns mowed at 2 to 3 inches will be competitive and resist disease and weed infestation. Lawns that are scalped or neglected will prove otherwise.
* Mow frequently; avoid letting the grass get too tall. Cut no more than one-third of the blade height at a time.
* Edging will define your landscape. For a nice manicured look, create a 4 inch trench between the lawn and landscape border.

Under the green hedges, after the snow,
There do the dear little violets grow;
Hiding their modest and beautiful heads
Under the hawthorn in soft mossy beds.

Sweet as the roses and blue as the sky,
Down there do the dear little violets lie;
Hiding their heads where they scarce may be seen,
By the leaves you may know where the violet hath been.
                    John Moultrie (1799-1874)

Insect and Weed control

* Apply a post-emergent broadleaf and grassy weed killer. Apply mid-month if you did not apply last month. Do not apply on newly seeded area.

Broad-leafed weeds
Buckhorn plantain *(Plantain lanceolata)*
Cinquefoil
Common chickweed *(Stellaria media)*
Dandelion *(Taraxacum officinale)*
English daisy *(Bellis perennis)*
Ground ivy *(Glechoma hederacea)*
Henbit *(Lamium amplexicaule)*
Knotweed *(Polygonum aviculare)*
Mouse-ear chickweed *(Cerastium)*
Plantain *(Plantago major)*
Potentilla
Purslane *(Portulaca oleraceae)*

Grassy weeds
Bermuda *(Cynodon dactylon)*
Bluegrass, annual *(Poa annua)*
Crabgrass *(Digitaris sanguinalis)*
Foxtail *(Setaria)*
Goosegrass *(Eleusine indica)*
Nimblewill *(Muhlenbergia*
           schreberi)
Nutgrass *(Cyperus esculentus)*
Quackgrass, dog-grass
           (Agropyron repens)

Garden Lore

• *A wet Good Friday and a wet Easter Day make plenty of grass, but very little hay.*
• *To ward off evil spirits, common purslane was scattered around beds for a safe nights sleep.*
• *To induce sleep field violets were positioned on the forehead.*
• *Chickweed closes its leaves before rain.*
• *To meet your future husband wear a four-leaf clover in the heel of your shoe.*
• *Place four-leaf clovers beneath the four corners of your bed to dream of your future husband.*

There was a child went forth Every day And the first object he look'd upon That object he became.
-Walt Whitman (1819-1892)

Sheep sorrel, red sorrel *(Rumex acetosella)*
Sheperd's purse *(Capsella bursa-pastoris)*
Prostrate spurge *(Euphorbia maculata)*
Thistle *(Cirsium)*
White clover *(Trifolium repens)*
Wild strawberry *(Fragaria vesca)*
Yarrow *(Achillea millefolium)*
Yellow wood sorrel *(Oxalis stricta)*

* Be sure not to use weed killer on newly seeded areas.

The grass of spring covers the prairies,
Then bean bursts noiselessly through the mould in the garden,
The delicate spear of the onion pierces upward,
The apple-buds cluster together on the apple-branches.
Walt Wittman (1819-1892)

Composting

A gush of bird-song, a patter of dew,
A cloud, and a rainbow's warning,
Suddenly sunshine and perfect blue-
An April day in the morning.
-Harriet Prescott Spofford (1835-1921)

* Now is a great time to start a new compost pile. Refer to page 145 for instructions.
* If you treat your lawn with an herbicide, do not include lawn clippings to compost pile if you plan to use compost within the next six weeks.

Water Ponds

Expect poison from the standing water.
-William Blake (1757-1827)

* This is a good time to clean your pond if needed. Remove plants that are in baskets, siphon the water and gently remove sediment in the bottom. Thin oxygenating plants to avoid clogging the pond.
* Before adding fish, let them acclimate in a plastic bag floating for a half-hour on the surface of the pond.
* Plan to shop for new aquatic plants around late April to early May.

Dance like nobody's watching;
love like you've never been hurt.
Sing like nobody's listening;
live like it's heaven on Earth.
-Mark Twain (1835-1910)

April Indoor Gardening

Every flower is a soul blossoming in nature.
-Gerard De-Nerval (1808-1855)

And April weeps – but,
O ye hours!
Follow with May's fairest
flowers.
-Percy Bysshe Shelley (1792-1822)

* As soon as night temperatures are above 55 degrees, houseplants can be moved outdoors. Move them to a shady location to adjust before moving to higher light. Keep them protected from wind until they have acclimated to the new surroundings. Fertilize with a liquid fertilizer such as 20-20-20 every other watering throughout the summer.
* Rotate houseplants so that each side receives the same light for even growth.
* African violets that are positioned in the south-facing window may need to be relocated to avoid leaf scorch as the sun gets more intense. Don't forget that African violets bloom best in small pots.
* Spring clean houseplants by rinsing dust away with water; remove spent flowers, dead and yellowing leaves. Those plants with soft fuzzy foliage like the African violet can be lightly brushed with a soft bristle brush or paint brush.
* Take cuttings from houseplants for extra outdoor plants this summer. These new tropical plants can be added to summer containers next month. Refer to page 122 for instructions.

African violet *(Saintpaulia)*
Aluminum plant *(Pilea)*, roots well in water
Aralia *(Fatsia japonica)*
Begonia
Burro's tail, donkey tail *(Sedum morganianum)*
Chinese evergreen *(Aglaeonema)*
Christmas cactus *(Schlumbergera bridgesii)*
Coffee plant *(Coffea arabica)*
Coleus
Dracaena
Dumbcane, mother-in-law's tongue *(Dieffenbachia amoena)*
English Ivy *(Hedra helix)*, roots well in water
Gloxinia *(Sinningia)*
Grape ivy *(Cissus)*

Hibiscus
Jade *(Crassula argentea)*
Madagascar jasmine *(Stephanotis floribunda)*
Nephthytis *(Syngonium)*
Peperomia
Philodendron
Poinsettia *(Euphorbia pulcherrima)*
Polka dot plant *(Hypoestes phyllostachya)*
Pothos, devil's ivy *(Raphidophora)*
Red-nerve, mosiac *(Fittonia verschaffeltii)*
Swedish Ivy *(Plectranthus australis)*, roots well in water
Wandering Jew *(Tradescantia zebrina)*, roots well in water
Wax vine, porcelain flower *(Hoya carnosa)*

* Pinch leggy houseplants to encourage new growth.
* Continue to repot plants that are root-bound.
* Apply liquid 20-20-20 fertilizer and fish emulsions to ferns.

May Garden Chore List

In the Garden:
- ❑ Apply 2 to 3 inches of mulch around plants to reduce weeds and retain moisture.
- ❑ Remove and destroy foliage on plant and ground that has succumbed to insects or disease to avoid spreading.

Flowers and Herbs:
- ❑ Plant summer containers, window boxes, and hanging baskets.
- ❑ Fertilize annuals weekly with a liquid fertilizer such as 20-20-20.
- ❑ Apply a granular fertilizer, such as 10-10-10, twice throughout the growing season.
- ❑ Stake flowering plants that get top heavy.
- ❑ Late summer and fall-blooming perennials can be dug and divided now.
- ❑ Pinch late summer and fall-blooming perennials when they are 6 inches tall.
- ❑ Plant or sow annuals to gardens.
- ❑ Thin and transplant self-sown annuals to desired location.
- ❑ Plant summer bulbs, corms, and tubers.
- ❑ Remove spent flowering stalks from bearded irises.

Seeds:
- ❑ Harden seedlings and transplant in the garden.
- ❑ Direct sow annual herbs to the garden.

Vegetables and Fruits:
- ❑ Provide supports for tomatoes, beans, and peas.
- ❑ Plant transplants and sow seeds.
- ❑ Watch for insects and control early in the season to reduce problems.
- ❑ Thin brambles and fruit on apples, plums, peaches, and pears trees.
- ❑ Harvest strawberries.

Trees and Shrubs:
- ❑ Finish pruning spring-flowering shrubs and trees after blooms fade and before new growth begins.
- ❑ Continue to prune dead, damaged, and diseased branches from plant material.
- ❑ Trim and shape hedges.

Lawn Care:
- ❑ Adjust mower to cut higher to allow grass to grow fuller, choke weeds, and shade roots from the hot summer sun.
- ❑ Apply post-emergent broadleaf herbicide.

Composting:
- ❑ Keep compost heap turned and damp.

Water Ponds:
- ❑ Lift and divide pond plants.
- ❑ Plant tender tropical plants.
- ❑ Feed established plants with an all-purpose fertilizer such as 10-10-10.

Indoors Plants:
- ❑ Divide and transplant houseplants.
- ❑ Move houseplants outdoors.
- ❑ Fertilize houseplants with liquid 20-20-20.

Chapter

3 *May Garden*

New flowery scents strewed everywhere,
New sunshine poured in largesse fair,
"We shall be happy now," we say.
A voice just trembles through the air,
And whispers, "May."
-Sarah Chauncey Woolsey (1835-1905)

What a great month! May is truly the month of flowers and gardeners couldn't be busier. Weeds seem to pop up everywhere, but who cares? Its prime gardening in Tennessee, when it isn't raining. The strong and poised tulip fades from the spring garden; romantic fragrances from peonies, irises and lily of the valley fill the air. The bulbs have completed their performance and it is time for perennials to take the stage. Nothing compares to the dripping pendants of bleeding hearts and the awesome spires of foxgloves. As poppies wave in the breeze, dames' rockets sweeten it. Someone once said, "let the delicious secret out to every breeze that roams about". May is truly a gardening month and there are not enough hours in the day for everything gardeners want to accomplish.

The time for Tennesseans has come to shop for annuals. Annuals are scene-savers as perennials wane and well worth the effort of annual planting. A trip to the garden center and bringing home flats full of beautiful flowers always brightens the day. Visit your local arboretum and public botanical gardens to get great ideas to bring to your yard. Pay close attention to color combinations and design. Take along a note pad and pen; as you are sure to find something you like and you will want to write it down.

General Maintenance

Earthworms are the intestines of the soil.
-Aristotle (384-322 B.C.)

Garden Lore

• *A bee flying around a child's head is considered good luck.*
• *The early settlers and Native Americans called the full moon in May the Flower Moon or Planting Corn Moon.*
• *It is considered good luck if a butterfly or lady bug lands on you.*
• *Upon catching a ladybug, release it and whatever direction it flies is the direction you should look for love.*
• *It is bad luck to kill a ladybug.*

• *If you wish to live and thrive, let the spider walk alive.*
-Mother Goose

• *Ladybug, ladybug, flyaway home. Your house is on fire, Your children all roam.*

Mulch

* Cultivate existing mulch to allow moisture to penetrate more easily.
* When soil temperatures are above 55 degrees apply 2 inches of mulch around plants to reduce weeds, retain moisture, aid in soil erosion, and soil temperature fluctuation. Keep mulch away from trunks and stems to reduce insect and disease problems.
* Apply mulch to damp soil to lock-in moisture.
* Remove weeds prior to mulching.
* Remove old mulch where disease spores or insects are present.
* Do not use sawdust as mulch. After sawdust decomposes, water is slow to penetrate.
* Use mulch to disguise soaker hoses for a more pleasing appearance.
* Many types of mulch to choose from:
  Grass clippings, 1 inch only, not chemically treated.
  Hard wood chips
  Pine needles
  Shredded bark
  Shredded deciduous leaves
* Hardwood mulch is attractive but it is not a good source of acid for acid-loving plants.
* Dark flowers show their color best when mulched with light-color mulch.
* Light-color mulch will reflect heat and dark mulch will absorb it.

Insects and Weed Control

Gardening is the purist of human pleasures.
-Sir Francis Bacon (1561-1626)

* ***Always*** identify the insect or disease before applying anything. Is it a beneficial insect?
* ***Always*** read the directions before applying anything. Buy or mix small amounts of products to minimize disposal.
* ***Always*** protect yourself by wearing gloves, mask, eye protection, and appropriate attire. Spray on a calm day.
* ***Always*** dispose of leftover chemicals in a safe manner. Spray leftover chemicals over an area away from drains, drainage ditches, and water sources. Be sure to clean the sprayer well after application is complete.
* ***Always*** store chemicals in a safe place out of the reach of children.

* Be cautious of insects before killing.

Beneficial insects:	Non-beneficial insects:
Bees	Aphid
Butterflies	Colorado potato bug
Earthworms	Cutworm
Ichneumon fly	Japanese beetle
Lacewing	Leafhopper
Ladybug	Plum curculio
Praying mantis	Scale
Spiders	Slug
	Spotted cucumber beetle

* Early detection is vital when controlling insects and disease. For example, finding very small bags of bagworms as they begin to form allows you to successfully treat them chemically. Waiting until the bags are close to full formation results in non-effectiveness of chemicals penetrating the impermeable bag barrier. Hand picking is your only recourse at this point.
* Take samples of any undetermined insect or disease to your local county extension office for identification and determining the best method of treatment.
* Watch for spider mites on flowers and shrubs and control with insecticidal soap.
* Spray rust, leaf spot, and powdery mildew with a fungicide or wettable sulfur.
* Keep watching for aphids and mealy bugs on plant material and wash away with soapy water. Follow with a high-pressure garden hose to wash away insects. If infestation is severe you may choose to use a commercial insecticide.
* Remove Japanese beetles with tweezers or fingers and put them in a jar of soapy water for their final swim.
* Remove and destroy foliage on plant and ground that has succumbed to insects or disease to avoid spreading. Do not compost.
* To reduce the amount of slugs in the garden bury jars into the soil and fill partially with beer for their final swim.

In-The-Garden Maintenance

More than anything,
I must have flowers,
always, always.
-Claude Monet (1840-1926)

* It is best to garden early in the morning or late in the afternoon from now until fall. The sun can be very damaging so don't forget to use sunscreen and drink plenty of water.
* Continue to cultivate soil and remove weeds before they flower and go to seed. You are preventing further spread of the weeds.
* **Emma Lou's weed tea:** Take young weeds and put them in a 5-gallon bucket with water. Let weeds steep for two weeks. Strain and water plants; they will love it. **Always** place buckets of fluid out of the reach of children.
* Avoid scorching new plants by placing them in full sun or high winds. New plants will adapt better if you start them in a shady, sheltered area to adjust prior to planting.

Garden Lore
• Keep a light jacket handy for the "Three Chilly Saints' Days". These days are named for May 11th, 12th, and 13th or the last blast of winter.
• May Day celebrations are mirrored after the Roman Goddess Flora's springtime celebration rituals for flowers and fruit called Florialia. Flowers were gathered and a birch maypole was erected. People danced around the pole honoring springtime and love.
• Wash your face with the dew of May and all year long you will have beauty.

•The first of May, the fair maid who, the first of May,
Goes to the fields at the break of day,
And washes in dew from the Hawthorne-tree,
Will ever after handsome be.
-Mother Goose

Beauty come, freckles go, dewdrops make me white as snow.
-Mother Goose

* Continue to protect tender plant material until after the last frost.
* Try using downed branches to stake tall plants.
* Keep your eyes open for the Tennessee state butterfly, the Zebra Swallowtail. Their wings are black and white stripped on a pale whitish green background. You can find the caterpillar residing in the paw paw tree. Often found sipping nectar from blossoms on blackberry, blueberry, lilac, redbud, verbena, and common milkweed.

Container Gardening

My only desire is an infusion with nature, and the only fate I wish is to have worked and lived in harmony with her laws.
                    -Claude Monet (1840-1926)

* Plant summer containers, window boxes, and hanging baskets.
* Fertilize containers and hanging baskets weekly with a liquid fertilizer such as 20-20-20.
* Apply a granular fertilizer, such as 10-10-10, twice throughout the growing season.
* Grow moss on garden accessories to give them an established look. Pour or paint a well-blended solution of moss, buttermilk or yogurt and water over anything that you want to antique. If possible place object in a cool, damp area of the yard until moss grows.
* Plant roses and trees in containers for the terrace or patio.
* Before planting, gently loosen roots from plant material if they have become root-bound.
* Choose dwarf varieties when planting vegetables in containers.
* Fill the base of large containers with foam peanuts or old plastic pots. This will create a lighter container and save on soil.

Container Gardening

If you have minimal space in your yard or you have no yard with a deck or patio, you can't go wrong with container gardening. Instant warmth and charm can be obtained easily with container gardening. A pot of flowers can brighten any spot. Containers can be used anywhere: next to steps, to show a grade change, mark an entryway or just a focal point to draw a person into your garden or onto a deck or patio. Use them in clusters anywhere to give your home a cottage feel.

Step 1 – Choosing a container:
* Choose containers larger than 12 inches in diameter and 10 inches deep. Make sure the container complements your home and garden style. It may be helpful to know where the containers will be placed after they have been potted.
* You will want to cover drainage holes in containers with any of the following items to increase drainage and to keep soil in the container.

Broken clay potshards	Rocks
Coffee filters	Window screen
Foam peanuts, packing material	

* Position containers within reach of a water hose.

Garden Lore

• *A cold & wet May is kindly and fills the barn with hay finely.*
• *Wet May, happy year.*
• *When the sun goes to bed red, 'twill rain tomorrow'.*
• *Shear your sheep in May and shear them all the way.*
• *Mist in May and heat in June, will bring all things into tune.*
• *A dry May and a rainy June put the farmer's pipe in tune.*
• *An open anthill indicates good weather; a closed anthill indicates a storm.*
• *Dust rising in dry weather is a sign of weather change.*
• *Cast not a clout till May be out.*

The earth laughs in flowers.
-Ralph Waldo Emerson (1803-1882)

Step 2 – Potting mix:

* If you are using last year's containers, freshen soil by adding vermiculite, fresh potting mix and a handful of all-purpose fertilizer such as 10-10-10 or 14-14-14.
* Work the soil to the base of the container.
* Choose a potting mix that is best suited for the plants you have chosen. Bags that have the ingredients on them will be better quality. Potting mixes are mostly peat and they dry very quickly. You can add a loam-or humus-based soil to help retain water.
* Change soil in containers every other planting or refresh every time.

Step 3 – Plant selection:

* Choose plants you like for a sunny or shady spot that also complement your home and garden style.
* Keep containers full of plants that share the same need for sun or shade.
* If your home is white, white flowers will go unnoticed. Use dark foliage and bright flowers with light-colored houses.
* If your home is a dark color, use plants with light foliage and pastel flowers.
* Red flowers will make the garden look closer and larger. A lot of commercial businesses follow this plan.
* Blue flowers will make the garden appear more distant.
* White flowers complement most color schemes.
* Make a list to take with you to the garden center. The selection of flowers is wonderfully broad. Evergreen plants are nice choices for year-round interest.
* Don't forget to use foliage and tropical plants for more interest among summer-flowering annuals.

Step 4–Planting:

* Always loosen root ball to help root-bound plants.
* Water plants well prior to planting.
* Choose a tall upright plant to use as the centerpiece or to use in the back if container will set against a wall.
* Plant low-growing and cascading plants around edge of containers.
* Plant mid-level plants in between the tall-and low-growing plants to fill spaces.
* Cram containers full of plants for a better display.
* Fill containers with soil leaving a 2-inch rim space to collect water.
* After watering, add soil to surface of container to areas that have settled.

Plant selection is endless for containers; here are some of my favorites.

Sun-loving uprights:

Asparagus fern *(Asparagus densiflorus)*
Canna
Dahlia
Dracaena spike
Dusty-miller *(Senecio cineraria)*
Geranium *(Pelargonium)*
Marigold *(Tagetes)*
Ornamental and native grasses

Shade-loving uprights:

Begonia
Caladium
Coleus (sun or shade)
Dracaena spike
Ferns
Impatiens
Rock rose *(Cistus)*

Trailing for sun:
  Alyssum *(Lobularia maritima)*
  Black-eyed Susan vine *(Thunbergia alata)*
  Geranium, Ivy-leaved *(Pelargonium peltatum)*
  Ivy *(Hedra)*
  Lantana
  Petunia, cascading
  Periwinkle *(Vinca major)*
  Sweet potato vine *(Ipomoea batatas)*
  Vervain *(Verbena)*

Trailing for shade:
  Bacopa
  Begonia, angel wing
  Fan flower *(Scaevola)*
  Fuchsia
  Impatiens
  Lobelia
  Plumbago (sun or shade)

Trees and shrubs to choose for containers:
  Evergreens, dwarf
  Hydrangea, 'Peegee' *(Hydrangea paniculata)*
  Japanese maple *(Acer japonicum)*
  Rose *(Rosa)*

Step 5 – Watering:
* Water thoroughly and regularly.
* Check containers and baskets daily for moisture loss. Use mulch for moisture retention and appearance (shredded bark, pine straw, gravel, small pinecones)

Step 6 – Fertilizing:
* All container plants will benefit from a flushing of water to reduce build-up of salts from fertilizer and hard water.
* When planting annuals in containers add an all-purpose slow-release fertilizer to the potting mix such as 10-10-10 or 14-14-14. Another application mid-summer will keep annuals looking great all season.
* Container plants need regular watering; therefore they need to be fertilized more often. Apply liquid fertilizer such as 20-20-20 weekly throughout the growing season.

Perennials and Biennials

* Deadheading is the term given to the removal of spent flowers. This practice encourages new flowers. Continue to deadhead throughout the growing season.
* Stake flowering plants that get top heavy such as foxgloves, balloon flowers, Shasta daisies, monkshood, veronica, and delphiniums.
* Peonies and delphiniums will benefit from a little dusting of lime around them.
* Late summer and fall-blooming perennials can be dug and divided now. Discard old hard center.
* Pinch late summer and fall-blooming perennials when they are 6 inches tall.
* Pinch terminal buds to promote branching to create a more compact

plant. This may delay blooms but proves to create more prolific blooming. This practice may also decrease the need for staking.

> Chrysanthemum
> Delphinium
> Garden Phlox *(Phlox paniculata)*
> Joe-pye weed *(Eupatorium fistulosum)*
> Michaelmas daisy *(Aster)*
> Showy stonecrop *(Sedum spectabile)*

* Cut candytuft and creeping phlox after blooming if they have overgrown their boundaries.
* Continue to train ground covers and vines as they are growing very quickly now.
* Vines and ground covers are easily propagated by layering. Refer to page 47 for instructions.
* When planting clematis remember they like their heads in the sun and feet in the shade. Keep newly planted clematis watered well throughout the season.
* Prune wisteria immediately after blooming.
* Thin and transplant self-sown perennials to desired location.
* Sow biennial seeds. Biennials live for two years and only bloom in the second.

Choose from my favorite list of perennials:

Shade-loving perennials:

> Beardtongue, dead man's bells *(Penstemon)*
> Bear's breeches *(Acanthus mollis)*
> Bergenia
> Bleeding heart, ladies' lockets *(Dicentra)*
> Bugleweed *(Ajuga reptans)*
> Cardinal flower *(Lobelia cardinalis)*
> Christmas rose *(Helleborus niger)*
> Columbine, granny's bonnets, meeting houses *(Aquilegia)*
> False spirea *(Astilbe)*
> Ferns
> Goats beard *(Aruncus dioicus)*
> Hardy begonia *(Begonia grandis)*
> Hosta, plantain lily, funkia
> Jack-in-the-pulpit *(Arisaema triphyllum)*
> Jacob's ladder, Greek valarian, ladder to heaven *(Polemonium caeruleum)*
> Japanese anemone
> Japanese painted fern *(Athyrium nipponicum)*
> Japanese spurge *(Pachysandra)*
> Lady's mantle *(Alchemilla mollis)*
> Lenton rose *(Helleborus orientalis)*
> Ligularia
> Lily-of-the-valley, wood lily, May lily, Our Lady's tears *(Convallaria)*
> Lungwort *(Pulmonaria)*
> Monkey grass, lily turf *(Liriope)*
> Monkshood *(Aconitum)*
> Solomon's seal, David's harp *(Polygonatum odoratum)*
> Sweet woodruff *(Gallium odoratum)*

Shade-loving biennials:

> Forget-me-not *(Myosotis sylvatic)*
> Honesty, money plant *(Lunaria annua)*

Love is the only flower that grows and blossoms without the aid of the seasons.
-Kahil Gibran (1883-1931)

If you have a mind at peace, and a heart that cannot harden, go find a door that opens wide upon a lovely garden.
-Author unknown

Garden Lore

The roots of Solomon's Seal, stamped while it is fresh and greene and applied, taketh away in one night or two at the most, any bruise, blacke or blew spots gotten by falls or women's wilfulness in stumbling up in their hastie husband's fists, or such like.
        -John Gerard (1545-1612)

Toad lily *(Tricyrtis hirta)*
Virginia bluebells *(Mertensia virginica)*

Sun-Loving Perennials:
Adam's needle, bear grass
    (Yucca filamentosa)
Artemsia
Bee Balm, Oswego Tea, bergamot
    (Monarda)
Blackberry lily, leopard flower
    (Belamcanda chinensis)
Black-eyed Susan *(Rudbeckia fulgida)*
Blanket flower *(Gaillardia)*
Butterfly weed *(Asclepias tuberosa)*
Candle larkspur, lark's heel
    (Delphinum elatum)
Candytuft, candied mustard,
    Billy-come-home-soon
    (Iberis sempervirens)
Chrysanthemum
Clematis, traveler's joy, old man's beard *(Clematis)*
Coral bells, alumroot *(Heuchera spp.)*
Cranesbill geranium *(Geranium sanguineum)*
Creeping phlox *(Phlox stolonifera)*
Dames' rocket, sweet rocket *(Hesperis matronalis)*
Daylily *(Hemerocallis)*
Garlic chives *(Allium tuberosum)*
Gayfeather *(Liatris spicata)*
Globe thistle *(Echinops ritro)*
Goat's beard *(Aruncus dioicus)*
Gooseneck loosestrife *(Lysimachia clethroides)*
Japanese anemone
Lady's mantle, lion's foot, bear's foot *(Alchemilla mollis)*
Lamb's ear *(Stachys byzantina)*
Michaelmas daisy, starwort, frost flower *(Aster)*
Pincushion flower *(Scabiosa)*
Pinks, carnation *(Dianthus)*
Phlox, creeping *(Phlox subulata)*
Phlox, garden *(Phlox paniculata)*
Primrose, cowslip, Jack-in-the-green *(Primula)*
Purple coneflower *(Echinacea purpurea)*
Red-hot poker, torch lily *(Kniphofia uvaria)*
Russian sage *(Perovskia)*
Shasta daisy *(Chrysanthemum x superbum)*
Showy stonecrop *(Sedum specabile)*
Soapwort, sweet Betty, bouncing bet *(Saponaria)*
Speedwell *(Veronica spicata)*
Thrift, sea pink, ladies cushion *(Armeria maritima)*
Tickseed, calliopsis *(Coreopsis)*
Vervain *(Verbena rigida)*
Whirling butterflies *(Gaura)*
Yarrow, squirrel tail nosebleed, old man's pepper *(Achillea)*

Sun-Loving Biennials:
Bellflower, Canterbury bells,
    bats in the belfry *(Campanula medium)*
Daisy, English, bonewort,
    bruisewort *(Bellis perennis)*
Foxglove, witches fingers, fairy
    gloves, dead men's bells, fairy
    thimbles, virgin's glove
    (Digitalis purpurea)
Hollyhock, alley orchids *(Alcea rosea)*
Sweet William *(Dianthus barbatus)*
Wallflower *(Cheiranthus)*

Annuals

*All sorts of flowers....
in goodly colours
gloriously array'd.*
-Edmund Spencer (1552-1599)

* Annuals have arrived at your garden centers and the colors are amazing. Annuals live, flower, form seed, and die in one season.
* Plant or sow annuals to gardens and containers when the danger of frost has past or when the soil temperature is above 60 degrees. Plant annuals early or late in the day to decrease transplanting stress. Overcast days are perfect, but not always available. Water plants before and after planting. Choose from my favorites for a great summer show.

African daisy, Star of the Veldt *(Osteospermum)*
Annual phlox *(Phlox drummondii)*
Annual statice *(Limonium sinuatum)*
Baby's breath *(Gypsophila elegans)*
Bells of Ireland, shell flower *(Moluccella laevis)*
Black-eyed Susan *(Rudbeckia hirta)*
Busy lizzy, lady's slippers, garden balsam, touch-me-not, jewelweed *(Impatiens balsamina)*
China aster *(Callistephus chinensis)*
China pink *(Dianthus chinensis)*
Cockscomb *(Celosia cristata)*
Cornflower, bachelor's button *(Centaurea cyanus)*
Dusty Miller, silver dust *(Senecio cineraria)*
Feverfew *(Chrysanthemum parthenium)*
Floss flower, painter's brush *(Ageratum)*
Four-o'-clock, marvel of Peru *(Mirabilis jalapa)*
Geranium *(Pelargonium)*
Gerbera daisy
Globe amaranth, bachelor's buttons *(Gomphrena globosa)*
Ladies' eardrops *(Fushia)*
Lantana
Lobelia
Love-in-a-mist, devil-in-a-bush, lady-in-the-bower *(Nigella)*
Love-lies-bleeding, chenille plant, kiss-me-over-the-garden-gate, tassel flower *(Amaranthus caudatus)*
Marigold *(Tagetes)*
Melampodium
Mexican aster *(Cosmos bipinnatus)*
Mexican sunflower *(Tithonia rotundifolia)*
Nasturtium, Indian cress, flame flower *(Tropaeolum majus)*
Painted nettle, Flame nettle *(Coleus)*
Parrots beak, lotus vine *(Lotus berthelotii)*
Periwinkle *(Vinca)*
Petunia
Pincushion flower *(Scabiosa)*
Poppy, California *(Eschscholzia californica)*
Poppy, corn, Iceland *(P. rhoeas, P. nudicaule)*
Rose moss, moss rose, sun plant *(Portulaca grandiflora)*

*When to the flowers so
   beautiful
The Father gave a name
There came a little blue-eyed
   one.
And timidly it came
And standing at the Father's
   feet
And gazing in His face
It said in a low and trembling
   tone
Yet with a gentle grace
"Dear Lord, the name Thou
   gives me
Alas I have forgot."
Kindly the Father looked Him
   down
And said, "Forget-me-not."*
-Anonymous

*We have a little garden, a
   garden of our own,
And everyday we water there
   the seeds that we have sown.
We love our little garden, and
   tend it with such care,
You will not find a folded leaf
   or blighted blossom there.*
Nursery rhyme

Garden Phenology

• When new growth appears on bur oaks, green ash and grapes, it is safe to plant tender vines, annuals, and perennials.

Garden Lore

• *When frogs are jumping about more than usual, expect a storm, But when they are piping in the evening, the next day will be fair.*

• *Calendula or "Mary's Gold" is considered sacred to many and is placed before holy statues.*

• *Plant African (Tagetes erecta) and French (Tagetes patula) marigolds to repel flies.*

When you have only two pennies left in the world, buy a loaf of bread with one, and a lily with the other.
—Chinese proverb

Do you see Christ in the passion flower? It's five petals and five sepals are the 10 apostles, the five stamens represent the wounds of Christ. The corona is the crown of thorns; the leaves are the hands of his harassers.

The passion flower, maypop, wild apricot or ocoee was chosen in 1919 for the Tennessee state wildflower by school children. The early Christian missionaries due to its resemblance to the Crucifixion named this prized flower of the Indians.

Sow passion flower vine to protect you and attract love.

Sage, Mexican bush, mealy-cup, scarlet (*Salvia*)
Snapdragon (*Antirrhinum majus*)
Snow-on-the mountain (*Euphorbia marginata*)
Spider flower (*Cleome hasslerana*)
Star cluster (*Penta*)
Stock, Brampton stock, gillyflowers, night violets (*Matthiola*)
Strawflower (*Helichrysum bracteatum*)
Sunflower (*Helianthus annuus*)
Sweet alyssum (*Lobularia maritima*)
Vervain (*Verbena*)
Zinnia, Brazilian marigold, youth-and-old-age (*Zinnia elegans*)

* For a greater impact, plant annuals closer together than recommended.
* If you are planting peat pots, be sure to bury the pot completely or tear the exposed rim to avoid drying of the peat pot on hot days.

* Annuals that do not require deadheading can save gardeners loads of work. Choose from:
Alyssum
Begonia
Coleus
Floss flower (*Ageratum*)
Impatiens
Lobelia
Love-in-a-mist (*Nigella*)
Sage (*Salvia*)
Spiderflower (*Cleome hasslerana*)
Vinca

* Pinch annuals such as zinnia, sage (*Salvia*), and petunia back to promote bushy growth when they are 4 to 6 inches tall.
* Thin and transplant self-sown annuals to desired location.

Bulbs, Corms, Rhizomes, and Tubers

... Iris, fair among the fairest, who, armed with golden rod, and winged with celestial azure, bearest, the message of some god.
-Henry Wadsworth Longfellow (1770-1850)

* Celebrate the state flower of Tennessee, the purple iris (*Iridaceae*). Named after the Greek goddess Iris, she was the goddess of the rainbow.
* Tender summer bulbs, corms, and tubers can be planted in the spring after your region's last frost date. These plantings should be completed by the mid-June. Plant bulbs twice as deep as bulbs and tubers are tall with exception of begonias and dahlias they need to be planted just below the surface of the soil.

Time to plant for summer beauty (* = *inches*)

	Planting Depth*	Spacing*
Angel wings (*Caladium*)	2	10
Blackberry lily (*Belamcanda chinensis*)	2	10
Calla lily (*Zantedeschia*)	4	12
Corn flag (*Gladiolus*)	6	4
Crocosmia	6	5
Dahlia	8	10 to 30
Elephant ear (*Caladium esculenta*)	8	24
Indian shot (*Canna*)	5	15 to 20
Iris	surface to 1	5 to 10
Lily (*Lilium spp.*)	Asiatic 6 to 8	15
	Oriental 3	15
Lily of the Nile (*Agapanthus*)	1 to 3	8 to 10
Lily-of-the-Valley (*Convallaria majalis*)	1 to 2	4
Peruvian daffodil (*Hymenocallis narcissiflora*)	3 to 5	12-18
Tuberose (*Polianthes tuberose*)	2 to 3	5 to 10
Yellow rain lily, Yellow fairy lily (*Zephyranthes sulphurea*)	1 to 2	3 to 4

* Plant gladiolus where they will be protected from the wind. Staking will help support these tall slender plants from the elements. Plant gladiolus every two weeks after last frost date until mid-June for a succession of blooms all season. The white gladiolus is hardier than any other color.
* Summer bulbs will need an application of 10-10-10 every 6 to 8 weeks throughout the growing season. Container grown bulbs can be fertilized weekly with liquid 20-20-20.
* Bulbs can be divided and transplanted when foliage has turned yellow.
* Plant late summer to fall-blooming bulbs as they become available.
> Autumn amaryllis, resurrection lilies, naked lilies, magic lily (*Lycoris squamigera*)
> Hardy cyclamen (*Cyclamen hederifolium*)
> Meadow saffron, autumn crocus, naked nannies, naked ladies, or Michaelmas crocus (*Colchicum speciosum*)
> Saffron Crocus (*Crocus sativus*)

* Have stakes available for tall-flowering lilies, peonies, dahlias, and gladiolus.
* It is best to provide support for dahlias before you plant them to avoid damaging tubers.
* Remove faded peony blooms as soon as they fade.
* Add a tree peony (*Peony suffruticosa*) to your landscape. Plant the graft union 6 inches below soil level.
* If it has been two years or more remove tulips after blooms fade; remove bulbs and foliage.
* Remove old flowering stalks from bearded irises.
* Try the remontant (reblooming) iris, they will produce irises again in the fall. You may want to choose fall appropriate color when buying this variety.
* Never deadhead small bulbs, which drop seed and spread. These small bulbs include grape hyacinth, pearls of Spain (*Muscari*), Siberian squill, cuckoo's boot (*Scilla*), and glory-of-the-snow (*Chionodoxa*).

A little rain and a little sun, and a little pearly dew, and pushing up and reaching out, then leaves and tendrils all about!   1800s song

*The garden with its little gate
of green,
Invites you to enter, and view
mysteries unseen,
Its vine laden bowers and
overhanging trees,
The air filled with sweetness,
the hum of the bees,
The flagged walks with iris
galore,
Of most beautiful coloring,
unknown before,
Pink, white, purple, yellow,
azure blue,
Mixed and mingled of every
hue,
You come away wondering,
can more beauty be seen
Than in the garden with its
little gate of green.*
                    Unknown

*Sweetness of Spring
memories bring
Of a place I long to be.
Land of Sunshine calls this
old heart of mine,
Come back to Tennessee.
Rocks and the rills deep
tinted hills,
Three's no spot so dear to me.
Where'er I roam still it's my
Home Sweet Home,
My own, my Tennessee.
When it's Iris time down in
Tennessee,
I'll be coming back to stay
Where the mockingbird sings
at the break of day
A lilting love song gay.
Where the Iris grows,
Where the Harpeth flows,
That is where I long to be.
There's a picture there that
lives in memory
When it's Iris time in
Tennessee.*
        Willa Waid Newman,
"When It's Iris Time In Tennessee"

Roses

Now I see the secret of the making of the best persons. It is to grow in the open air, and to eat and sleep with the earth.
    -Walt Whitman (1819-1892)

* If rain is scarce, keep roses watered so they receive at least 1 inch a week.
* Roses can still be planted or transplanted this month.
* Apply mulch to conserve water and reduce weeds.
* Add cow manure to rose bushes.
* Scatter crushed eggshells around rose bushes to deter slugs.
* Deadhead repeat flowering roses or cut to encourage more flowering.
* When cutting roses use a wide 45-degree angle; cut ¼ inch above an outward facing branch with a five-leaf cluster.
* Remove sucker growth that sprouts below the grafted union.
* Prune climbers, ramblers, and old roses that bloom once a year immediately after they bloom.
* Continue spray program to control black spot, mites, and powdery mildew.
* Continue to keep gardens weed free.

Herbs

Forget not that the earth delights to feel your bare feet and the winds long to play with your hair.
    -Kahlil Gibran (1883-1931)

* Plant warm-weather transplants after the last frost has passed.
* Plant marigolds for color in your herb garden.
* Direct sow these annual herbs to the garden after the last frost:
    Basil, sweet *(Ocimum basilicum)*
    Calendula *(Calendula officinalis)*
    Coriander *(Coriandrum sativum)*
    Fenugreek *(Trigonella foenum-graecum)*
    Nasturtium *(Tropaeolum majus)*

* If you like tarragon choose the "French tarragon;" it will give you the best flavor.
* Cut chives as needed for cooking to have freshness all season. Allow some to flower, otherwise continue to deadhead to decrease reseeding.
* Cut lovage all season and use in dishes that call for celery.
* Avoid planting fennel too close to vegetables; bad chemistry.
* Avoid planting different varieties of mint in the same garden. They will cross-pollinate and alter flavor, unless you remove the blooms.
* Keep weeds out of thyme or the weeds will take over.
* No garden should be without basil. Basil is a four-way win as it purifies air, deters flies and mosquitoes, stimulates the appetite, and flavors food.
* Add a container of mint to the porch to deter flies.
* Add color, scent, and flavor to your salad by growing, decorating, and eating the blooms of these favorite edible plants; be cautious that no chemicals have been applied.
    Bachelor's button *(Centaurea cyanus)*
    Bee balm *(Monarda)*, citrus
    Begonia stems, substitute for rhubarb
    Borage *(Borago officinalis)*, cucumber flavor
    Carnation *(Dianthus)*
    Cattails *(Typha* spp.)

Chive *(Allium schoenoprasum)*
Chrysanthemum, mild or bitter
Clary sage *(Salvia sclarea)*
Common milkweed *(Asclepias syriaca)*
Coriander *(Coriander sarivum)*
Dandelion *(Taraxacum officinale)*
Daylily *(Hemerocallis)*
English daisy *(Bellis perennis)*
Fuschia, sharp lemon flavor
Gardenia
Garlic, *(Allium sativum)*
Geranium *(Pelargonium)*, variety of scents
Gladiolus *(Gladiolus hortulanus)*
Hibiscus
Hollyhock *(Alcea rosea)*, sweet
Honeysuckle *(Lonicera)*, sweet
Hyssop *(Hyssopus officalis)*
Impatiens
Lavender *(Lavandula)*
Leek *(Allium porrum)*
Lemon *(Citrus limon)*
Lilac *(Syringa vulgaris)*
Marigold *(Tagetes)*, tarragon flavor
Marjoram *(Origanum vulgare)*
Marsh mallow *(Althaea officinalis)*
Mint *(Mentha)*
Mustard *(Brassica* spp.)
Nasturtium *(Tropaeolum majus)*, peppery flavor
Orange *(Citrus sinensis)*
Oregano *(Origanum vulgar)*
Pansy *(Viola wittrockiana)*
Peony *(Paeonia lactiflora)*
Petunia, mildly sweet
Plum *(Prunus* spp.)
Pot marigold *(Calendula officinalis)*, tangy
Primrose *(Primula vulgaris)*
Rose or rose hips *(Rosa)*, pleasing to the nose
Rosemary *(Rosmarinus officinalis)*
Rose-of-Sharon *(Hibiscus syriacus)*, mildly sweet
Sage *(Salvia)*
Snapdragon *(Antirrhinum majus)*
Spiderwort *(Tradescantia virginia)*
Squash *(Cucurbita* spp.), pleasing to the eye
Strawberry *(Fragaria ananassa)*
Sunflower *(Helianthus)*, eat the seeds or boil the buds
Thyme *(Thymus)*
Tulip *(Tulipa)*, slightly sweet
Violet *(Viola odorata)*, apple flavor
Water hyacinth *(Eichhornia crassipes)*
Water lily *(Nymphaea odorata)*
Winter savory *(Satureja montana)*
Yucca *(Yucca* spp.)

Never make the mistake of departing from nature, imagining to better by yourself…for art is embedded in nature.
And the artist who can extract it has it.
  -Albrecht Durer (1471-1528)

Garden Lore

• *Set sage in May and it will grow always.*
• *He that would live for aye should eat sage in May.*
• *Orange bergamot in your wallet will attract money.*
• *Rosemary, basil, fennel, rue or witch bane was planted by the front door to keep witches and evil away.*
• *Use crushed rue leaves around pet bedding to deter fleas.*
• *Plant thyme to attract fairies and St. John's wort to keep fairies away.*
• *Place rosemary under your pillow to deter evil dreams.*
• *Protect your infant from evil by placing a bundle of rosemary over its crib.*
• *Rosemary or "brides herb" was used in wedding ceremonies to deter evil.*
• *Rub anise leaves on your face to remove freckles.*
• *Grow caraway to protect your home from thieves.*
• *Chew on dill to cure hiccoughs.*

Do not eat from this list of plants and flowers!

Autumn crocus (*Colchicum autumnale*)
Azalea
Bloodroot (*Sanguinaria canadensis*)
Boxwood (*Buxus spp.*)
Burning bush (*Euonymus spp.*)
Buttercup (*Ranunculus spp.*)
Butterfly weed (*Asclepias spp.*)
Caladium
Calla
Carolina jasmine (*Gelsemium sempervirens*)
Castor bean (*Ricinus communis*)
Christmas rose (*Helleborus niger*)
Clematis
Daffodil (*Narcissus spp.*)
Delphinium
Four o'clock (*Mirabills jalapa*)
Foxglove (*Digitalis purpurea*)
Heavenly bamboo (*Nandina domestica*)
Hyacinth
Hyacinth bean (*Dolichos lablab*)
Hydrangea
Iris
Ivy (*Hedera helix*)
Lantana
Lily-of-the-valley (*Convallaria majalis*)
Lobelia
Mistletoe (*Phoradendron spp.*)
Morning glory (*Ipomoea violacea*)
Oleander (*Nerium oleander*)
Periwinkle (*Vinca spp.*)
Sweet pea (*Lathyrus spp.*)
Trumpet flower, chalice vine (*Solandra spp.*)
Windflower (*Anemone*)
Wisteria
Wolfsbane, monkhood (*Aconite*)

* Harvest mint for the Kentucky Derby mint juleps.

Aunt Sharon's Mighty Mint Julep
1) Create simple syrup with 1 cup granulated sugar and 1 cup water; bring to boil.
2) Add mint leaves (10 or 15).
3) Cool and remove leaves.
4) Pack julep cup with crushed ice.
5) Add 1 tablespoon of mint syrup and 1 ¼ oz. of Kentucky bourbon.
6) Top-off with water; lightly stir.
7) Garnish with a fresh sprig of mint and a sprinkle of powdered sugar.
8) Use a short straw to keep your nose close to the fresh mint.

Seeds

He who knows what sweets and virtues are in the ground, the plants, the waters, the heavens, and how to come to these enchantments- is the rich and royal man.
-Ralph Waldo Emerson (1803-1882)

* Harden seedlings and transplants in the garden after the last frost has passed. This process should take about 2 weeks. Begin with 2 hours a day and leave plants out a little longer each day.
* Soak seeds in water overnight if they have a hard shell; this will speed germination. Some examples are:

> Cup-and-saucer vine *(Cobaea scandens)*
> Four-o'clock *(Mirabilis jalapa)*
> Hyacinth bean *(Dolichos lablab)*
> Mealy-cup sage *(Salvia farinacea)*
> Moonflower *(Ipomoea alba)*
> Morning glory *(Ipomoea tricolor)*
> Nasturtium *(Tropaeolum majus)*
> Sweet pea *(Lathyrus odoratus)*

* Sow warm-weather annual flower seeds directly to the garden after danger of frost has past. New seedlings will perish if they dry-out before they become established.
* Sow annual vines. These annual vines will need a guide. Use light string or twine to direct the vine in a preferred direction.

> Black-eyed Susan vine *(Thunbergia alata)*
> Hyacinth bean *(Dolichos lablab)*
> Japanese hop *(Humulus japonicus)*
> Moonflower *(Ipomoea alba)*
> Morning glory *(Ipomoea purpurea)*
> Nasturtium *(Tropaeolum spp.)*
> Scarlet runner bean *(Phaseolus coccineus)*

* Save seeds to sow after torrential rains wash away the seeds you just planted or to fill in voids that didn't germinate.
* Thin seedlings that were sown directly to the garden when they are 2 to 4 inches tall to ensure each plant grows to its potential. Read seed packets for preferred spacing of plants. Thin by snipping weaker seedlings to avoid soil disturbance.
* Pinch seedlings to create bushy plants.
* Keep seed garden damp to ensure maximum germination.
* Mulch seedlings when they are 4 inches tall.
* It is best to clean seed-starting supplies now rather than wait until January.

Garden Lore

• *Pluck not the flower if you cherish the seed.*
• *If you can sit on the ground with your trousers down, its safe to sow your seeds.*

Garden Phenology

• *When maple trees have full-size leaves, sow morning glories.*

Garden Lore

• *Chew on a mint leaf to cure sores in the month.*
• *Rub garlic on skin that has been exposed to poison ivy.*
• *Rub mint leaves on the dining table to increase the appetites of your guests.*
• *Dried lady's bedstraw has a sweet fragrance when dried. This makes it the perfect choice when stuffing a mattress.*
• *Scatter bay leaves and pennyroyal on pantry shelves to deter roaches and flies.*
• *Hang bundles of mint and tansy in the house to deter flies.*
• *Rub tansy leaves on pets to help repel fleas.*
• *Create your own moth, spider, and mice repellent with sachets made of dried lavender and tansy. Cut thin cotton material into squares; create a pile of dried herbs and use ribbon or raffia to secure.*
• *Mary Magdolin used lavender oil to wash Jesus' feet.*

Garden Lore

• *Do not plant dill too close to carrots; bad chemistry.*

In May get a weed-hook, a crotch and a glove,
And weed out such weeds, as the corn do not love.
For weeding of winter corn, now it is best;
But June is the better for weeding the rest.
-Thomas Tusser (1515-1580)

Vegetables

Who loves a garden still his Eden keeps?
Perennial pleasure plants, and wholesome harvest reaps.
-Amos Bronson Alcott (1799-1888)

* Harden indoor-grown seedlings in a sheltered area outdoors. This process should take about two weeks.
* Thin seedlings sown early in the spring.
* Add Epsom salts to water when planting tomatoes and peppers to supply magnesium sulfate; 2 tablespoons to 1 gallon water.
* After tomatoes and peppers get their first buds apply Epsom salts again. Create a foliar spray; 1/2 tablespoons Epson Salts per 1 quart water. This application will create larger vegetables.
* Add 1 to 3 banana peels to soil around tomatoes and peppers for natural potassium and phosphorus.
* Provide supports for tomatoes, beans, and peas before they grow too big.
* Marigold roots release a toxin that kills root nematodes. Knowing this, plant marigolds among vegetables to protect them.
* When you have noticed that half of the foliage on shallots, garlic, and onions have flopped over, stop watering and allow the bulbs to dry. After a few weeks you can harvest, cure, and store in a cool dry place.
* Harvest broccoli before flowers open.
* Harvest lettuce from the outside leaves first. The inner leaves will continue to mature and produce more leaves.
* Plant vegetable transplants. Remember, most vegetables require at least 6 hours of sun.
>
> Asparagus crowns, (1 year old perennial)
> Broccoli
> Brussels sprouts
> Cabbage
> Cauliflower
> Cucumber
> Eggplant
> Onion sets
> Peppers
> Potatoes, 2 eye pieces
> Rhubarb crowns (perennial)
> Squash
> Sweet potato slips
> Tomato (snip side shoots and plant first set of leaves at soil level.)

* Sow vegetable seeds after last frost date.
>
> Beans, bush and pole, lima
> Beets
> Cabbage
> Carrots
> Chard
> Corn, sweet (Plant in blocks for better pollination, choose one variety for best flavor.)
> Cucumber

Endive
Kale
Kohlrabi
Lettuce
Mustard
Okra
Parsnips
Peas, late
Potatoes, Irish
Pumpkin
Radish
Rutabaga
Squash, yellow, summer
Zucchini

* Grow vegetables, such as zucchini, squash and pumpkins around root crops such as beets, carrots, and onions as a natural mulch.
* Lightly cover sown carrots with straw to protect seeds and seedlings from heavy rains.
* Fertilize corn when it is planted and again when it is knee-high.
* After cucumbers begin to bloom, fertilizer with 10-10-10, repeat every three weeks.
* Carrots are light feeders; be cautious of heavy fertilizing.
* Don't grow beans too close to onions, leeks, shallots, or garlic; bad chemisty.
* Continue to plant lettuce and salad crops for successive harvest.
* Harvest rhubarb by gripping base of the stalk and firmly pull stalk away from crown. Give a twist to remove stalk from crown. Dispose of leaves since they are toxic.
* Watch for insects and control early in the season to reduce problems.
* Plant herbs to control insects in the vegetable garden. The following list is often found in popular literature about gardening. Try the combinations and see what you think.

Anise repels aphids
Basil repels flies, aphids, asparagus beetles, and mosquitoes
Borage deters tomato hornworms
Catnip deters flea beetles
Chives repel aphids, decreases mildew on cucumbers and
  pumpkins,
Coriander repels aphids and spider mites
Elderberry repels aphids, carrot flies, and cucumber beetles
Garlic deters potato bugs and Japanese beetles
Geraniums deters Japanese beetles, corn earworms, and cabbage
  moths
Horsetail deters slugs and snails
Hyssop deters cabbage moths
Ivy deters corn wireworms
Marigolds deter cucumber beetles and tomato hornworms
Mint repels aphids, beetles, ants, and cabbage moths
Parsley repels asparagus beetles
Rosemary deters cabbage moths, bean beetles, and carrot flies
Rue deters Japanese beetles

Garden Phenology

• *When foxgloves bloom, expect the Mexican bean beetle larvae.*
• *When elm leaves are the size of a penny, plant kidney beans.*
• *When the shadbush flowers, plant potatoes.*
• *When dogwoods are at their peak and daylilies begin to bloom, it is time to plant tomatoes, corn, cabbage, spinach, peppers, and carrots.*
• *Plant corn and cabbage when oak leaves are the size of a dime or when apple blossoms begin to fall.*
• *When lilac blooms fade, plant cucumbers, corn, squash, and beans.*
• *Plant beets, Irish potatoes, bush beans and carrots when dandelions and wild violets are in bloom. Plant pole beans two weeks later.*
• *Set out tomato transplants when the first ladybug appear.*

Garden Phenology

• *When peach and plum trees are in full bloom, plant hardy crops.*

What I enjoy is not the fruits alone, but the soil itself, its nature and its power.
-Cicero (106-43 B.C.)

Sage deters cabbage moths, carrot flies and tomato hornworms
Tansy deters cucumber beetles, Japanese beetles, squash bugs, ants, and aphids.
Thyme deters cabbageworms
Wormwood repels cabbageworms, deters flea beetles, and carrot flies

* Wrap aluminum foil or felt around the stalks of cabbage and broccoli to prevent cutworms from eating stems.
* Use garden space wisely by planting cucumbers and melons among corn.
* Plant radishes and garlic around cucumbers, melons, squash, peas, and beans to repel insects.
* Sow beans with eyes down for better germination. Since beans are top-heavy, heel soil around base of plants for support, after beans are actively growing.
* Harvest spinach, peas, lettuce, onions, kale, and kohlrabi.
* May 15 celebrate the feast day of St. Isidore, patron saint of the farmer.

Fruit

Hail, bounteous May, that dost inspire
Mirth and youth and warm desire!
Woods and groves are of thy dressing,
Hill and dale doth boast thy blessing.
John Milton (1608-1674)

* Remove sucker growth and weeds from around fruit trees and apply mulch. Keep mulch away from trunk.
* Remove flowers from new strawberry plants to encourage better root development and increase development of runners. Deadheading now will give you more fruit next year.
* Tuck straw under strawberry plants to keep fruit clean and to conserve water.
* Protect berries from birds by covering with protective netting.
* Thin brambles and fruit on apples, plums, peaches, and pear trees.
* For larger berries, prune cane tips on brambles.
* Train grape vines.
* Sow seeds of cantaloupe, muskmelon, and watermelon directly to the garden after last frost date.

Beneath these fruit-tree boughs that shed
Their snow-white blossoms on my head,
With brightest sunshine round me spread
Of spring's unclouded weather,
In this sequestered nook how sweet
To sit upon my orchard-seat!
And birds and flowers once more to greet,
My last year's friends together.
William Wordsworth (1770-1850)

My beloved spake, and said unto me,
Rise up, my love, my fair one and come away.
For, lo, the winter is past,
The rain is over and gone;
The flowers appear on the earth;
The time of the singing of birds is come,
And the voice of the turtle is heard in our land;
And the fig tree putteth forth her green figs,
And the vines with the tender grape give a good smell.
Arise, my love, my fair one, and come away.
-The Song of Solomon 2:10-13

Trees and Shrubs

Come ramble awhile through this exquisite weather
Of days that are fleet to pass,
When the stem of the willow shoots out a green feather,
And buttercups burn in the grass!
        -Edgar Fawcett (1847-1904)

* Finish pruning spring-flowering shrubs and trees after blooms fade and before new growth begins. Prune no more than 1/3 of entire plant at one time.

> Beautybush *(Kolkwitzia amabilis)*
> Deutzia
> Flowering cherry *(Prunus)*
> Flowering quince *(Chaenomeles)*
> Forsythia
> Lilac *(Syringa)*
> Magnolia
> Mock orange *(Philadelphus)*
> Mountain laurel *(Kalmia latifolia)*
> Pieris
> Pyracantha
> Rhododendron and azaleas
> Spirea, spring bloomers
> Summersweet *(Clethra)*
> Viburnum
> Weigela

* Prune winterkilled branches from crape myrtles. Prune to green wood after new growth begins.
* Continue to prune dead, damaged, and diseased branches from plant material.
* Trim and shape hedges such as yew, hemlock, and arborvitae.
* Remove sucker growth from lilac.
* Now that the chance of frost has passed, prune boxwoods, topiaries, and holly shrubs.

*Since 1947 the Tennessee state tree has been the yellow poplar or tulip poplar *(Liriodendron tulipifera)*. A member of the magnolia family, its blooms are unique with yellow-green petals and an orange inner covering.

The maple puts her corals on in May,
While loitering frosts about the lowlands cling...
        -James Russell Lowell (1819-1891)

Garden Lore

• *Sow morning glories with melons to help melons germinate; good chemistry.*
• *Plant nasturtiums under apple trees to decrease aphids.*
• *"Blackberry winter" is a mild cold spell that arrives as the blackberries bloom.*
• *In the middle of May comes the tail of winter.*

• *Days before Ascension Thursday (Rogation Days) were set-aside for days of prayer to ensure a bountiful harvest. Farmers would go into the orchard and sing:*
  Stand fast, root; bear well, top;
  God send us a yowling sop!
  Every twig, apple big,
  Every bough, apple enow,
  Hats full, caps full,
  Fill quarter sacks full!

• *If honeysuckle is brought into the house, a wedding will soon be announced.*
• *Place honeysuckle in the bedroom to promote erotic dreams.*
• *To protect from drowning, Irish immigrants carried a piece of ash.*
• *The small branches of the May tree or English Hawthorne were used to make the crown of thorns that Christ wore.*
• *Use elder leaves to deter flies and wasps.*
• *Don't make a birch broom in May or you will sweep your family away.*
• *When dogwoods bloom, it will frost no more.*

To the fairy land afar
Where the Little People are;
Where the clover-tops are
*   trees,*
And the rain-pools are the
*   seas,*
And the leaves, like little
*   ships,*
Sail about on tiny trips;
And above the Daisy tree
Through the grasses,
High o'er head the Bumble
*   Bee*
Hums and passes.
*   -Robert Louis Stevenson (1850-*
*   1894)*

Crow on the fence,
rain will go hence,
Crow on the ground,
Rain will come down.

Who bends a knee
Where violets grow
A hundred secret
Things shall know.
*   -Rachel Field (1894-1942)*

Garden Lore

• *Blooms of the dandelion or wild*
endive will close before a rain
shower.
• *"The devil's milk pail" refers to the*
white sap of the dandelion. This
white sap used to be a remedy for
removing warts.
• *Make your wishes come true by*
rubbing the white sap of a dande-
lion on your skin
• *Who doffs his coat on a winter*
day will gladly put it on in May.

Lawn Care

Whatever a man's age, He can reduce it several years by putting a bright-colored flower in his buttonhole.
*   -Mark Twain (1835-1910)*

Maintenance

* Adjust mower to cut higher to allow grass to grow fuller, choke weeds, and shade roots from the hot summer sun.

Insect and Weed Control

* Depending on when you first applied a pre-emergent herbicide, a second application can be made if your problem is serious with crabgrass or annual bluegrass. (Wait at least 8 weeks between these applications).
* Weed control can be done using liquid or granular. Granular must be applied to damp lawn with no chance of rain for two days and temperatures need to be above 65 degrees for this application to work properly.
* If you have a grub or insect problem, now is a great time to apply an insecticide.

I know, blue, modest violets,
Gleaming with dew at morn,
I know the place you came from
And the way that you are born.
When God cut holes in heaven,
The holes the stars look through,
He let the scraps fall down to earth --
The little scraps are you.
*   -Anonymous*

Composting

We can never have enough of nature.
*   -Henry David Thoreau (1817-1862)*

* Keep compost heap turned and damp. Air and moisture will speed decomposition.
* If the pile is not hot and steamy you may need to add water or absorb excess moisture by applying leaf matter, sawdust or shredded newspaper.

Water Ponds

When you put your hand in a flowing stream, you touch the last that has gone before and the first of what is still to come.
-Leonardo da Vinci (1452-1519)

* Lift and divide large clumps of pond plants. Divide when new growth is midway between water and container.
* Replant tender tropical plants that you overwintered when water temperature reaches 70 degrees.
* Try these Tennessee hardy aquatic and waterside plants. Choose from marginal or bog, floating plants, and lilies:

> Anacharis *(Egeria densa)*, oxgenating
> Arrow arum *(Pelrandra virginica)*, bog or marginal
> Arrowhead *(Sagittaria latifolia)*
> Bog bean *(Menyanthes trifoliata)*
> Butterfly fern *(Salvinia rountrundifolia)*, floater
> Canna, water *(Thalia dealbata)*, bog or marginal
> Cardinal flower *(Lobelia cardinalis)*, bog or marginal
> Cattail *(Typha spp.)*, bog or marginal
> Four-leaf water clover *(Marsilea mucronata)*, floater
> Golden club *(Orontium aquaticum)*, bog or marginal
> Greater spearwort *(Ranunculus lingua)*
> Iris, (Japanese, Luisiana, yellow or blue flag), bog or marginal
> Lizard's tail *(Saururus cernuus)*, bog or marginal
> Lotus *(Nelumbo spp.)*, floater
> Marsh marigold *(Caltha palustris)*
> Myriad leaf *(Myriophyllum verticillatum)*
> Pickerel rush *(Pontederia cordata)*, bog or marginal
> Sweet flag, also in variegated *(Acornus calamus)*, bog or marginal
> Water arum *(Calla palustris)*
> Water dragon, lizard's tail *(Saururus cernuus)*
> Water lily *(Nymphaea)*, floater
> Water milfoil *(Myriophyllum spp.)*, oxgenating
> Water plantain *(Alisma plantago-aquatica)*
> Water violet *(Hottonia palustris)*

* Feed established plants every three weeks with an all-purpose fertilizer such as 10-10-10 (1 tablet per gallon pot).

* It would be wise to stay away from these over agressive water plants:
> Bamboo
> Chameleon plant *(Houttuynia cordata)*
> Duckweed
> Horsetail *(Equisetum hyemale)*
> Water hyacinth *(Eichhornia crassipes)*

May
Indoor
Gardening

Flowers are my music.
-Sir Thomas Arnold (1795-1842)

* If you kept the poinsettia from Christmas go ahead and repot. Set it outside in a protected area that receives dapple rays of sun throughout the day.
* Divide and transplant houseplants that have become too large or leggy.
* As soon as the last frost has past, amaryllis bulbs can be moved outdoors for the summer. Set pots outside or transplant bulb to shade garden for the summer. Lightly feed bulbs monthly with a liquid 20-20-20 fertilizer throughout the summer. Decrease fertilizer and water as summer passes to prepare for dormancy.

June Garden Chore List

In the Garden:

- ❑ Apply water to gardens if rainfall is inadequate
- ❑ Apply a pre-emergent weed preventer to gardens.
- ❑ Fertilize gardens early this month with a light application of 10-10-10.

Flowers and Herbs:

- ❑ Add fall-blooming plants to your landscape.
- ❑ Divide spring-blooming perennials after blooms fade.
- ❑ Remove cool-weather annuals and replace with warm-weather annuals.
- ❑ Pinch annuals to create compact plants with more blooms.
- ❑ Trim bulb foliage that has turned yellow.
- ❑ Bulbs can be divided and transplanted after their foliage has turned yellow.
- ❑ Complete summer bulb planting.
- ❑ Remove spent flowers to encourage more blooms.

Seeds:

- ❑ It's not too late to sow annual seeds.

Vegetables and Fruits:

- ❑ Harvest vegetables as they ripen.
- ❑ Use row covers to prevent insect damage to young plants.
- ❑ Practice crop rotation to decrease insects and disease.
- ❑ Try successive planting.
- ❑ Thin fruit 6 to 8 inches apart on fruit trees.

Trees and Shrubs:

- ❑ Plant trees and shrubs.
- ❑ Wait to transplant trees and shrubs this fall.
- ❑ Prune hedges.
- ❑ Take softwood cuttings from new growth on trees and shrubs.

Lawn Care:

- ❑ Raise lawn mower to 2.5 to 3 inches and stay there until fall.
- ❑ Do not fertilize cool-season lawns until mid-October.
- ❑ Spot kill broadleaf and grassy weeds with a squirt bottle of post-emergent herbicide.

Composting:

- ❑ Add spent flowers and foliage to compost pile.
- ❑ Turn compost pile more frequently as weather warms.
- ❑ Keep compost pile moist to speed decomposition.

Water Ponds:

- ❑ Top-up pond with fresh water.
- ❑ Remove dying debris and deadhead plants before they fall into the water.

Indoors Plants:

- ❑ Fertilize houseplants with liquid 20-20-20.

Chapter 4
June Garden

A noise like of a hidden brook
In the leafy month of June,
That to the sleeping woods all night
Singeth a quiet tune.
    -Samuel Taylor Coleridge (1772-1834)

As the ever so elegant iris fades, June brings a kaleidoscope of color to the landscape. Roses reign with grace and charm, as hydrangeas continue to steal the show. Daylilies naturalize along road banks and the fields are full of chicory and Queen Anne's lace. The sun reddens as the sky grows hazy, and we frown on the sticky muggy days that lie before us.

Time spent in the garden grows shorter, due to the growing heat of summer. It's best to find yourself there early in the day and late in the evening to capture your peace of mind. Everyone needs a garden in his or her life. Plants continue to be great companions that always listen. It is amazing how soil, seeds and water can create beauty, fragrance, and serenity. Being in the garden can be just as rewarding as working in it. This hobby brings positive results for those who experience it.

With our daytime temperatures rising every month we must create our gardens to thrive in heat. This month jot down a few notes on what plants can take the heat and plants that should be avoided. After summer solstice, comes a time of celebration for gardeners and a time to bless the land. Midsummer's Day marks the halfway mark between planting and harvest; gardeners can breath easier as the garden season hits a downward slide.

Observe National Garden Week and World Environment Day in your area and attend some activities to educate you and your family. This is also a good time to lie in your hammock, sip lemonade, and observe your garden from a different point of view. Take time to breathe deeply and smell the life that nature provides. When you hear crickets sing and fireflies light up the night, summer is here.

General Maintenance

Garden Lore

Water is the eye of a landscape.
-Vincent Stuckey Lean (1820-1899)

• *Gray evening sky, not one day dry.*
• *A leak in June brings harvest soon.*
• *A cold wet June spoils the rest of the year.*
• *The early settlers and Native Americans called the full moon this month the Strawberry Moon or Rose Moon. It is so low in the sky you can almost pick it.*
• *When the dew is on the grass, rain will never come to pass.*
• *When grass is dry at morning light, look for rain before night.*

Water

* Apply water to gardens if rainfall is inadequate. One inch of water is necessary every week. Less frequent, deep watering will allow roots to grow deeper. Deep roots are more likely to survive a drought than shallow roots. Remember, plants are 90% water.
* Try to avoid wetting foliage when watering. Overhead watering will increase spread of disease.
* Don't forget to monitor those plants placed under eaves and tall evergreens.
* Water at dusk and dawn to conserve water.
* New plants will need more water than established plants. Soaker hoses are very helpful when watering a new or existing garden. Monitor water by placing a pan under the soaker hose.

In-The-Garden Maintenance

All my hurts my garden spades can heal.
- Ralph Waldo Emerson (1803-1882)

* War of the vines starts this month. They seem to come from everywhere and grow on everything. Vines need to be kept clear unless you can identify them and choose to keep them.
* Keep gardens weed-free; remove weeds before they bloom and set seed or they will multiple fast. Use a scuffle hoe, stirrup hoe or your hands to remove weeds, roots, and all. Weeding is easier if the soil is damp.
* Reapply a pre-emergent weed preventer to borders to prevent weed seeds from germinating. Do not apply where you would like plants to reseed themselves.
* Stake asters, foxgloves, delphiniums, lilies, and hollyhocks to prevent flopping over.
* Wait to mow wildflower meadow when seedpods are empty.
* Cultivate soil to increase oxygen and reduce weeds.
* Fertilize gardens early this month with a light application of 10-10-10.
* Enjoy the evenings and watch for the firefly or lightning bug. The firefly has been named one of the Tennessee state insects. Loved by children everywhere, they use their rhythmic flashes of light to attract a mate.

That beautiful season the summer!
Filled was the air with a dreamy and magical light;
And the landscape lay as if new
Created in all the freshness of childhood.
-Henry Wadsworth Longfellow (1807-1882)

Container Gardening

If the day and the night are such that you greet them with joy, and life emits a fragrance like flowers and sweet-scented herbs…. that is your success.
    Henry David Thoreau (1817-1862)

* Container gardens, window boxes and raised beds will need monitoring for moisture loss during the next few months.
* Use ice cubes in hanging baskets and containers for a slow-drip watering method.

Perennials and Biennials

*The butterfly is a flying flower,
The flower a tethered butterfly.*
    -Ecouchard Le Brun (1729-1807)

* It is not too late to add fall-blooming plants to your landscape.
    Chrysanthemum
    Goldenrod (*Salidago*)
    Joe-Pye weed (*Eupatorium fistulsum*)
    Michaelmas daisy (*Aster*)
    Showy stonecrop (*Sedum spectabile*)
    Toad lily (*Tricyrtis*)

* Pinch tips of all runners on wisteria to reduce climbing and control growth.
* Divide spring-blooming perennials after blooms fade.
* Try a new favorite perennial in your garden maybe the perennial of the year.
* Prune ground covers to keep in shape.
* Continue to water new clematis vines deeply throughout the season to ensure survival.
* Complete transplanting of self-sown perennials to desired location.
* As daylily blooms fade, remove entire stalk to base of plant.
* Take stem cuttings from these perennials: Refer to page 122 for instructions
    Baby's breath (*Gypsophila paniculata*)
    Bellflower (*Campanula*)
    Boltonia
    Candytuft (*Iberis*)
    Catmint (*Nepeta x faassenii*)
    Coreopsis
    Cransbill geranium
    Crysanthemum
    Garden phlox (*Phlox paniculata*)

Garden Lore

• *Much wind brings rain.*
• *Count the stars inside the halo of the moon to know the number of days until rain.*
• *Northern air brings weather fair.*
• *June damp and warm does the farmer no harm.*
• *If the bees stay at home, rain will soon come. If they fly away, fine will be the day.*
• *Till the soil on Midsummer's Day, not feast aye famine will come your way.*
• *Wash your face with the dew on Midsummer's Day to capture youth and beauty.*
• *Walking through the Midsummer's Day dew will protect your feet from getting chapped.*
• *A busy hoe gathers no rust.*

A rusty hoe in June is a sure sign of a poor gardener.
    -Genesee Farmer (1838)

*A nation that destroys its soils destroys itself.
Forests are the lungs of our land,
purifying the air and giving fresh strength to our people.*
    -Franklin D. Roosevelt (1882-1945)

Garden Lore

• *Carry chicory for good luck!*

• *If Ivy grows on a maiden's grave, she died of love; if no ivy grows, her soul is not at rest.*

• *Grow ivy on your home to repel evil.*

• *Maidenhair ferns were believed to be the hair of Venus. A potion was created to help ladies develop beauty, grace, and love.*

• *Put a daisy under your pillow to dream of true love.*

• *When jasmine forms its buds, the girls begin to feel the urge of love.*

• *Verbena hung over the front door will protect you and your family from evil.*

• *White sweetclover (Melilotus alba) can be grown and harvested for clothing sachets or potpourri. Its sweet fragrance will deter moths as well as freshen your wardrobe.*

Goodnight, fair yarrow,
Thrice goodnight to thee;
I hope before tomorrow's
     dawn
My true love I shall see.
            -Mother Goose

Goldenrod (*Solidago*)
Pink turtlehead (*Chelone lyonii*)
Pinks (*Dianthus*)
Plumbago (*Ceratostigma plumbaginoides*)
Russian sage (*Perovskia atriplicifolia*)
Sage (*Salvia*)
Showy stonecrop (*Sedum spectabile*)
Soapwort (*Saponaria x lempergii*)
Sneezeweed (*Helenium*)
Snow-in-summer (*Cerastium tomentosum*)
Spike speedwell (*Veronica spicata*)
Vervain (*Verbena*)
Wall rock cress (*Arabis caucasica*)
Wisteria
Wormwood (*Artemisia*)
Yarrow (*Achillea*)

Vines:

Clematis
Climbing hydrangea (*Hydrangea anomala subsp. petiolaris*)
Ivy (*Hedra*)
Porcelain vine (*Ampelopsis brevipedunculata*)

Garden Lore

• *Early American farmers called ferns 'devil brushes.' The ferns were dried during the Mid-summer's bonfire and hung in the home to protect the family from summer storms. Farmers would also burn ferns to induce rain upon their crops. The silver nitrate that is produced by the burning leaves was thought to bring rain.*

• *On St. John's Eve or Mid-Summer's Eve search for a common fern. Legend holds that it is in bloom at night and he who has possession of it will find a hidden treasure. If you eat the seeds of the fern you will become invisible.*

• *Early American maidens would pick three or four thistles. They would cut the tips and name each thistle after their admirers. After sleeping with the thistles under her pillow, the thistle showing new growth was the man for her.*

• *Yarrow (Devil's plaything or Devil's rattle) was also consulted for love. Upon finding the first spring yarrow, preferably during a new or waxing moon, pick a bloom and say:*
Yarrow, sweet yarrow, the first I have found!
In the name of my lady, I pluck from the ground.
As father loved mother, taking her for his dear,
In my own dreams tonight, may my true love appear?

• *Place yarrow under your pillow to bring the love of your life to your dreams. If you dream of yarrow, beware!*

• *Hang a bundle of yarrow over your wedding bed for love to last at least seven years.*

• *If you can put yarrow in your hat and fly, you are most likely a witch.*

-In France the corn poppy or Flanders poppy
(Papaver rhoeas) was widely used on the
graves of fallen solders.

In Flanders fields the poppies blow
Between the crosses, row on row
That mark our places; and in the sky
The larks, still bravely, singing, fly
Scarce heard amid the guns below.

We are the Dead. Short days ago
We lived, felt dawn, saw sunset glow,
Loved and were loved, and now we lie
In Flanders fields.
       -Fallen soldier, Lt.-Col. John McCrae

Garden Lore

- If a lady picks seven different wildflowers on Midsummer's Eve Day and walks home quietly and backwards, she may dream of her future husband if she places the bundle under her pillow.
- Young ladies who rub pansies across their eyes will fall in love at next sight.
- Place calendula petals under your bed to ward-off evil.
- To relieve the itch from poison ivy, rub affected area with the juice from touch-me-nots *(Impatiens)*.

Annuals

Gently steed our spirits, carrying with
them dreams of flowers.
      -William Wordsworth (1770-1850)

* Completely remove cool-weather annuals such as pansies and replace with warm-weather annuals such as vinca or sage.
* Pinch annuals to create compact plants with more blooms.
* Annuals in containers will need to be watered daily if not twice a day.
* Complete transplanting self-sown annuals to a desired location.
* Work toward completion of planting warm-weather annuals.
* Reapply 10-10-10 or 14-14-14 to annual flowerbeds. Space applications 6 to 8 weeks apart.
* During wet summers, apply Epsom salts to water when watering plants to compensate for magnesium and iron being leached from of the soil.

Bulbs, Corms, Rhizomes, and Tubers

A bird in the boughs sang "June,"
And "June" hummed a bee
In a bacchic glee
As he tumbled over and over
Drunk with the honey-dew.
      -Clinton Scollard (1860-1932)

* Bulbs can be divided and transplanted after their foliage has turned yellow. Stop watering bulbs after leaves turn brown. If you use a soaker hose in your garden, move the hose away from the bulb site until next spring.
* Trim bulb foliage that has turned yellow. This will immediately improve the appearance of your garden. Always trim dead foliage at the soil line. Remove dead foliage and put in your compost pile or discard. Pulling and yanking dead foliage can injure bulbs.

Shall I sing of
happy hours
Numbered by opening
and closing flowers?
  -Hartley Coleridge (1796-1849)

As is the gardener, such is the garden.
      -Hebrew

Garden Lore

• *Deliver a proposal of marriage the Victorian way by giving an armload of irises.*

• *The three petals of the iris are symbols of faith, wisdom, and valor on the Fleur-de-lis or Flower of Louis VII of France.*

* Prune faded flower stocks from Siberian and bearded irises to the rhizome.
* Bearded irises can be divided and transplanted after blooms fade.
* Complete summer bulb planting except continue to plant gladiolus for successive summer blooms.
* Give summer-blooming bulbs a liquid fertilizer such as 20-20-20.

> *Where flowers bloom so does hope.*
> -Lady Bird Johnson (b.1912)

Roses

> *…I know a little garden-close*
> *set thick with lily and red rose,*
> *Where I would wander if I might*
> *From dewy dawn to dewy night…*
> -William Morris (1834-1896)

* Cultivate soil shallow and gently beneath roses.
* Prune one-third of old canes on once-blooming ramblers and climbers after blooms fade.
* Remove crossed canes and twiggy growth to increase airflow.
* Remove spent flowers to encourage more blooms. Cut above an outward facing bud with five leaflets.
* Remove sucker growth.
* To decrease spider mites wash under-side of leaves with water twice a week when daytime temperatures are hot. Removing lower leaves will also decrease spider mites and decreases black spot.
* Continue spray program to control black spot, mites, and powdery mildew.
* Watch for Japanese beetles, which can devour both leaves and flowers. In the early morning before they become really active, using a small bucket of soapy water, tap them so they fall into the bucket and drown.
* Add 2 inches of woody mulch if needed to conserve water.
* Secure climbing roses as they produce new canes. Use a stretchable material or jute tied loosely around canes.

> *It is the month of June,*
> *The month of leaves and roses*
> *When pleasant sights salute the eyes,*
> *And pleasant scents the noses.*
> -Nathaniel Parker Willis (1806-1867)

> *I remember, I remember,*
> *The roses, red and white,*
> *The vi'lets, and the lily-cups,*
> *Those flowers made of light.*
> -Thomas Hood (1799-1845)

> *I saw the sweetest flower*
> *Wild nature yields,*
> *A fresh blown musk-rose*
> *'twas the first that threw*
> *its sweet upon the summer;*
> *graceful it grew….*
> - John Keats (1795-1821)

> *A Sepal, petal, and a thorn*
> *Upon a common summer's morn,*
> *A flash of dew, a bee or two,*
> *A breeze*
> *A caper in the trees,*
> *And I'm a rose!*
> -Emily Dickinson (1830-1886)

> *A thorn defends the rose, harming only those who would steal the blossom.*
> -Chinese proverb

*Send a silent, personal message the way the Victorian's did by using the language of leaves and flowers or Florigraphy.

Aloe.................................*Healing*
Amaranth ....*With affection*
Amaryllis.............................*Pride*
Anemone ....*Unfading love*
Angelica ....*Inspiration*
Apple blossom.......................*Preference*
Aspen..................................*Fearlessness*
Aster ....*Variety, afterthought, fidelity, love*
Azalea ....*Temperance, womanhood*
Baby's breath ....*Pure heart, festivity, gaiety*
Basil ....*Love or hate*
Bay.....................................*Victory, strength*
Bee balm ....*Virtue*
Beech ....*Tolerance*
Begonia ....*Beware*
Bells-of-Ireland ....*Whimsy, good luck*
Bittersweet ....*Truth*
Bleeding heart ....*Love*
Bluebell ....*Constancy*
Borage.................................*Bravery*
Buttercup.............................*Cheerfulness, riches*
Caladium..............................*Great joy and delight*
Calendula ....*Winning grace, joy*
Calla lily, white ....*Sophistication, seduction*
Camellia ....*Perfected loveliness, gratitude*
Carnation, pink ....*Maternal love, beauty, pride*
Carnation, purple ....*Capriciousness*
Carnation, red ....*Deep love*
Carnation, red (light) ....*Admiration*
Carnation, striped..................*Refusal of love*
Carnation, white....................*Symbol of democracy, pure love, good luck*
Carnation, yellow ....*Fascination or rejection*
Cattail.................................*Peace*
Chamomile............................*Wisdom, patience*
Cherry ....*Composure*
Chestnut bud........................*Readiness to learn*
Chicory................................*Self love*
Chrysanthemum, red ....*Love*
Chrysanthemum, white ....*Truthfulness*
Chrysanthemum, yellow..........*Cheerfulness or slighted love*
Clematis ,,,,.........................*Mental beauty*
Clover, shamrock...................*Good luck, light-heartedness*
Columbine............................*Resolution*
Coriander ....*Lust*
Cornflower, bachelor's button ..*Delicacy, felicity, unity*
Crocus.................................*Cheerfulness*
Cyclamen ....*Shyness, modesty*
Dahlia..................................*Good taste*
Daisy...................................*Innocence, simplicity, gentleness, loyal love*

Garden Lore

Legend holds that all roses were once thornless. As Cupid kissed the sweet smelling blossom, he was stung on his lip by a bee. Cupid took revenge and shot arrows at the bee creating thorns on roses.

A rose becomes more beautiful between two thorns.
                        -John Lyly (1554-1606)

*Mary, Mary, quite contrary,
How does your garden grow?
Silver bells and cockle shells
And pretty maids all in a row.*
                        -Mother Goose

Dandelion..............................*Wishes come true*
Dead leaves...........................*Sadness*
Dill ....*Good cheer, survival*
Dogwood...............................*Durability*
Dusty miller...........................*Happiness, industriousness*
Elm ....*Reliability*
Eucalyptus.............................*Protection*
Evergreen bough ....*Everlasting life*
Fennel ....*Worthy of all praise*
Fern......................................*Discretion, fascination, sincerity*
Fern, asparagus ....*Airy grace*
Feverfew................................*Good health, warmth, flirt, protection*
Fir ....*Time*
Forget-me-not.........................*Remembrance, true love, good memories*
Forsythia ....*Anticipation*
Foxgloves ....*Insincerity*
Freesia ....*Innocence*
Fuchsia.................................*Good taste*
Gardenia...............................*Secret love, ecstasy*
Geranium, red ....*Comfort, beauty without virtue*
Geranium, scented ....*Happiness*
Gladiolus ....*Generosity, strength of character*
Goldenrod ....*Encouragement, precaution*
Grape hyacinth ....*Birth*
Grass ....*Submission*
Hawthorne ....*Hope*
Heather ....*Admiration, wishes come true,*
Heliotrope ....*Faithfulness, devotion*
Hemlock................................*You will be my death*
Hibiscus ....*Delicate beauty*
Holly ....*Love, friendship, eternal life*
Hollyhock ....*Ambition*
Honesty.................................*Honesty*
Honeysuckle...........................*Devoted affection, bonds of love, generosity*
Hyacinth................................*Sport, game, play, loveliness*
Hydrangea.............................*Thanks for understanding, boastfulness*
Hyssop ....*Deter evil*
Iris..*Faith, wisdom, and valor, a message for thee*
Iris, yellow............................*Passion*
Ivy..*Wedded love, constancy, trustfulness, fidelity*
Jasmine ....*Grace, elegance*
Larkspur ....*An open heart*
Laurel leaves.........................*Glory, perseverance*
Lavender ....*Devotion, luck, success, happiness*
Lilac ....*Youthful innocence, romance*
Lily, orange...........................*Hatred*
Lily, white..............................*Purity, virginity*
Lily-of-the-valley ....*Sweetness*
Linden branches....................*Romance*
Magnolia ....*Perseverance, sweetness, love of nature*
Marigold................................*Remembrance, grief*
Marjoram ....*Joy, happiness*

Mint ....*Warmth of feeling, protect from illness*
Mistletoe.................................*Fertility*
Mock orange ....*Deceit, counterfeit*
Morning glory.........................*Affection*
Moss.......................................*Charity*
Moss rose ....*I admire you from afar, voluptuous love*
Morning glory.........................*Affection*
Myrtle.....................................*Love, marriage*
Narcissus ....*Respect, chivalry, regard, egotism*
Nasturtium ....*Patriotism*
Oak leaves..............................*Heroism, hospitality*
Oleander ....*Beware*
Olive branch...........................*Peace*
Orange blossoms.....................*Bridal festivities, chastity, thoughts, loving thoughts*
Orchid, pink ....*Pure affection, beauty*
Oregano ....*Happiness*
Palm leaves ....*Victory*
Pansy ....*Good thoughts of you*
Parsley....................................*Merriment*
Passion flower ....*Faith*
Peach blossom ....*Captive heart*
Peony ....*Wedded bliss, aphrodisiac*
Peppermint ....*Warmth, cordiality*
Petunia ....*Don't despair, your presence soothes me*
Phlox......................................*Proposal of love, agreement*
Pine..*Hope*
Plum Blossoms.......................*Fidelity*
Poppy, red ....*Consolation*
Primrose ....*Youth*
Ranunculus, white ....*Overpowering interest in you*
Rosa, centifolia, cabbage rose ..*Ambassador of love*
Rose, Amethyst ....*I will love you forever*
Rose, coral..............................*Longevity, admiration, desire*
Rose, cream............................*Perfection*
Rose, golden...........................*Jealousy*
Rose, lavender ....*Rarity, love at first sight*
Rose, orange...........................*I love you with enthusiasm*
Rose, peach ....*Immortality, modesty*
Rose, pink ....*Grace, beauty, youth, innocent love*
Rose, red ....*I love you, passion*
Rose, rose. ....*Pride, shyness*
Rose, white.............................*Silence, keep my secret, beauty and respect, birth*
Rose, white/pink......................*Two roses of two different colors; unity, commitment*
Rose, yellow ....*Friendship, I love another, joy, jealousy*
Rose, a single ....*Simplicity, perpetual love*
Rose bud ....*Hope, innocence*
Rosemary................................*Remembrance*
Rudbeckia ....*Justice*
Queen Anne's lace..................*Protection*

Rosemary is for remembrance
Between us day and night,
Wishing that I may always
  have
You present in my sight.
            -British song

Sage	Domestic virtue, skill, household, faith, immortality
Snowdrops	Hope, purity
Southernwood	Constancy
Spurge	Welcome
Statice	Remembrance, gratitude
Straw	Agreement
Straw, broken	Broken agreement
Sunflower	Pride, respect, sunshine
Sweet basil	Best wishes
Sweet pea	Delicate pleasures, birth, goodbye
Sweet William	Gallantry
Tarragon	Lasting involvement
Taxus, yew	Continued life
Thistle	Sternness
Thyme	Courage, strength
Tuberose	Dangerous pleasures
Tulip	Consuming love, fame, symbol of the rich
Tulip, pink	Love, imagination
Tulip, red	Declaration of love, ardent love
Tulip, variegated	Beautiful eyes
Tulip, white	Lost love
Tulip, yellow	Hopeless love
Verbena	May you get your wish
Veronica	Fidelity
Violet	Modesty, faithfulness
Weeping willow	Sorrow and bereavement
Wheat	Fertility
Yarrow	Health, healing
Zinnia	Thoughts of an absent friend

Where are the dear, old-fashioned posies,
Quaint in form and bright in hue,
Such as grandma gave her lovers
When she walked the garden through?
            -Ethel Lynn Beers (1827-1879)

There's rosemary, that's for remembrance;
pray, love, remember; and there is pansies,
that's for thoughts.
            -William Shakespeare (1564-1616),
            Hamlet, IV, 5, 174

Dreaming of nature:

To dream of………
- Acorns – Brings good luck
- Daisies – If it's spring or summer it brings good luck
- Daisies – If it's fall or winter it brings bad luck
- Flower garden – brings happy love, home life and foretells great joy
- Green peas bring happiness. Dried peas bring marriage.
- Neglected garden – means you are neglecting yourself
- Oak tree- means you will live a long and successful life
  For newlyweds this dream can mean successful marriage and lots of children.
- Roses – receiving a rose in a dream means you are going to be deceived by a friend
  If it is springtime, a bouquet of roses means you will find love.
  If it is winter, a bouquet of roses means you will not find love.
  To dream of the entire rose bush means a wedding will be announced.
- Vegetable garden – means good things are on their way

Cutting Flowers

* If your garden doesn't supply everything for your arrangements you can go to a florist to complete your ideas.
* Choose vases that are clean and complement your home or occasion.
* Harvest flowers early in the day when the temperatures are still cool. Keep freshly cut flowers away from sun and heat.
* Place fresh cut flowers and foliage into water immediately. Choose flowers that have firm petals, and have buds that show a little color. These buds have a great shot at developing.
* Before arranging it's best to let the flowers rest in a cool dark space.

Tips:
* Cut flowers at an angle to increase larger area for water uptake. Re-cut every 2 to 3 days to encourage more water uptake.
* Make sure your pruners, scissors, or knife is sharp to get a nice clean cut. Don't smash stems or cut with blunt scissors; this will keep water out of stems
* Remove foliage that touches the water.
* Change water daily to prevent bacteria buildup.
* Use cut flower food packets – Feeds flowers
                                Reduces bacteria
                                Encourages buds to open
                                Lengthens the life of flowers
        Or, use a cap full of bleach to fight bacteria

Garden Lore

- *Send an upside-down or a withered bouquet to reject a proposal.*
- *Legend tells us that Mary's tears, as Jesus carried the cross, became pink carnations.*
- *English lore says if the petals fall from a just cut red rose, bad luck.*
- *Because the cattalya orchid means mature charm, it has become the favorite corsage to give on Mother's Day.*
- *Victorian legend says to include ivy in your bridal bouquet. This ivy should be rooted and planted as a memorial of your special day.*
- *Give a spider flower to your love if you want to elope.*
- *Wearing a corsage over your heart means feelings are mutual. Wearing a corsage over your bosom means friendship.*

Garden Lore

• *Seeds are a symbol of fertility; this is why we throw rice or birdseed on newlyweds.*

* Use luke-warm water – Has less oxygen in it
  Prevents air bubbles in the stem
  Encourages blooms to open
  Exception to luke-warm water will apply
  to spring bulbs; they prefer cool water.
* Don't place arrangements next to ripening fruit. Fruit emits a hormone called ethylene gas that will age flowers and leafy vegetables; bad chemistry.
* Always remove spent flowers; they also will age surrounding flowers.
* Place arrangements out of drafts and cold areas.
* Keep arrangements out of direct sunlight and away from heaters.
* Try foliage such as hosta, iris, and equisetum for arrangements.
* Keep roses and tulips wrapped in newspaper in a bucket of water to protect stems.
* Don't mix daffodils (*Narcissus*) with other flowers; bad chemistry.

Herbs

How miraculous that growing on my little plot of land are plants that can turn the dead soil into a hundred flavors as different as horseradish and thyme, smells ranging from stinkhorn to lavender.

John Seymour (1849-1923)

* Herbs enhance the flavor of any dish. To get the best flavor cut herbs after the dew has dried on the leaves in the morning. It's best to harvest herbs on a cool day before the plant blooms. After herbs bloom they lose the amount of oil that once concentrated in the leaves.
* Harvest lavender for sachets. It is best to harvest before the florets open.
* Remove flower cluster from basil to encourage new leafy growth for harvesting.
* Try successive planting of parsley to have constant harvest until fall.
* Is your oregano for real? True Greek oregano (*Origanum heracleoticum*) blooms white whereas its double – marjoram (*Origanum marjorana or Origanum vulgare*) blooms mauve. Actually there are 40 some varieties of oregano.
* Harvest herbs, leaves, stems, seeds and roots.
* Harvest herbs for tea such as mint, chamomile, bergamot (also called bee balm), lavender, and lemon verbena.

> *1 cup hot water*
> *2 to 3 teaspoons of fresh crushed leaves*
> *Steep 5 minutes*
> *Drain*
>   *Enjoy*

Shall I compare thee to a summer's day?
Thou art more lovely and more temperate:
Rough winds do shake the darling buds of May,
And summer's lease hath all too short a date.
-William Shakespeare (1564–1616)

The earth laughs in flowers.
-Ralph Waldo Emerson (1803-1882)

Garden Lore

• As rosemary is to the spirit, so lavender is to the soul.
• (Artemisia absinthum), or wormwood in the shoes will ensure safe travel.
• Children used to create necklaces out of magical angelica to deter evil.
• Since Aphrodite created the smell of oregano this symbol of happiness has led many to crown bride and grooms with oregano as well as burial wreaths.

St. John's wort
• An onion planted on St. John's night will grow and grow to a farmer's delight.
• On St. John's day, pick elderberries to ward-off witches.
• The red juice that is squeezed from the leaves and flowers of St. John's wort (*Hypericum perforatum*) is thought to represent the blood of John the Baptist.
• Place a sprig of St. John's wort under your pillow on St. John's Eve and St. John will visit you in your dreams and bless you for another year.
•Hang St. John's wort on the front door to deter evil.
• Burn St. John's wort, wormwood, and mugwort in your Midsummer bonfire to protect you from witches and to help you see fairies.

Lavender
• If lavender grows well in the garden, the girls of the house will never marry.
• Lavender is for lovers. Not only is it an aphrodisiac, if you place lavender under your sheets you and yours will not fight and you will have more restful sleep.
• Charms were created out of lavender to protect home and families against evil spirits.
• Irish brides wore lavender in their garters to protect them from evil spirits on their wedding day.
• After lavender had be bundled and dried it was burned to sanitize rooms where sick people stayed.

Basil
• At the beginning of each season, place a piece of basil in the corners of your home to bring wealth.
• If a young girl places basil in her bedroom window it means she is looking for love.
• If a man accepts a gift of basil from a woman he will fall in love with her.

Lavender blue and rosemary green,
When I am king, you shall be queen,
Call up my maids at four of the clock,
Some to the wheel, and some to the rock,
Some to make hay, and some to shell corn,
And you and I shall keep the bed warm.
                    -English 1600's

As for the garden of mint, the very smell of it alone
recovers and refreshes our spirits,
as the taste stirs up our appetite for meat.
   Gaius Plinius Secundus a.k.a. Pliny the Elder (c.23-79 A.D.)

Garden Lore

• It was believed that if you create an archway out of brambles you could cure an ill person by passing him under the archway.
• Chew on blackberry leaves to relieve mouth sores.
• Make a tea out of blueberry leaves to avoid hair loss. Don't drink it! Create a rinse and massage it on the scalp.
• If you swallow a watermelon seed it will grow in your stomach.

Legend says, when Satan was thrown out of heaven wherever his right foot stepped, smelly onions grew, and wherever his left foot stepped, stinky garlic sprouted.

Seeds

To own a bit of ground, to scratch it with a hoe, to plant seeds, and watch the renewal of life, this is the commonest delight of the race, the most satisfactory thing a man can do.
-Charles Dudley Warner (1829-1900)

* It's not too late to sow annual seeds. You won't be disappointed by their late summer color.

Alyssum (*Lobularia maritima*)
Annual phlox (*Phlox drummondii*)
Annual statice (*Limonium sinuatum*)
Black-eyed Susan (*Rudbeckia hirta*)
Blanket flower (*Gaillardia pulchella*)
Celosia, cockscomb (*Celosia cristata*)
China aster (*Callistephus chinensis*)
China pink (*Dianthus chinensis*)
Cornflower, bachelor's button (*Centaurea cyanus*)
Cosmos (*Cosmos bipinnatus*)
Feverfew (*Chrysanthemum parthenium*)
Four-o'clock (*Mirabilis jalapa*)
Garden balsam, touch-me-nots, jewelweed (*Impatiens balsamina*)
Globe amaranth (*Gomphrena globosa*)
Love-lies-bleeding (*Amaranthus caudatus*)
Marigold (*Tagetes*)
Mexican sunflower (*Tithonia rotundifolia*)
Nasturtium (*Tropaeolum majus*)
Rose moss (*Portulaca grandiflora*)
Snapdragon (*Antirrhinum majus*)
Snow-on-the mountain (*Euphorbia marginata*)
Spider flower (*Cleome hasslerana*)
Strawflower (*Helichrysum bracteatum*)
Sunflower (*Helianthus*)
Zinnia (*Zinnia elegans*)

* Clean seed flats and store.

Vegetables

Sleep thyself in a bowl of summertime.
-Virgil (c. 70-19 B.C.)

* Harvest vegetables as they ripen. Harvest leafy vegetables, squash, and cucumbers after the dew has dried; about mid-morning. The sugar content is highest in the afternoon on corn, peas, and tomatoes so they should be harvested then.
* Thin seedlings to allow each plant to grow to its potential. Try using scissors to thin seedlings to avoid injury to surrounding roots.
* Use row covers to prevent insect damage to young plants.
* Control vines such as squash and cucumbers, by using lawn fabric staples to hold and direct new growth.
* Mound soil around potato plants that are not ready for harvest.

Mounding the soil will protect tubers from sunlight, which will turn them green. These are not safe to eat. When tops have died it will be time to harvest.
* Dry conditions produce better tasting corn and potatoes.
* Mound the soil around the base of corn stalks to help anchor plant during high winds.
* Continuous picking of beans will encourage production of more beans.
* Remove suckers from tomato plants as well as excess foliage to allow more water and sun to go toward ripening fruit and less to foliage.
* Stop cutting asparagus and rhubarb towards the end of the month. Leave plants to grow into ferns until the end of the season to store food for next year.
* Remove spent vegetables and add to compost pile.
* Use dry grass clippings around most vegetables as mulch.
* Add hair from your last haircut or sprinkle blood meal to deter animals from the garden.
* Apply used coffee grounds around carrots to deter root maggots.
* Practice crop rotation to decrease insects and disease.
* Lime dusted on vegetables may deter Japanese beetles.
* After the spring harvest, cultivate the soil, sow seeds, and set more transplants. Try successive planting of your favorite vegetables to have a constant harvest from now until fall.

Transplants:

> Eggplants
> Peppers
> Tomatoes

Seeds:

> Beans, bush, pole, lima,
> Corn, sweet
> Cucumbers
> Okra
> Onion sets (Onions need twice as much fertilizer as other
>   vegetables.)
> Peas, crowder
> Peppers
> Pumpkin
> Squash
> Sweet potato slips

 *Fruit*　　Long about knee-deep in June, 'Bout the time strawberries melt on the vine.
　　　　　　　　-James Whitcomb Riley (1849-1916)

* If a natural thinning process doesn't take place go ahead and thin fruit to 6 to 8 inches apart on fruit trees to encourage larger remaining fruit. There will be another natural thinning process in about a month.
* Prune excessive raspberry and blackberry canes to the ground after fruit production; with exception to ever-bearing. To control boundaries, do not allow plants to grow outside of an 18-inch wide row.

Garden Lore

• *When shelling peas, if you find a single pea in a pod it will bring good luck.*
• *If you find nine peas in a pod, you can throw one of the peas over your shoulder and make a wish.*
• *To relieve a sick person from fever, place an onion, cut in half, under their bed.*
• *Lettuce and cabbage have long been eaten to reduce drunkenness as well as an aphrodisiac.*
• *Eat lettuce to induce childbirth.*
• *If it rains on June 8, a wet harvest will follow.*

The even-ash leaf in my hand,
the first I meet shall be my
*   man.*
The even-ash leaf in my glove,
the first I meet shall be my
*   love.*
The even-ash leaf in my
*   bosom,*
the first I meet shall be my
*   husband.*
*   -Mother Goose*

•*Upon finding an even ash leaf,*
which is a sign of good luck, repeat
this chant:
   Even ash, I do thee pluck,
   Hoping thus to meet good luck.
   If no good luck I get from thee,
   I shall wish thee on the tree.

•*It was often thought that the*
aspen tree could cure someone
who was ill. The ill person would tie
a lock of their hair in the branches
and repeat:
   Aspen tree, aspen tree,
   Shake and shiver
   Instead of me.

Life without love is like a tree
without blossom and fruit.
*   -Khalil Gibran (1883-1931)*

* Keep suckers and water sprouts pruned from fruit trees.
* Continue to train grape vines.
* Sow seeds or plant transplant for watermelon, muskmelon and cantaloupe.
* When foliage on melons begins to crawl, spray with a mixture of water and borax; 2 tablespoons per 1 gallon of water. This application will create stronger and sweeter fruit.
* After harvest, strawberries will decline into a semi-dormant state. Set mower on highest setting and mow tops of strawberries and fertilize with 10-10-10.
* Keep lemons mixed in the fruit bowl to prolong freshness.
* Create a natural room freshener. Fill a pot with water, lemon, apple or orange peels, and cinnamon sticks. Simmer for at 30 minutes or longer.

Trees and Shrubs

In June 'tis good to lie beneath a tree
While the blithe season comforts every sense,
Steeps all the brain in rest, and heals the heart,
Brimming it o'er with sweetness unawares.
*   -J.R. Lowell (1819-1891)*

* Plant trees and shrubs that are in containers or burlapped. Water regularly throughout the season.
* Wait to transplant trees and shrubs this fall.
* Prune shrubs after the first flush of new growth, keep hedges wider at the base to allow sun to reach entire hedge.
* Prune new growth on evergreens (candles) such as pines, firs, and spruces to thicken structure; cut one-third of new growth.
* Prune shrubs with hand pruners to obtain a natural look and use shears for a formal appearance.
* Prune these trees now that their leaves have fully developed.   These trees "bleed" sap if pruned in the spring.
   Birch *(Betula)*
   Cottonwood *(Populus deltoides)*
   Dogwood *(Cornus)*
   Elm *(Ulmus)*
   Fir *(Abies)*
   Locust *(Robinia pseudoacacia)*
   Maple *(Acer)*
   Pine *(Pinus)*
   Spruce *(Picea)*
   Willow *(Salix)*
   Yellowwood *(Cladrastis lutea)*

* As your landscape fills, make decisions on troubled trees & shrubs. Sometimes it is best to remove and replace plants.
* Plant shrubs you received on Mother's day in a nice shady protected area of your garden.

* Take softwood cuttings from new growth on these trees and shrubs:
Refer to page 122 for instructions.

Shrubs:

> Abelia
> Bayberry *(Myrica pensylvanica)*
> Bluebeard *(Caryopteris)*
> Bodinier beautyberry *(Callicarpa bodinieri)*
> Boxwood *(Buxus)*
> Burning bush *(Euonymus alata)*
> Butterfly bush *(Buddleia davidii)*
> Carolina allspice *(Calycanthus floridus)*
> Chokeberry *(Aronia)*
> Cotoneaster
> Crape myrtle *(Lagerstroemia indica)*
> Deutzia
> Forsythia
> Fothergilla
> Heavenly bamboo *(Nandina domestica)*
> Holly *(Ilex)*
> Hydrangea *(macrophylla and H. paniculata)*
> Japanese barberry *(Berberis thunbergii)*
> Japanese kerria *(Kerria japonica)*
> Japanese pieris *(Pieris japonica)*
> Lace shrub *(Stephanandra incisa)*
> Mock orange *(Philadelphus coronaris)*
> Redvein enkianthus *(Enkianthus campanulatus)*
> Rhododendron, azalea
> Rose-of-Sharon *(Hibiscus syriacus)*
> Scarlet firethorn *(Pyracantha coccinea)*
> Summer-sweet *(Clethra alnifolia)*
> Viburnum
> Virginia sweetspire *(Itea virginica)*
> Weigela
> Winter-hazel *(Hamamelis)*

Trees:

> Bald cypress *(Taxodium distichum)*
> Cherry, flowering *(Prunus serrulata)*
> Crab apple *(Malus floribunda)*
> Dogwood *(Cornus spp.)*
> Gingko biloba, male trees only
> Japanese snowbell *(Styrax japonicus)*
> Juniper *(Juniperus)*
> Maple *(Acer spp.)*
> Smoke tree *(Cotinus coggygria)*
> Tulip tree *(Liriodendron tulipifera)*
> Willow *(Salix)*

* Listen for the whistle of the Tennessee state game bird, the bobwhite
quail. Also known as a partridge, this bird can be found foraging for insects and vegetation near forest openings.

Garden Lore

• If leaves are turned upward on cottonwoods, expect rain.

• Place a birch branch over your front door to protect your family from evil.

• Elder branches are buried with loved ones to protect them from the devil.

• Mountain ash and taxus were planted in graveyards to keep the dead from returning. Due to this belief, many coffins were made from ash. Cypress wood was also a choice for coffins because it is very slow to decompose.

• Hawthorns are thought to bring good luck to their owners.

• Wands made from the hawthorn tree will bring love, protection and fertility.

• Because the oak tree is sacred and the symbol of strength to many, oak was burned on the Midsummer's Eve bonfire.

*By the breath of flowers
Thou callest us from city
  throngs and cares,
Back to the woods, the birds,
The mountain streams,
That sing of thee-
Back to free childhood's heart,
Fresh with the dews of
  tenderness.*
  -Felicia Dorothea Browne Hemans
  (1793 - 1835)

...Ring ye the bells,
  to make it wear away,
And bonfires make all day;
And dance about them,
And about them sing,
That all the woods may
    answer,
and your echo ring.
    Edmund Spencer (1552-1599)
    "Epithalamion"

Lawn Care

Not every soil can bear all things.
    -Virgil (c. 70-19 B.C.)

Maintenance

* Keep new lawns watered. Established lawns may turn brown if rain is scarce. The grass will go dormant but usually survives. You can apply 1 inch of water a week, or ½ inch twice a week, to keep it green when rain does not provide water.
* Raise lawn mower to 2.5 to 3 inches and stay there until fall. Tall grass will keep the roots cool to beat the summer heat and discourage weeds.
* Mow regularly and allow clippings to stay on the lawn. These clippings will break down into useable nitrogen for your lawn.
* Sections of lawn that are full of naturalized bulbs, can now be mowed.

Fertilize

* Do not fertilize cool-season lawns until mid-October.

Insect and Weed Control

* Spot kill broadleaf and grassy weeds with a squirt bottle of post-emergent herbicide.

Composting

Earth knows no desolation. She smells regeneration in the moist breath of decay.
    -George Meredith (1828-1909)

* Add spent flowers and foliage to compost pile.
* Turn compost pile more frequently as weather warms.
* Keep compost pile moist to speed decomposition.

Water Ponds

Opportunity is missed by most people because it is dressed in overalls and looks like work.
    -Thomas A. Edison (1847-1931)

* Top-up pond with fresh water if weather has been hot and windy.
* Early summer is the best time to plant tender and tropical water plants.
* Remove dying debris and deadhead plants before they fall into the water.
* Algae can be reduced by adding more floating plants and decreasing the sun exposure to the water.

Garden Lore

• *The ashes from the Midsummer's Eve bonfires were mixed with water and used to bless the sick.*
• *Weddings on and around summer solstice were preformed under oak trees because they are a symbol of endurance and strength.*
• *When the forest murmurs and the mountain roars, then close your windows and shut the doors.*

In the meadow- what is in the meadow?
Bluebells, buttercups, meadowsweet,
And fairy rings for children's feet,
In the meadow.
    Mother Goose

June Indoor Gardening

With a few flowers in my garden,
half a dozen pictures and some books,
I live without envy.
  -Lope de Vega (1562-1635)

•*When the down of a dandelion contracts rain will soon fall.*
•*Wet June, dry September.*
•*Fairy rings are rings of tall, dark green grass that circle toadstools. These rings were created by dancing fairies. Stepping into the ring may cure an illness.*
•*When the dew is on the grass, rain will never come to pass.*

* Now that you are outside all the time, do not forget about the indoor houseplants; keep them watered and fertilized with liquid 20-20-20.
* Take leaf cuttings from African violets. Place cuttings or plants in a north or northeast-facing window.
* Optimum leaf growth on African violets is horizontal. If the leaves are growing any other direction you should move the plant to another location.
* Watch for insects and disease throughout the summer.
* Summer sun is more intense, more direct, and less filtered. Using sheers in your windows will help filter the sun for the low-light plants left indoors. Normally the extra indoor light benefits sun-loving tropical plants.

The Sun, as common, went abroad,
The flowers, accustomed, blew,
As if no soul the solstice passed
That maketh all things new.
  -Emily Dickinson (1830-1886)

I hear thy presence in the whispering air,
The lifting leaf, the honey-bee's low tune,
The drowsy hum of insects everywhere;
The world is full of thee, O peerless June.
  -Mary E. Hobbs (c. 1870)

July Garden Chore List

In the Garden:
- ❑ This month is too hot to add plants to your landscape.

Flowers and Herbs:
- ❑ Continue to fertilize containers and hanging baskets weekly with a liquid fertilizer such as 20-20-20.
- ❑ Reapply 10-10-10 to all containers and gardens.
- ❑ Deadhead perennials to promote new blooms.
- ❑ Complete pinching fall-flowering perennials by mid-July to allow time to form flower buds prior to fall.
- ❑ Pinch or cut leggy annuals to keep a more compact and healthy appearance.
- ❑ Make a list of bulbs you need for fall.
- ❑ Side-dress herbs with compost.

Seeds:
- ❑ Sow seeds now for a succession of late summer flowers.

Vegetables and Fruits:
- ❑ Harvest crops daily to promote new vegetables for late season picking.
- ❑ Heel in soil around root crops to avoid sun scorching.
- ❑ Remove spring crops that have completed production and replant for fall harvest.
- ❑ Plant strawberries.
- ❑ Prune apple and pear trees to allow more sun to penetrate through the tree to ripen fruit.

Trees and Shrubs:
- ❑ Prune topiaries and espaliers.
- ❑ Remove sucker growth from trees and shrubs.
- ❑ Water new trees and shrubs deeply on a regular basis.

Lawn Care:
- ❑ Allow lawn to go dormant if regular watering is not easily performed.
- ❑ Lay sod if you need grass for summer.
- ❑ Treat lawn for insects if there is a problem.

Composting:
- ❑ Turn compost pile and continue to keep it damp.
- ❑ Do not add foliage to your compost pile that shows signs of diseases or insects.

Water Ponds:
- ❑ Top ponds with water as necessary.
- ❑ Feed fish regularly.
- ❑ Thin floating plants when they cover more than 2/3 of the pond surface.

Indoors Plants:
- ❑ Beware of scorching plants that are directly in front of windows.
- ❑ Fertilize houseplants regularly with liquid 20-20-20.
- ❑ Repot indoor plants as needed.
- ❑ Stop watering amaryllis at the end of July.

Chapter 5

July Garden

*Whoever makes a garden
Has, oh so many friends!
The glory of the morning,
The dew when daylight ends.*
Douglas Mallach (1705-1765)

As we welcome the "dog days" of summer along with the loud shrill of cicadas, the haze only hides the true beauty in the fields. The fields are alive with chicory, Queen Anne's lace, thistles, and morning glories. Even rolls of hay give decoration to a freshly mowed field. Gardens appear lush but are exhausted from heat. Garden phlox and black-eyed Susan's add much needed color to the landscape. Steamy mornings fade to humid days and muggy evenings, and though July is the month of fireworks and watermelon, we tend to wish it away. Through drought or thunderstorm the crickets never fail to sing this month and as children, we remember those muggy evenings brought fireflies and what good is summer without fireflies?

The heat can be overwhelming, but there is plenty to do outside. Weeds will take over if you take a break this month. Unfortunately weeds love the heat. July is all about controlling growth, supporting growth and shaping your garden.

If you need an escape from the heat, spend time planning your fall garden. If you like working in the heat, now is a great time to install your next garden. This new garden can be prepared and amended now for fall planting. Visit your local arboretum or botanical garden to get some new landscaping ideas.

In-The-Garden Maintenance

Take care of your garden
And keep out the weeds,
Fill it with sunshine
Kind words and kind deeds.
        -Henry Longfellow (1807-1882)

Garden Lore

• *Never carry a cultivating hoe into the house. If you do, carry it out again, walking backwards to avoid bad luck.*

• *If it rains on the first "Dog Day" (July 3ʳᵈ), it will rain for forty days.*

• *The early settlers and Native Americans called the full moon in July the Ripe Corn Moon or Hay Moon.*

• *Evening red and morning gray, two sure signs of one fine day. Evening gray and morning red put on a hat or you'll wet your head.*

• *A sunshiny shower, last half an hour.*

• *Rub insect sting with marigold blossom to alleviate the pain.*

* Due to the heat of the season, concentrate on weed control and general cleaning in shaded areas of your yard. Save the sunny work for early morning or late afternoon.

* This month and next are too hot to add plants to your landscape. If you wait until September you will not have to water as much.

* Take the time to jot down thoughts on your summer garden and the plant material you may want to add this fall.

* Did you know that south of the equator vines climb right to left? North of the equator they climb left to right?

* If you don't have a cold frame, now would be a great time to build one or repair the one you have. You can extend the growing season by almost eight weeks.

* If you have a cold frame, now is a great time to clean it out so it will be ready for fall use.

Summer afternoon.... summer afternoon; to me
those have always been the two most beautiful
words in the English language.
        -Henry James (1843-1916)

St. Swithin's Day, if thou
  dost rain,
For forty days it will remain.
St. Swithin's Day, if thou
  be fair,
For forty days 'twill rain
  na mair.
        -Mother Goose

Container Gardening

A piece of sky and a chunk of the earth lie lodged in the heart of every human being.

-Thomas Moore (1478-1535)

* Container plants dry more quickly than bedding plants. Terra cotta pots lose water very quickly and may need water twice a day. Allow water to drain through soil and drainage hole to ensure thorough watering.
* Continue to fertilize containers and hanging baskets weekly with a liquid fertilizer such as 20-20-20.
* Reapply 10-10-10 or 14-14-14 to containers.

July

When the scarlet cardinal tells
Her dream to the dragonfly,
And the lazy breeze
Makes a nest in the trees,
And murmurs a lullaby,
It is July.

When the tangled cobweb pulls
The cornflower's cap awry,
And the lilies tall
Lean over the wall
To bow to the butterfly,
It is July.

When the heat like a mist veil floats,
And poppies flame in the rye,
And the silver note
In the streamlet's throat
Has softened almost to a sigh,
It is July.

When the hours are so still that time
Forgets them, and lets them lie
'Neath petals pink
'til the night stars wink
At sunset in the sky,
It is July.

-Susan Hartley Swett   (1843-1907)

Garden Lore

• *Gazing balls were thought to scare away witches who came to steal plants. Upon gazing, they would see their ugliness and run away empty handed.*

When evening comes, you say, 'It will be fair weather, for the sky is red,' and in the morning, "Today it will be stormy, for the sky is red and overcast'.

Matthew 16:2 - 3

Garden Lore

• *Joe Pye, an American Indian, considered his weed to be an aphrodisiac.*
• *To deter snakes from your home scatter a barrier of Solomon's seal.*
• *A weed caught in time saves nine.*
• *To scatter seeds of tickseed (Coreopsis) was thought to deter ticks and bed bugs.*
• *The red hibiscus speaks. If worn behind the left ear, you desire a lover. If worn behind the right ear, you are already spoken for. If worn behind both ears, you have a lover and want another.*
• *Basil is a love token in Italy. Young men would wear a sprig of basil behind their ear if they were ready for love and marriage.*
• *In the Middle East crushing daisies and mixing with oil was used to cover grey hair.*
• *An open anthill indicates good weather; a closed hill, an approaching storm.*

If you truly love Nature, you will find beauty everywhere.
  -Vincent Van Gogh (1853-1890)

I like to go out on a walk and with each plant and flower talk.

    16th century

Perennials and Biennials

I love the sweet, sequestered place,
The gracious roof of gold and green,
Where arching branches interlace
with glimpses of the sky between
              -Anonymous

* Deadhead perennials to promote new blooms.
* Remove brown leaves on lamb's ears to promote not only better appearance but new growth as well.
* Divide and replant oriental poppies. If they don't need to be divided, just cut brown foliage and fill the void with summer annuals.
* Dig, divide, and propagate bleeding heart when foliage disappears which indicates dormancy.
* Cut spent flower stalks on plants such as Shasta daisy, hosta, daylilies, and coral bells.
* Train and prune stray sprigs on these vines:
    Climbing hydrangea (*Hydrangea anomala subsp. petiolaris*)
    Ivy (*Hedera*)
    Wisteria

* Many perennials and biennials will benefit from having weak stems cut to the ground. This thinning will also allow for more air circulation and reduce disease.
    Bee balm (*Monarda didyma*)
    Garden phlox (*Phlox paniculata*)
    Hollyhock (*Alcea rosea*)
    Michaelmas daisy (*Aster*)
    Sneeze weed (*Helenium*)

* Complete pinching fall-flowering perennials by mid-July to allow time to form flower buds prior to fall.
    Blanket-flower (*Gaillardia*)
    Cyrsanthemum
    Delphinium
    Fleabane (*Erigeron*)
    Garden phlox, summer phlox (*Phlox paniculata*)
    Joe-Pye weed (*Eupatorium fistulosum*)
    Michaelmas daisy (*Aster*)
    Purple coneflower (*Echinacea*)
    Russian sage (*Perovskia*)
    Showy stonecrop (*Sedum spectabile*)

* Shear faded blooms from coreopsis and baby's breath and they should rebloom.
* Continue to supply supports for tall perennials and vines.

And I beseech you, forget not to informe yourselfe
as diligently as may be, in things that belong to gardening.
      John Evelyn (1620-1706)

The Lord God planted a garden
In the first white days of the world;
And placed there an angel warden,
In a garment of light unfurled.
So near to the piece of heaven,
The hawk might nest with the wren;
For there in the cool of the even,
God walked with the first of men.

And I dream that these garden closes,
With their shade and their sun-freckled sod,
And their lilies and bowers of roses
Were laid by the hand of God.
The kiss of the sun for pardon,
The song of the birds for mirth,
One is nearer God's heart in a garden
Than anywhere else on earth.
                    -Dorothy Frances Gurney (1858-1932)

Eagle of flowers! I see thee stand
And on the sun's noon-glory gaze
With eye like his, thy lids expand,
And fringe their disk with golden rays.
            -James Montgomery (1771-1854)

* Pinch or cut leggy annuals to keep a more compact and healthy appearance. This will stretch bloom time until September or October.
* Make a list of annuals that are doing well this summer and the plants that are not doing so well can be eliminated from your list next year.
* Crush dry seedpods on cool-weather annuals to help seeds fall to the ground. These seedlings will supply the garden with early flowers next spring.
     Larkspur *(Consolida ambiqua)*
     Love-in-a-mist *(Nigella damascena)*

If you would have a lovely garden,
you should live a lovely life.
                    -Shaker saying

Garden Lore

• *The first frost comes three months past the first cicada shrill.*
• *When the sunflower raises its head rain will come.*
• *If you place marigold in your mattress, you will have visionary dreams.*
• *If you place marigold under your mattress it will make whatever you dream come true.*
• *Bees will not swarm, Before a near storm.*
• *Never trust the sky In the month of July.*

Garden Phenology

• *When morning glory vines begin to take off and climb, expect Japanese beetles.*

I come to the velvet, imperial crowd,
The wine-red, the gold, the crimson, the pied-
The dahlias that reign by the gardenside.
-Edith Matilda Thomas (1854-1925)

With statues on the terraces
and peacocks strutting by;
but the glory of the garden lies
in more than meets the eye.
-Rudyard Kipling (1865-1936)

Bulbs, Corms, Rhizomes, and Tubers

I have a garden of my own,
But so with roses overgrown,
And lilies, that you would it guess
to be a little wilderness.
Andrew Marvell (1621-1678)

* Make a list of bulbs you need for fall and start shopping for them at your local garden center. Remember to list those bulbs you will need for winter forcing.
* For optimum bloom size, replant and separate irises every three years. The best time to replant is after the flowers fade through late summer. Irises do not require a lot of moisture.
   1) Dig clumps and discard old central rhizomes.
   2) Replant the outer young rhizomes.
   3) Trim leaves to create a 6-inch fan of foliage for nourishment.
   4) Plant rhizomes on the surface of the soil preferably on a mound.

* Plant the last group of gladiolus to have blooms until frost.
* When cutting gladiolus, leave three leaves on the stem to aid in bulb nutrition.

The dahlia you brought to our isle
Your praises forever shall speak:
Mid gardens as sweet as your smile,
And colour as bright as your cheek.
-Lord Holland to Lady Webster, early 1800's

Roses

Roses do comfort the heart.
-William Langham (1756-1830)

* Continue spray program to control black spot, mites, and powdery mildew.
* Hand pick Japanese beetles and drop them in a container of soapy water.
* Keep roses well watered throughout the hot season. Water deeply!
* Increase in pruning increases plant vigor.
* Remove leaves with black spots from plant and the ground below.
* Deadhead hybrid tea, grandiflora, floribunda, miniature, repeat-blooming shrubs, and climbers to encourage more blooms.
* Prune roses that bloom once a year after they bloom.
* After they bloom, cut tall canes on hybrid teas to 3 feet. Always cut above an outward facing eye at a five-leaf leaflet.

Herbs

Perfumes are the feelings of flowers.
-Heinrich Heine (1797-1856)

* If you grow basil, don't allow the plant to form blooms; this will decrease the flavor in the leaves. Removing blooms will encourage new growth.
* Harvest basil, mint, thyme, oregano, rosemary, lavender, and sage for drying. Hang herbs upside down in a cool place.
* Harvest herb leaves, stems, seeds, and roots.
* Lavender is most fragrant just prior to flowers opening, which makes then the best time to harvest.
* Harvest seeds from dill, coriander, and fennel.
* Trim straggly plants such as rosemary and sage. Use the trimmings as cuttings and create new plants.
* Clip sage and thyme as they flower.
* Sow parsley for fall and winter harvest.
* Side-dress herbs with compost.
* Try scouring pots and pans with horsetail or pewterwort foliage *(Equisetum)* as our ancestors did.
* Make your own natural fungicide from horsetail *(Equisetum).*
    -Chop horsetail into tiny bits and add water.
    -Bring water to boil, reduce and simmer for 2 hours.
    -After cooling, strain and pour into squirt bottle.
* Create your own herbal hair rinse. Boil 4 cups of water and add up to 1 tablespoons of herbs. Use one or try a combination of herbs. Simmer for ½ hour; cool and strain. Apply to hair for ½ hour. Choose from these:
    Chamomile to soften
    Lavender to stimulate growth
    Marigold to lighten
    Parsley for luster
    Rosemary to darken

And where the marjoram once, and sage and rue'
And balm and mint, with curled-leaved parlsey grew,
And double marigold, and silver thyme,
And pumpkins 'neath the window used to climb;
And where I often, when a child, for hours,
Tried through the pales to get the tempting flowers.
-John Clare (1793-1864)

If a man be anointed with the juice of rue, the poison of wolfsbane (aconite), mushrooms, or toadstools, the biting of serpents, stinging of scorpions, spiders, bees, hornets, and wasp will not hurt him.
-John Gerard (1564-1637)

 Garden Lore

• *Where the mistress is master, parsley grows faster.*
• *Planting rue near basil or sage can be fatal for these plants.*
• *Garlic is as good as ten mothers.*
• *To avoid hay fever sleep with fresh mint under your pillow.*
• *Deter ants from the house by creating a barrier with catnip blossoms.*
• *Hang fennel over your door and stick some in the keyhole to protect you from witches.*
• *When spiders build new webs, the weather will be clear.*
• *In the sixteenth century, lavender was used as a remedy to cure passions of the heart.*
• *Having trouble falling asleep? Do as the early colonists did and take a sprig of fennel to church. This fragrant herb will keep you awake during a long sermon.*
• *Since Venus, Roman goddess of love, was in charge of love, she created marjoram, and she made wreaths to place on the heads of brides and grooms.*
• *Marjoram can also be planted at a love ones' grave to ensure a happy departed soil.*
• *Hang chives in the rafters of your house to prevent bad luck.*
• *Before windows had screens, pots of basil were used to line the sill to deter flies.*
• *Place fennel in keyholes to keep unwanted ghosts out.*
• *Legend holds that tears shed by Helen of Troy turned into thyme.*

Garden Lore

• *If you have a sunburn, place cucumber slices over skin to relieve inflammation and pain.*

• *Never plant cabbage near rue.*

• *Dog days bright and clear*
Indicate a happy year.
But when accompanied by rain,
For better times our hopes are vain.

• *In July, shear your rye.*

• *In this month of July, eschew all wanton bed-sports, and of all things forbear lettuce.*

• *When the cow tries to scratch its ear,*
It means a shower is very near;
When it thumps its ribs with it tail,
Look out for thunder, lightning, and hail.

Seeds

> *A morning glory at my window satisfies me more than the metaphysics of books.*
> *-Walt Whitman (1819-1892)*

* Collect and sprinkle seeds of hollyhocks, larkspur, nigella, and foxgloves after the blooms fade and plant dies.

* Sow seeds now for a succession of late summer flowers. They bloom until the first hard frost. This means you could have cut flowers at Thanksgiving. Try seeds of cosmos, zinnias, celosia, cleome, and tithonia. Bloom time should arrive around 6 to 10 weeks after planting. Late summer sowing requires more watering. Apply 20-20-20 liquid fertilizer when seedlings emerge. Apply fertilizer regularly throughout entire season for best results. You may want to plant seeds a little deeper than you did in the spring to keep them moist for germination. Water seedlings lightly as needed.

Vegetables

> *It does not matter how slowly you go, as long as you do not stop.*
> *-Confucius (c. 551-479 B.C.)*

* Harvest crops daily to promote new vegetables for late season picking.

Asparagus–Harvest before spear tips begin to open.

Beans–Pick green beans when pods are 4 inches long. Pods should be smooth. For sweeter beans, harvest in the morning. Harvest daily to increase production.

Beets–Harvest when beets are 2 inches in diameter.

Broccoli and cauliflower–Cut when flower heads are hard and firm.

Carrots–Harvest carrots when foliage is dark green and lush. Remove foliage to keep carrots moist. Don't harvest too soon, optimum flavor is reached at maturity. Harvest sweet baby carrots when the root is the diameter of your pinky finger.

Corn–When silk has turned brown and ears feel full, it's time to pick corn. Press thumbnail into kernels and look for a white fluid rather than clear.

Cucumbers–For cucumbers to slice, harvest at 6 inches long. For pickling, harvest cucumbers when they are 3 to 4 inches long.

Eggplant–Harvest eggplant while the skin is shiny and firm. You may need to prop produce up with a brick or clay pot to reduce weight pulling on plant.

Onions–When stalks begin to fall on shallots, onions, and garlic, bend remaining foliage and stop watering. After one to two weeks dig bulbs, remove soil, and dry for a few days. Do not wash. Store with foliage braided or cut stems; store in mesh bags. Cure by placing in a dark, dry, airy place for about 2 weeks.

Peas–Pick fat pods before they dry-up. Look for white residue around stems.

Peppers–Withhold water from peppers if you want them to be "hot".

Potatoes–Decrease watering potatoes when foliage begins to die back. To help potatoes thicken skin wait 2 weeks before harvest. Keep potatoes covered with soil to avoid burning, greening by the sun.

Snap Peas–Harvest snap peas when pods are fat and crisp. Keep mature pods harvested to encourage more production.

Squash–Harvest when stem begins to turn from green to brown. Store in a cool, dark place for about one month to sweeten.

Sweet Potatoes–Sweet potatoes with dark skin tend to have a sweeter flavor and great texture. Stop fertilizing this month.

Tomatoes–Remove suckers to promote a fuller plant. Withhold water from tomatoes up to a week before harvest for optimum flavor. Pick when color begins to change from orange to red. Ripen off the vine. Never store in the refrigerator, bad chemistry.

Zucchini–Pick zucchini when they are 5 inches long. Large zucchini tends to lack flavor.

* Heel in soil around root crops such as carrots, potatoes, and onions to avoid sun scorching. This will prevent root crops from developing a green color.

* Remove spring crops that have completed production and replant for fall harvest. Prepare gardens by tilling and amending the soil. If you plan to wait before sowing your next crop, plant a cover crop or "green manure". The use of cover crops will prevent soil erosion, prevent soil compaction, and return nutrients to depleted soil in the form of humus. Cover crops also discourage weeds from occupying empty gardens.

> Buckwheat
> Clover
> Crown vetch
> Mustard
> Oats
> Ryegrass, annual

* When sowing cool-weather crops in July for fall harvest, sow seed just a little deeper than recommended on the package to help protect seed from intense sun.

* Remove tips on runner beans as they reach the top of their support.

* Remove yellowing leaves and side shoots from tomatoes.

* Plant pumpkin seeds now to have Jack-o-lanterns for Halloween (takes 90 to 110 days to mature from germination).

* Try successional gardening by planting repeat crops every two weeks. This will allow you to harvest crops in September and October. Choose disease resistant seeds that germinate and mature quickly. You can continue to sow seeds or transplants from July through mid-August for fall crops.

> Beans
> Beets
> Brussels sprouts
> Carrots
> Cucumbers
> Lettuce
> Squash
> Turnips

*Yellow Butterflies
Over the blossoming virgin
  corn,
With pollen-painted faces
Chase one another in
  brilliant throng.*
        -Hopi Indian song

Garden Lore

• *Celebrate the harvest on July 23rd, which is the feast day of St. Phocus the patron saint of gardeners and farmers.*

• *Corn should be knee-high by Fourth of July.*

• *If carrots go to seed, expect bad luck for the family.*

• *An apple a day keeps the doctor away.*

• *Determine whom you shall marry by twisting an apple stem. Repeat the names of those you admire and when the stem breaks away from the apple that is the chosen husband for you.*

• *Split an apple in half to determine how many children you will have; just count the seeds.*

You've got to go out on a limb sometimes because that's where the fruit is.
 -Will Rogers (1879-1935)

A melon and a woman are hard to know.
 French

---

* Side-dress tomatoes, peppers, and okra again with a general fertilizer such as 10-10-10.
* As tomatoes, peppers, and eggplants bloom, apply Epsom salts to provide magnesium. Apply one pint to each plant (2 tablespoons Epsom salts to one gallon water).
* Place a slice of onion over insect bite to relieve itching and swelling.
* Use an all-purpose fertilizer such as 10-10-10 on corn as ears began to form.
* Continue to plant:
    Seeds:
    Beans, bush, pole, lima
    Beets
    Corn, sweet (up to mid July)
    Cucumbers
    Okra
    Onion sets (onions need twice as much fertilizer as
      other vegetables).
    Pumpkin
    Rutabaga
    Squash

    Transplants:
    Eggplant
    Peppers
    Sweet potato slips
    Tomato

There is a garden in her face,
Where Roses and white lilies grow;
A heav'nly paradise is that place
Wherein all pleasant fruits do grow.
 -Thomas Campion (1567-1620)

* If needed, spray borer control on ornamental peach and cherry trees.
* Plant strawberries.
* Harvest raspberries when they are rich in color and pull away easily from the stem.
* Prune dying fruit canes on blackberries after they have been harvested.
* Tip: prune new vigorous growth to create a denser hedge with increased fruit production.
* If you grow melons horizontally prop them on a support or lay them on a bed of straw to reduce rotting. As soon as melons have three or four fruit sets begin to remove new fruit sets. This will direct more energy to the existing fruit which will benefit sizing greatly.
* Melons become sweeter in the hot dry sun. Don't over water and don't water near the base of the stem. To discourage rot mound soil around stem area to allow water to drain away. Harvest when stem has withered.
* Prune apple and pear trees to allow more sun to penetrate through the tree to ripen fruit.
* Prune espalier and cordon fruit trees to maintain desired shape.

Trees and Shrubs

O to lie in the ripening grass
That gracefully bends to the winds that pass,
And to look aloft the oak leaves through
Into the sky so deep, so blue!
-William Roscoe Thayer (1859-1923)

* During the summer, shrubs are busy making and storing food for next year. They can handle pruning now but they will not have the same growth spurt as they did this spring. Now is a good time to get shrubs in bounds.
* Prune topiaries and espaliers this month, before they lose their shape.
* Try your own espalier. Add a few of these Tennessee hardy trees and shrubs to your fall shopping list:

> Bearberry *(Arctostaphylos uva-ursi)*
> Bristle-cone pine *(Pinus aristata)*
> Convexleaf Japanese holly *(Ilex crenata 'Convexa')*
> Cornelian cherry *(Cornus mas)*
> Cotoneaster *(Cotoneaster horizontalis, C. divaricata)*
> Crabapple *(Malus astrosanguinea, M. 'Dorothea', M. 'Red Jade')*
> Creeping juniper *(Juniperus horizontalis)*
> Dogwood *(Cornus kousa)*
> Forsythia
> Japanese maple *(Acer palmatum 'Dissectum Atropurpureum',*
>   *A.'ornatum')*
> Japanese snowball *(Viburnum plicatum)*
> Korean Stewartia *(Stewartia korena)*
> Magnolia, saucer & star
> Silver Japanese white pine *(Pinus parviflora 'glauca')*
> Yew *(Taxus)*

* Watch for borers on dogwood, birch, lilacs, and ornamental peach trees and treat as needed.
* Fertilize acid loving plant material once more before mid-August with an acid based-fertilizer than contains iron.
* Remove sucker growth from trees and shrubs.
* Overgrown shrubs can be thinned by removing one-third of the older stems to the ground.
* Cut old wood on mock orange to the ground if it has become overgrown.
* Water new trees and shrubs deeply on a regular basis.
* Never use a string trimmer around trees trunks. The scratches it creates exposes the tree to infection and disease.

-Beware of an oak it draws the stroke,
Avoid an ash it courts the flash.
Creep under the thorn, it will save you
from harm.
-Mother Goose

Garden Lore

• *Collect hazel branches prior to a storm to protect your house from lightning.*
• *Hang an evergreen branch in the rafters of your new home for good luck.*
• *Planting a hedgerow of English yew (Taxus) was thought to protect the dead.*
• *Carry an acorn for good luck and longevity.*
• *Keep an acorn in all the windows to repel lightning.*

Brown and furry
Caterpillar in a hurry
Take your walk
To the shady leaf, or stalk,
Or what not,
Which may be the chosen
  spot.
No toad spy you,
Hovering bird of prey pass by
  you;
Spin and die,
To live again a butterfly.
  Christina Georgina Rossetti
  (1830 -1894)

Garden Lore

• *When the dandelion is in the puff-ball stage, pick it and blow on it hard. The remaining seeds on the stem determine how many children you will have.*

Lawn Care

Breathless, we flung us on the windy hill, laughed in the sun, and kissed the lovely grass.
-Rupert Brooke (1887-1915)

Maintenance

* Allow lawn to go dormant if regular watering is not easily performed. Most lawns will rebound after drought conditions pass.
* Lay sod if you need grass for summer. Sowing grass now is very tiring due to constant watering.

Insect and Weed Control

* Remove fallen leaves and debris from plant material suspected of having insects or diseases. Discard affected plant material and do not add to compost pile.

Composting

Fix'd like a plant on his peculiar spot,
To draw nutrition, propagate, and rot.
-Alexander Pope (1688-1744)

* Turn compost pile and continue to keep it damp. Aeration and moisture will speed decomposition.
* Do not add foliage to your compost pile that shows signs of diseases or insects as well as invasive plant material.
* When adding foliage to your compost pile, think healthy.

Water Ponds

* Top ponds with water as necessary.
* Hot weather decreases the oxygen levels in still water. The use of a fountain or cascade will oxygenate the water. A running water hose can be helpful to increase oxygen in the pond.
* Feed fish regularly.
* Fertilize lilies and lotus twice a month during growing season.
* Thin floating plants when they cover more than 2/3 of the pond surface.
* Use a rake to remove blanketweed from surface of pond. This weed is a slimy algae that will grow profusely if not controlled.

I'm glad the sky is painted blue
And the Earth is painted green
With such a lot of nice fresh air
All sandwiched in between.
Unknown

July
Indoor
Gardening

* Remember to water plants with room temperature water. Cold water is shshshshocking!
* Beware of scorching plants that are directly in front of windows.
* Fertilize houseplants regularly throughout the growing season with liquid 20-20-20 to ensure vigorous new growth.
* Cut branches on poinsettia if you still have it. Leave three or four leaves on each stem and remove the rest. This pruning will create a more compact plant. Fertilize with liquid 20-20-20 throughout the growing season.
* Continue to repot indoor plants as needed.
* Stop watering amaryllis at the end of July. Move bulbs to a dry location with a temperature around 70 degrees for storage until first of September. Bulbs should be moved to a location in September that will provide temperatures around 50 degrees for 3 months or until new growth emerges.

August Garden Chore List

In the Garden:
- ❏ Remove weeds in the garden before they bloom and set seed.
- ❏ Review your perennial beds for fall work.

Flowers and Herbs:
- ❏ Continue to deadhead flowers to promote new blooms.
- ❏ Trim daylilies to 6 inches for a better appearance.
- ❏ Prune ground covers to keep them in bounds.
- ❏ Cut straggly growth on annuals.
- ❏ Propagate annuals now before daylight starts decreasing.
- ❏ Plant chrysanthemums to add color to the garden this fall.
- ❏ Divide and transplant lilies after foliage turns yellows.
- ❏ Harvest herbs for drying.

Seeds:
- ❏ Collect seeds to sow and give away from your favorite perennials, biennials, and annuals.
- ❏ Sow biennial seeds in rows and transplant this fall.
- ❏ Sow perennials and cool-weather annuals in flats for transplanting next month.

Vegetables and Fruits:
- ❏ Harvest vegetables as they mature.
- ❏ Remove the tops and suckers on tomato plants.
- ❏ Remove excessive foliage from pumpkin plants.
- ❏ Harvest gourds for fall decorations.

- ❏ Plant and sow vegetables for fall and winter harvesting.
- ❏ Start a new strawberry patch this month.
- ❏ Renovate existing strawberry patch.

Trees and Shrubs:
- ❏ Stop fertilizing trees and shrubs.
- ❏ Give hedges and topiaries a final trim early in the month.
- ❏ After summer-blooming shrubs have bloomed, they can be pruned for shape.

Lawn Care:
- ❏ Lawn renovation is most successful in late August and early September.
- ❏ Over-seed or reseed as needed.
- ❏ Keep the mower set on the high setting until weather cools.

Composting:
- ❏ Moisten and aerate compost to speed decomposition.
- ❏ Shred or cut debris into small pieces to allow fast decomposition.

Water Ponds:
- ❏ Top ponds with water.
- ❏ Keep oxygen available to fish by running a water hose in pond or establishing a fountain.

Indoors Plants:
- ❏ Prune overgrown houseplants.
- ❏ Start moving amaryllis into a cool, dry, dark place for 3 months.

Chapter 6
August Garden

Loud is the summer's busy song:
The smallest breeze can find a tongue,
While insects of each tiny size
Grow teasing with their melodies,
Till noon burns with its blistering breath
Around, and day lies still as death.
-John Clare (1793-1864)

As summer gives away to fall, the scents of the garden grow stronger. Morning glories blanket everything within reach and gardens seem to flourish. As sure as fruit ripens on trees, the heat rises to a new level this month. The heat-loving sunflowers stand tall as if reaching for more sun and abandoned farmhouses, guarded by hollyhocks and ironweed, are brought to life by the colors of the season.

Desperately seeking a sense of summer before fall arrives, we tend to forget the yard and focus on vacations and family time. While we slip away for summer fun our gardens grow out of control. Time spent in the garden seems to disappear; it is too hot to enjoy. If you can brave the dry heat and humidity it's time to discard the dying and rejuvenate the exhausted. It is time to look at the voids in the landscape and plant some fall color and interesting foliage plants.

Create an evening or shade garden that can be enjoyed this time of year. Choose lightly colored or white flowers and variegated foliage. This bright color scheme will enhance the bearable summer evenings. There are many annuals that come in white that add brightness to an evening garden. While evenings may be the only relief in the garden you will appreciate this garden more than most.

In-The-Garden Maintenance

Show me your garden and I shall tell you who you are.
-Alfred Austin (1835-1913)

Garden Lore

- *For every fog in August, There will be a snowfall in winter.*
- *If a cold August follows a hot July, It foretells a winter hard and dry*
- *If the first week of August is unusually warm, the coming winter will be long and white.*
- *If the 24th of August be fair and clear, then hope for a prosperous Autumn that year.*
- *If St. Lawrence Day be fair, so will Autumn.*
- *Rainbow in the morning, travelers take warning.*
- *Rainbow at night, traveler's delight.*
- *Italian saying: Watch for tears of St. Lawrence this month. (Tears are meteor showers).*
- *When you hear the locust, the first frost is six weeks away.*
- *The early settlers and Native Americans called the full moon in August the Corn Moon.*

* Although August is much too stressful to plant, prune, and fertilize, we do it anyway. It is important to remove flower stalks and dying foliage from spent plants before you transplant new ones. Do not let soil dry completely until cool, wet weather arrives. Removing stalks and dying foliage reduces insect and disease problems and does not affect root development at this point. Food reserves reach the roots while foliage is green, not once it has declined.
* Continue to remove weeds in the garden before they bloom and set seed. This month is the best time to spray perennial weeds that live in your garden. The food produced by leaves descends into the root system (or crown in the case of herbaceous plants) this month, replenishing its reserves for vigorous root growth (and hence support of top growth) for the next year. The chemical you spray in August will equally be translocated to the root system, weakening it. It may take a couple years to get total kill, but August is a good month to work on this problem.
* There will be seasonal interest plants on sale at the garden centers. These plants will supply late summer and early fall color.

Nature soon takes over if the gardener is absent.
-Penelope Hobhouse (b.1929)

Perennials and Biennials

The brilliant poppy flaunts her head Amidst the ripening grain, And adds her voice to swell the song That August's here again.
-Winslow Homer (1836-1910)

* Review your perennial beds for fall work. You will want to dig, divide, and transplant perennials before soil temperatures drop below 50 degrees. Perennials take 6 to 8 weeks to get a good start after replanting.
* Continue to deadhead perennials to promote new blooms.
* Many perennials will produce new attractive foliage if you cut spent foliage. Cutting may even encourage a second flush of blooms.
* Trim daylilies to 6 inches for a better appearance. Dig and divide crowded daylilies every 3 years for better flower show and replant young and vigorous stock.
* Add humus and cow manure to Japanese iris (*Iris ensata*) beds.
* Prune ground covers to keep them in bounds.
* Transplant Oriental poppies this month.
* Cutting spent stalks on delphiniums may encourage a new flower stalk for early fall.

Garden Lore

• *Take a pinch of garden soil with you on vacation. Put it in your coffee to avoid getting homesick.*

* Cut and dry flowers for arranging.

    Artemisia

    Astilbe

    Baby's breath *(Gypsophila paniculata)*

    Bells of Ireland *(Molucella laevis)*

    Cockscomb *(Celosia)*

    Delphinium

    Forget-me-not *(Myosotis sylvatica)*

    Gay-feather *(Liatris spicata)*

    Ghost plant, white mugwort *(Artemisia lactiflora)*

    Globe amaranth *(Gomphrena globosa)* Harvest while blooms are perfectly round or when it matures in an oval form.

    Globe thistle *(Echinops ritro)*

    Lamb's ear *(Stachys byzantina)*

    Larkspur *(Consolida ambiqua)*

    Lavender *(Lavandula)*

    Love-in-a-mist pods *(Nigella)*

    Ornamental onion, chives *(Allium spp.)*

    Pearly everlasting *(Anaphalis spp.)*

    Queen Anne's lace *(Daucus carota)*

    Sea Holly *(Eryngium spp.)*

    Sneezewort *(Achillea filipendulina)*

    Statice *(Limonium sinuatum)*

    Strawflower *(Helichrysum bracteatum)*

    Yarrow *(Achillea spp.)*

    Zinnia

Annuals

No occupation is so delightful to me as culture of the earth, no culture comparable to that of gardening… But though an old man, I am but a young gardener.
    -Thomas Jefferson (1743-1826)

* Cut straggly growth on annuals.

* Continue to deadhead annuals to promote longer bloom time.

* Cut and dry flowers for arranging.

    Bells of Ireland *(Moluccella laevis)*

    Cockscomb *(Celosia)*

    Everlasting, immortelle *(Xeranthemum annuum)*

    Globe amaranth *(Gomphrena globosa)*

    Gomphocarpus *(Asclepias fruticosa)*

    Honesty *(Lunaria annua)*

    Prince's feather *(Amaranthus cruentus)*

    Quaking grass *(Briza maxima)*

    Scabious, paper moon *(Scabiosa stellata)*

    Statice, sea lavender *(Limonium sinuatum)*

    Strawflower, everlasting *(Helichrysum bracteatum)*

* Propagate annuals now as daylight starts decreasing and the days get cool. These new plants will brighten your winter and be ready for

Open afresh your round of starry folds,
Ye ardent marigolds.
    -John Keats (1795-1821)

Garden Lore

• *When sunflowers lift their heads rain is sure to fall.*
• *When the stars begin to huddle, the earth will soon become a puddle.*
• *The blade-shape foliage of the bearded iris and gladiolus represent Mary's piercing pain with the death of Jesus.*
• *Palm leaves represent someone who dies for a cause.*

spring containers. Take stem cuttings of coleus, impatiens, fuchsia, begonias, heliotropes, iresine, red thread (*Alternathera*), and geraniums.

1) Cut a healthy stem, with a sharp sterile blade ½ inch below a leaf node.
2) Remove leaves from the base of 4-6 inch stems (1-2 inch bare stem).
3) Remove flowers and buds.
4) Dip stem in rooting hormone.
5) Put stem in potting mix and place a plastic bag over entire container and stem cutting.
6) Keep soil moist; not too wet. Water from saucer to uptake water from the bottom.
7) Place container in a bright window with indirect sunlight.
8) In about one month remove bag and new cutting should be rooted.
9) Fertilize every 10 days with liquid fertilizer such as 20-20-20.

* Plant chrysanthemums to add color to the garden this fall. Choose plants with closed flower buds for prolonged blooming. Use chrysanthemums as annuals in your landscape and don't rely on them to survive USDA hardiness zone 6.
* Flowering cabbage and kale add nice color this time of year. Every garden needs pansies to be added this month.
* Continue to monitor moisture loss, especially in containers and hanging baskets.

Bulbs, Corms, Rhizomes, and Tubers

If one indulges in extravagant earthmoving and planting, valuing colorful effects, then (a garden) becomes like a fetter, a mere cage.

-Wen Zhenheng (1585-1645)

* Check garden centers for fall-blooming bulbs that can be planted now and bloom this season. Buy bulbs for winter forcing.
* After you purchase bulbs, keep them in a cool, dry, dark place until you are ready to plant. Plant them as soon as you can.
* Plant hardy amaryllis or magic lily bulbs (*Amaryllis belladonna*) for foliage growth next spring. You will have to wait until next August to get flowers.
* Divide and transplant lilies after foliage turns yellows.
* Continue to dig, divide, and transplant bearded, Japanese, and Siberian irises this month. Discard old rhizomes and the rhizomes that bloomed this year. Replant young new rhizomes. Japanese and Siberian irises thrive in moist soil.
* Crowding of tubers and rhizomes will decrease blooming; therefore, most rhizomes and tubers will need to be divided every 3 to 4 years.

Roses

There is simply the rose; it is perfect in every moment of its existence.
                                    -Ralph Waldo Emerson (1803-1882)

* Continue spray program to control black spot, mites, and powdery mildew.
* Continue to deadhead roses to promote more blooms.
* Last week of August is the last date to cut hybrid tea canes to get a fall bloom.
* Prune shrub roses to shape, but do not prune climbers that bloom on old wood. New growth on climbers will set flowers for next year.
* Buy roses on August 23rd; the feast day of Rose of Lima. As a child, Rose supported her family by selling flowers. St. Rose is now the patron saint of florist.

Herbs

Let thy kitchen be thy apothecary;
And, let foods be your medicine.
                                    Hippocrates (c. 460-377 B.C.)

* Pinch leggy herbs to create a more compact plant.
* Stop pruning lavender to prevent new growth from being killed by a hard frost. Wait until spring to rejuvenate lavenders.
* Basil can be fed with liquid 20-20-20 or slow-release granular fertilizer such as 10-10-10 to encourage more foliage for harvesting into fall. Keep blooms removed to increase flavor and allow more energy to be spent on leaf production.
* Harvest herbs for drying:
    Harvest herbs in the morning while oils are still fresh to increase flavor and aroma.
    Gather small bunches of young green leaves and hang bundles stem side up in brown paper bags. Allow the stems to stick out about 1 inch. Use a rubber band or raffia around stems and paper bag.
    Place bags in a moist-free closet and check every week until they are dry. Never dry herbs on a metal surface.
    Store crushed herbs in a dark glass bottles to retain color.
    Harvest herbs leaves, stems, seeds, and roots.
* Try freezing herbs for later use. Adding them to butter, freezing, then cutting the herbed butter into usable portions and refreezing works nicely.
* Serve tasty cold beverages by freezing herbs in ice cubes.
* Freeze chopped herbs in ice cube to be used later in soups.
* If you are allergic to ragweed, do not choose chamomile as your tea. These plants are in the same family.
* Chew fennel, parsley, and seeds of dill for a natural breath freshener.
* Alkaline-lovers such as lavender, sage, hyssop, and rosemary will benefit from a small application of lime to keep them growing well into fall.
* Propagate herbs from new growth for winter indoor plants. Take cuttings from:
    Oregano (*Origanum vulgare*)
    Rosemary (*Rosmarinus officinalis*)
    Scented geraniums (*Pelargonium spp.*)
    Thyme (*Thymus*)

* Celebrate the harvest of herbs on St. Fiacre's Day; he is the patron saint of gardeners and florists. Fiacre was very experience with herbal healing.

That which we call a rose
By any other name would
smell as sweet.
    -Romeo and Juliet, Act 2, sc. 2
    William Shakespear (1564-1616)

Garden Lore

• *Reduce the amount of fleas in and around your home by spraying rue water.*
• *Ward-off evil spirits by placing a sprig of rosemary under your pillow.*
• *Rosemary grows best where the woman is more dominant than her mate.*
• *If you are in love, stay away from parsley or bad luck will come your way.*
• *The garden is a poor man's apothecary*
• *Unmarried ladies could change their luck by chewing on parsley 3 times a day for 3 weeks.*
• *Italians once lined graves with parsley to keep away the devil.*

Lore

Seeds

* Collect seeds to sow and give away from your favorite perennials, biennials, and annuals. Put seeds in an envelope and label them by name, date, color. If you are saving seeds remember heat and moisture will ruin them. Store seeds in labeled airtight containers. Use silica gel packets to absorb moisture and store in the refrigerator.
* Sow biennial seeds in rows and transplant this fall wherever needed.
> Canterbury Bells (*Campanula medium*)
> Foxglove (*Digitalis purpurea*)
> Hollyhock (*Alcea*)
> Honesty, money plant (*Lunaria annua*)
> Sweet William (*Dianthus barbatus*)
> Wallflower (*Cheiranthus cheiri*)
* Sow perennials and cool-weather annuals in flats for transplanting next month.

Vegetables

Sweet, sweet, sweet
Is the wind's song,
Astir in the rippled wheat
All day long.
  Ellen M. H. Cortissoz (- 1933 d.)

* The scorching weather in August requires constant watch for the need for water and removal of weeds that compete for water.
* Harvest vegetables when mature; do not allow mature vegetables to stay on plants.
* Remove the tops on tomato plants and remove suckers to allow remaining energy to go toward ripening the remaining fruit.
* Remove excessive foliage from pumpkin plants to allow more sun through for ripening.
* Dig potatoes after the tops have died.
* Harvest gourds for fall decorations.
* Time to plant and sow vegetables for fall and winter harvesting.

Transplants:

Beans, bush	Kale
Broccoli	Lettuce, head & bibb
Cabbage	Mustard
Cauliflower	Squash, summer

Seeds:

Beets	Mustard
Carrots	Onions, winter
Chard	Peas, snow
Endive	Radishes
Kale, collards	Rutabaga, perennial
Kohlrabi	Spinach
Lettuce, loose, bibb	Turnips

* Thin seedlings that were sown last month.

Garden Lore

• *After Lammas Day (August 1ˢᵗ) or "loaf-Mass," corn ripens as much by night as by day.*
• *If cornhusks are thicker than usual, a cold winter lies ahead.*
• *If corn blades twist up, expect rain.*
• *Raw wet tobacco will draw the venom from an insect's sting.*
•*Onionskin very thin, mild winter coming in.*
Onionskin thick and tough, coming winter cold & rough.
• *Dry August and warm does harvest no harm.*
• *No weather is ill,*
If the wind be still.
• *The shaper the blast,*
The sooner 'tis past.
• *After a storm comes a calm.*
• *If St. Bartholomew's day (August 24ᵗʰ) be fair and clear,*
Then hope for a prosperous autumn that year.

What wondrous life is this I lead!
Ripe apples drop about my head;
The luscious clusters of the vine
Upon my mouth do crush their wine;
The nectarine and curious peach
Into my hands themselves do reach;
Stumbling on melons, as I pass,
Ensnared with flowers, I fall on grass.
-Andrew Marvell, (1621-1678)
Thoughts in a Garden

* Harvest fruits as they ripen. Harvest pears before they ripen and store in a cool place and cover with newspaper. When pears ripen on the tree the fruit texture is coarse.
* Withhold water one week before harvesting cantaloupe, muskmelon, and watermelons. This dryness creates sweeter fruit.
* Keep melons off the ground by laying them on a thin board. This should reduce rot and wireworms.
* Repeat borer spray if needed on peach and cherry trees about one month past the July application.
* Continue to keep blueberry bushes covered with a lightweight bird netting to keep birds away.
* Start a new strawberry patch this month.
* Renovate strawberry patch by thinning old plants, pulling weeds, and fertilizing one last time with 10-10-10.
* Considered a vegetable to many, the "love apple" or tomato is the Tennessee state fruit.

The sun, with all those planets revolving around it and dependent upon it, can still ripen a bunch of grapes as if it had nothing else in the universe to do.
-Galileo (1564-1642)

Make sure of your reapers,
get harvest in hand
the corn that is ripe,
doth but shed as it stand.

Garden Lore

• *August sunshine and bright nights ripen grapes.*
• *After licking the knuckles of your right hand, place an apple seed on each knuckle. Name the seeds. The seed that hangs on the longest will have the name of your future husband.*
• *Name two apple seeds. Place them either on each temple or on each eyelid. The one that hangs on the longest will name your future husband.*
• *Cut an apple into three pieces and rub the cut side on a wart. After you have said "Out wart, into apples", you must bury the apple pieces and when the apple decays the wart will disappear.*

Garden Lore

• *The Cherokee as chewing gum used the sweet gum sap.*
• *To get rid of chills, tie a string around a persimmon tree.*
• *To bring thunderstorms, Hercules would stir a pool of water with an oak branch.*
• *Oak trees are believed to provide safe havens and homes for many varieties of fairy. If you walk passed an oak tree you should turn your coat inside out to shield from their magic.*
• *Lay seven grains of wheat on a four-leafed clover to see fairies.*
• *Use a forked stick made of hazel wood to find water or a buried treasure.*
• *A man who carries a bag of holly leaves and berries will have better luck attracting a woman.*

Trees and Shrubs

Ah in the thunder air
How still the trees are!
And the lime-tree, lovely and tall, every leaf silent
hardly looses even a last breath of perfume.
-David Hubert Lawrence (1885-1930)

* Stop fertilizing trees and shrubs. Decreasing food will prepare plants for winter.
* It is about one month too soon to plant new trees and shrubs. Now is a great time to decide what and where new plants will be planted or transplanted.
* Give hedges and topiaries a final trim early this month to give them plenty of time to grow before the first frost. Only prune trees and shrubs that need to be shaped.
* Deadhead crape myrtles *(Lagerstroemia indica)* after blooms fade to encourage new blooms.
* After summer-blooming shrubs have bloomed, they can be pruned for shape.

> Hydrangea, oak-leaf *(Hydrangea quercifolia)*,
>   Bigleaf *(H. macrophylla)*
> Potentilla
> Summer-sweet *(Clethra alnifolia)*

* Prune side shoots on pyracantha that have grown on a wall to allow berries to be more visible this winter.
* Try propagating by layering shrubs this month. Refer to page 47 for instructions.

> Azalea *(Rhododendron)*
> Bottlebrush buckeye *(Aesculus parviflora)*
> Flowering quince *(Chaenomeles speciosa)*
> Japanese Pieris *(pieris japonica)*
> Juniper *(Juniperus)*
> Lilac *(Syringa)*
> Oak-leaf hydrangea *(Hydrangea quercifolia)*
> Rose-of-Sharon *(Hibiscus syriacus)*
> Tree peony *(Paeonia suffruticosa)*
> Witch hazel *(Hamamelis)*

* Continue to water new plantings and evergreens deeply if rain is scarce to prepare them for fall and winter.
* Keep an eye out for red spider mites on evergreens and treat accordingly. Spider mites will cause bronzing of needles and are problematic during hot dry weather.
* Spray for borers on peach, birch, and dogwood trees.
* Watch for bagworms on evergreens. Handpick and destroy.
* An application of iron chelate or iron sulfate may be needed if leaves are turning yellow on needled and broad-leafed evergreens.

The Oak is called the king of trees,
The Aspen quivers in the breeze,
The poplar grows up straight and tall.
The peach tree spreads along the wall,
The sycamore gives pleasant shade,
The willow droops in watery glade,
The fir tree useful timber gives,
The beach amid the forest lives.
-Sara Coleridge (1802-1852)

Turn your cloaks
For fairy folks
Are in old oaks
-British

You will find something more in woods than in books.
Trees and stones will teach that which you can never learn
from masters.
-St. Bernard of Clairvaux (1090-1153)

Summer, summer, summer, the soundless
footsteps on the grass.
-John Galsworthy (1867-1933)

Maintenance

* Lawn renovation is most successful in late August, early September.
* Dethatching is best performed on lawns with more than 1/3 to 3/4 inch thatch build-up.
* Over-seed or reseed as needed.
* Weed control now reduces work next spring.
* Mid-August to late September is the #1 time to seed Kentucky bluegrass, fescue, or perennial rye grass. If you miss this opportunity, don't expect miracles with mid-February through mid-March seeding; it's tough to get lawns established with spring seeding.
* If you dare to kill undesirable grass here is a method:
   • Buy a product that kills what you want to get rid of and apply once a week for two weeks. (Always use as directed on package)
   • Reapply if grass is not dead.
   • Removing dead grass is not required if you are renting a seed slitter or machine capable of seeding grass seed.
   •Reseed 10 days after 2nd application.

* For areas you want to seed, without using a machine, dethatching is required to help seed contact the soil. The slits made by a dethatching machine offer a good place for new seeds to drop and germinate.
* You can dethatch by raking with an iron tooth rake or by renting a thatcherizer. It is wise to choose the same grass seed that you already have established on the lawn to ensure a good match. After seeding, rake lightly to get seed-to-soil contact. Use straw if area is bare of grass, and water daily for the next 3 to 4 weeks.

* If the lawn is dry, postpone mowing until after you water or after it rains. Mowing when conditions are dry will only open the lawn to increased stress.

* Keep the mower set on the high setting until weather cools. Tall grass protects roots from the heat and reduces weed invasion.

Insect and Weed Control

* Control white grubs by applying insecticide before beetle eggs hatch and grubs appear. If you did not control grubs last fall now is a good time to control them.

* If grass has not grown due to lack of moisture, the weeds will still need to be mowed before they flower and set seed.

Composting

All nature wears one universal grin.
-Henry Fielding (1707-1754)

* Continue to moisten and aerate compost to speed decomposition.

* Add spent annuals to compost pile.

* Shred or cut debris into small pieces to allow fast decomposition.

* Don't add weeds with seed heads to your compost pile.

Water Ponds

Buttercups nodded and said "Goodbye!"
Clover and daisy went off together,
But the fragrant water lilies lie
Yet moored in the golden August weather.
- Celia Thaxter (1835-1894)

* Top ponds with water as needed.

* Don't forget to feed the fish. Fish will eat less as the water temperature grows warmer.

* Remove fading flowers and dying foliage before they fall into the water.

* Keep oxygen available to fish by running a water hose in pond or establishing a fountain.

Water is the driving force of nature.
-Leonardo de Vinci (1452-1519)

August Indoor Gardening

Half the interest of a garden is the constant exercise of the imagination.
Alice Morse Earle (1851-1911)

* Prune overgrown houseplants. Houseplants that have spent the summer outside should be shaped.
* Inspect houseplants for insects and disease before bringing them back indoors.
* Protect houseplants that are spending the summer outdoors from direct sun.
* Bring Christmas cactus (*Schlumbergera bridgesii*) and poinsettias (*Euphorbia pulcherrima*) indoor to prepare them for the holidays. Give the Christmas cactus a room temperature close to 55 degrees (in other words, the coolest room in your house with a window). Give the poinsettia 65 to 70 degree room temperature. Both plants require at least six weeks of 14 hours of darkness every day until late September. Place plants every day in an area they will receive 4 hours of direct light or 10 hours of sunlight. Apply 0-10-10 liquid fertilizer this month and next to boost buds on these plants.
* Near the end of the month, start moving pots of amaryllis into a cool 50 to 60 degree dry, dark place (basement) for 3 months. Lay pots on their sides and allow bulbs to dry. If you planted them in the garden, dig, rinse, and let them dry for a few days in the shade before storing. Do not water. Remove browning foliage and do not remove green foliage. Green foliage will fuel bulbs for next bloom.

Grow where you are planted.
-unknown

September Garden Chore List

In the Garden:
- ❏ Create new and replenish established gardens.
- ❏ Do a soil test on flower and vegetable gardens.
- ❏ Cultivate gardens to prepare for next season.

Flowers and Herbs:
- ❏ Clean the garden by removing spent plant material.
- ❏ Fall mulching is not necessary.
- ❏ Create autumn displays in containers.
- ❏ Cut herbaceous peonies after their foliage begins to die.
- ❏ Perennial planting and transplanting this month is ideal.
- ❏ Transplant self-sown biennials and perennials to a desired location.
- ❏ Establish a spring garden by sowing or planting cool-weather annuals.
- ❏ Purchase or order bulbs for winter forcing and fall planting.
- ❏ Deadheading roses should be discontinued around Labor Day to allow roses to prepare for winter.
- ❏ Secure climbing roses with twine.

Seeds:
- ❏ Sow biennial seeds in cold frame or directly to the garden.
- ❏ Harvest mature seeds.

Vegetables and Fruits:
- ❏ Sow cover crops or "green manure" where land is fallow.
- ❏ Remove spent foliage and over-ripe vegetables and apply to compost pile.
- ❏ Plant cool-weather vegetables.
- ❏ Finish planting strawberries, blueberries, and brambles.

Trees and Shrubs:
- ❏ It's too late to prune.
- ❏ Trees and shrubs can be planted until the ground freezes.
- ❏ Wait to transplant deciduous trees and shrubs when leaves start to change colors.

Lawn Care:
- ❏ Seed early this month to allow grass to establish before the onset of winter.
- ❏ Aerate the lawn as needed to discourage compact soil.
- ❏ Remove fallen leaves before they accumulate.

Composting:
- ❏ Start a compost pile in a well-drained area.

Water Ponds:
- ❏ Remove debris from pond.
- ❏ Feed fish high-protein feed to build reserves before winter.
- ❏ Dig and divide water plants.

Indoors Plants:
- ❏ All tropical plants should be brought indoors.
- ❏ Stop fertilizing houseplants.

Chapter 7

September Garden

O sweet September, thy first breezes bring
The dry leaf's rustle and the squirrel's laughter,
The cool fresh air whence health and vigor spring
And promise of exceeding joy hereafter.
-George Arnold (1834-1865)

Not until the Harvest Moon appears in our sky, do we realize that summer is drawing to an end and nature begins its resting period. The garden season wanes as cool weather approaches. Evenings arrive earlier creating shorter days and the weather is perfect with its low humidity. The sun is still hot and frost is at least a month away. As the foliage dies, we can only see the possibilities for spring. It's not goodbye, it's goodnight for many plants and they are sure to return to please us again and again. The goldenrod is one of the last to perform in nature's flower show as well as asters, showy sedum, and ornamental and native grasses. September prepares us, as well as plant material for the fall approaching. The air becomes refreshing and that favorite sweater resurfaces again.

Although the gardening season may soon end, it's time for renewal in our landscape. You may feel like the garden is fading, but it's only preparing for winter. It is time to change things around by digging and dividing to create a more pleasing display for next year. Removal of annuals is a hard mental garden chore; they seem to display extra color and beauty just before their inevitable end.

Whether it is color, form, or design, there is relief knowing that next year the garden will be better. Change is out of the gardener's control and if the garden looked perfect this year, you can't count on it next year to do the same. Find time this month to take notes on how your garden did or did not do. It's time to manicure our gardens and prepare for cool weather. It's time to cultivate, harvest, and create spring color with bulbs and pansies.

General Maintenance

Garden Lore

• *If it's fair on September 1ˢᵗ, it will be fair the entire month.*
• *When spiders weave their webs by noon, fine weather is coming soon.*
• *When spider webs in air do fly, the weather will soon be very dry.*
• *The early settlers and Native Americans called the full Moon this month the Harvest Moon, Corn Moon or Barley Moon.*
• *It's bad luck to carry flowers onto an airplane.*

Soil

* Fall is a great time to create new and replenish established gardens. Roots grow best in the fall making this an important time to amend the soil, propagate, and plant.
* A soil test can be done any time of year on flower and vegetable gardens as well as your lawn. It is recommended that you get your test results before you apply fertilizer or lime to your soil. Contact your local county extension office for details. Testing now will allow you to get results and amend soil before spring.

-Using a hand trowel, dig 12 to 15 scoops of soil from different areas of your garden or lawn, depending on what you are testing. It is recommended to collect separate soil samples for each major growing area. Mix the scoops together and keep only about 2 cups of combined soil for testing. Spread the two cups of soil on a newspaper to dry it for a couple days before packaging it to send or deliver. Put soil sample in bag or plastic container and take it to your local county extension office.

* Cultivate gardens to prepare for next season. Cultivating allows oxygen into soil spaces which is required for roots.
* Fall plowed soil will dry easier and can be worked earlier in the spring.

In-The-Garden Maintenance

* Start a compost pile. Refer to the composting on page 145.
* Begin cleaning the garden by removing spent plant material. Add debris to compost pile unless there is an insect or disease problem on foliage; then discard.
* Leave plants that contribute to the winter scenery. These plants will make the winterscape more interesting.

Astilbe
Black-eyed Susan (*Rudbeckia fulgida*)
Chinese lantern (*Physalis alkekengi*)
Honesty, money plant (*Lunaria annua*)
Ornamental and native grasses
Russian sage (*Perovskia atriplicifolia*)
Showy stonecrop (*Sedum spectabile*)
Spiky sea holly (*Eryngium*)

* The more weeds you pull now, especially before seeds mature, the less you will have next spring.
* Take advantage of fall clearance sales and stock-up on tools and supplies for next year.
* Clean mold and or moss from bricks with ½ cup bleach to one gallon of water; scrub with a brush and rinse.
* Aside from aesthetic reasons fall mulching is not necessary. It is best to wait until ground temperatures become cold and stay cold to allow plant material to prepare for winter before applying mulch.   Mulching when soil temperatures are still warm will only delay plants from preparing for winter.

Container Gardening

Mares eat oats and doe's eat oats,
And little lambs eat ivy,
Kids will eat ivy too,
Wouldn't you?
                              Mother Goose

* Time to change containers and create autumn and winter displays. Replace window boxes with kale or ornamental cabbage, mustard greens, chard, conifers, small-broadleaf evergreens, and dwarf shrubs. Severe winter temperatures (less than 0 degrees) may kill root systems exposed to temperature fluctuations (above-ground plantings). Cut branches may be a more economical approach than live material. Roadside shop for arrangement materials such as teasels, red seed heads from the sumac tree, and ornamental and native grasses for indoor and outdoor arrangements.
* Stay away from terra-cotta pots for winter interest. Terra-cotta pots will crack during winter freeze.
* Plant spring-blooming bulbs among the fall decorations for spring color.
* Continue to fertilize container annuals with 20-20-20.

Perennials and Biennials

Lift up your boughs of Vervain blue,
Dip't in cold September dew;
And dash the moisture, chaste and clear
O'er the ground and through the air.
                              -Unknown

* Defining perennials to aid in fall cleaning:
Herbaceous plants-Plants that die to the ground every year such as:
    Bleeding heart (*Dicentra spectabilis*)
    Coreopsis
    Daylilies (*Hemerocallis*)
    Hosta
    Japanese anemone
    Peony (*Paeonia*)
    Purple coneflower (*Echinacea purpurea*)

September

The goldenrod is yellow;
The corn is turning brown
The trees in apple orchards
With fruits are bending down.

The gentian's bluest fringes
Are curling in the sun:
In dusty pods the milkweed
Its hidden silk has spun.

The sedges flaunt their harvest,
In every meadow nook;
And asters by the brookside
Make asters in the brook.

From dewy lanes at morning
The grapes' sweet odors rise;
At noon the roads all flutter
With yellow butterflies.

By all these lovely tokens
September days are here,
With summer's best of weather
And autumn's best of cheer.
                 -Helen Hunt Jackson (1830-1885)

***Semi-herbaceous plants*-**Upper foliage dies and basal growth stays green throughout winter. Cut dead foliage only on perennials such as:

      Black-eyed Susan (*Rudbeckia fulgida*)

      Goldenrod (*Solidago*)

      Shasta daisy (*Chrysanthemum x superbum*)

Evergreen perennials such as these listed keep their foliage and should not be cut in the fall.

      Adam's needle (*Yucca filamentosa*)

      Candytuft (*Iberis sempervirens*)

      Coral bells (*Heuchera x brizoides*)

      Creeping Phlox *(Phlox stolonifera)*

      Lady's-mantle (*Alchemilla mollis*)

***Woody perennials*-**These perennials have exposed leaf buds. They need to be pruned in the spring and not in the fall.

      Butterfly bush (*Buddleia davidii*)

      Lavender (*Lavandula*)

      Russian sage (*Perovskia atriplicifolia*)

* If in doubt about pruning perennials, cut only dead or damaged foliage.
* Cut spent foliage on perennials; compost dead foliage unless there are signs of insects or disease. Avoid leaving spent foliage in gardens; sanitation is important to reduce overwintering of insects and disease.
* Cut herbaceous peonies after their foliage begins to die to reduce overwintering disease. Dispose of all peony foliage; do not add to compost pile. Do not prune tree peonies *(Peony suffruticosa)*.
* Cut bloom scapes on daylilies to 2 inches above the ground and cut foliage to 6 to 8 inches. If it is time to divide, replant at least two fans per clump and space clumps about 18 inches apart.
* Trim groundcovers if needed to control takeover and growth into areas where other plants are more valuable. Remove choking vines, such as ivy, from plant material.
* Plant perennials for fall color and interest; choose from:

      Chrysanthemums

      Japanese Anemone

      Ornamental and native grasses

      Russian sage (*Perovskia atriplicifolia*)

      Showy stonecrop (*Sedum spectabile*)

* Create a moon garden. Here are some of my favorite plants that will light up the night by the light of the moon.

Tall plants: Clematis (white)

          Climbing roses (white)

          Coneflower (white)

          Moonflower vine

          Russian sage

Medium plants: Artemisia, silver mound

             Asiatic lilies or trumpet lilies (white)

             Cosmos (white)

             Dahlias (white)

Delphinium (white)
Foxglove (white)
Hosta (variegated)
Lavender
Tulips (white)

Short or border plants: Alyssum (white)
Dusty Miller
Impatiens (white)
Lamb's ear
Pansies (white)
Salvia (white)

* Plant Christmas roses (*Hellebores niger*) and lords and ladies (*Arum*) for late winter interest in your garden.
* Perennial planting and transplanting this month is ideal. Wait until a cool cloudy day or late in the day. Water plants well before digging and keep soil moist to aid root reestablishment after planting. Perennials need a few months of root growth before the ground freezes to survive the winter.
* Try transplanting Oriental poppies this month; remember their foliage shrinks so you may get more than you think.
* Crowding of roots can decrease blooming; therefore most perennials need to be divided every 3 to 5 years. Decrease in blooms is a sure sign that the plant is crowded.
* Transplant self-sown biennials and perennials to a desired location.
* Goldenrod has lots of lore behind it. It was thought that masses of goldenrod in the field pointed the way to a hidden treasure or maybe a water source. It was often planted near the front of the house to bring good luck. It is often blamed for allergies, while ragweed is the culprit.

There are flowers enough in the summertime,
More flowers than I can remember—
But none with the purple, gold, and red
That dyes the flowers of September
-Mary Howitt (1799-1888)

* Add chrysanthemums to your landscape. They can be planted and possibly survive the winter or just treat them as annuals and use in containers. No other plant says fall like the chrysanthemum.
* Establish a spring garden by planting cool-weather annuals.
Johnny-jump-ups (*Viola tricolor*)
Kale, ornamental cabbage (*Brassica oleracea*)
Pansy (*Viola x wittrockiana*)
Snapdragon (*Antirrhinum*)
* Cool-weather annuals require cool weather to grow and 5 hours of sun daily for best results. Planting cool-weather annuals in the fall will increase root development over winter and the spring flower show will be maximized.
* Continue to fertilize annuals with liquid 20-20-20.
* Harvest seeds from annuals for drying, saving, and sharing.

* Continue to extend blooming season by removing faded blooms from marigolds, cosmos, zinnias, and sage.
* Cut annuals to soil level when they die. Leave the roots in the ground to add organic matter for nourishing the soil.
*Propagate warm-weather annuals now as daylight starts decreasing and the days get cool. Take cuttings of coleus, impatiens, fuchsia, begonias, and geraniums. Treat as houseplants this winter and you will have next summer beauties. Refer to page 122 for instructions.

* Save costly geraniums (*Pelargonium*) three different ways.

   1. Trim plant and grow indoors with good sunlight. Keep soil moist and feed throughout winter with a diluted liquid fertilizer such as 20-20-20.
   2. Remove spent blooms and store geranium out of its container in a cool, dark place (50 to 55 degrees). Store in paper bag or just hang upside down. Don't water. If stems start to shrivel, mist lightly.
   3. Take soft stem cuttings to create new plants. Refer to page 122 for instructions.

Bulbs, Corms, Rhizomes, and Tubers

* The success of a spring garden is fall planting. With little effort from the gardener, bulbs are sure to reward you in the spring.
* Purchase or order bulbs for winter forcing and fall planting.
* Bulb buying guide:
   Bulbs should be solid and heavy
   Firm all over with no soft spots or bruises
   No mold or discoloration
   No dark spots
   Base should be firm
   No holes
   No signs of insects
   Stay away from bulbs that have already sprouted
   Inspect bulbs like produce (onions)
   Loose papery covering is okay

* When planting bulbs think large quantity. Mass coloring is more dramatic.
* For mass planting, bulbs in a bag are ideal, but quality will be less.
* Stay away from mixed color bulbs. Bulbs look better planted in a mass of one or two complimentary colors.

* Don't forget to complement your house color when choosing bulbs.
* Plant these bulbs in early fall due to bulbs blooming in late winter to early spring.

> Crocus
> Crown imperial, Persian lily, tears of Mary (*Fritillaria imperalis*)
> Daffodil *(Narcissus)*
> Grape Hyacinth, pearls of Spain *(Muscari)*
> Hyacinth (*Hyacinth orietalis*)
> Snowdrop, Candlemas bells (*Galanthus*)
> Star flower *(Ipheion uniflorum)*
> Winter aconite (*Eranthis*)

* Plant bulbs in late fall (by Thanksgiving) that bloom later in spring.

> Lily (*Lilium*)
> Tulip (*Tulipa*)– pay special attention to early, middle or late season bloomers

* To get the most out of your bulbs, as well as many plants, create a hillock or berm in the center of landscape borders to have optimum viewing of all flowers. Position the berm to slope the border or bed toward the viewer.
* If you are not sure which end of the bulb is the top, plant bulbs on the their sides.
* Plant bulbs in the back or middle of a border. When the bulb foliage dies it is hidden by other plants.
* Dig and divide crowded crocuses, scillia sibiricas, and glory-in-the-snow (*Chionodoxas)*.
* Cover the bulb garden with chicken wire to deter squirrels. Remove chicken wire in late winter.
* Prepare to dig tender bulbs as soon as they have been frost bitten. Make a plan for curing and storage. Refer to October bulbs for instructions.

> Banana trees (*Musa*)
> Begonias (store cool and dry at 45 degrees)
> Canna (hardy in USDA zone 7)
> Caladium, angel wings
> Calla Lily (*Zantedeschia*)
> Dahlia (Dig after frost has blackened leaves)
> Elephant ears (*Philodendron domesticum*)
> Gladiolus
> Tuberose (*Polianthes tuberosa*)

* Daffodils and crocus get better over the years, where tulips decline after the first year. For the best show, tulips are best replaced every two years.

Forcing Bulbs

* Forcing bulbs to bloom earlier than nature intended will allow you to have fresh spring flowers in the gray of winter. When fall arrives and bulbs are available it is time to pot bulbs to force for late winter indoor blooming. By subjecting potted bulbs to darkness and temperatures near freezing for several months to mimic the outdoors, you can have spring

flowers indoor during winter. After a root system has been established and pots are brought into a warm and bright window, they will bloom.

* All bulbs will differ on the weeks of cold storage, but generally it will take 8 to 15 weeks for roots in the cold and about 3 weeks in the window to bloom. Tulips may take up to 15 weeks of cold to root, where paperwhites *(Narcissus tazetta)* need only 3 weeks to root.

* A cold period can be obtained by using an extra refrigerator, cold frame or digging a 2 inch trench outside. Line trench with straw and then pots of bulbs. After pots are placed in the trench, cover with straw or leaves. Keep pots moist.

* Amaryllis and paperwhites are in the same family and are not hardy outdoors. They do not need a cold period to prepare for forcing.

Bulb	Weeks of cold 40° to 50°F	Weeks to bloom	# Plants in 6 inch pot
Amaryllis	none	6-8	1
Crocus	15	2-3	6-10
Daffodils *(Narcissus)*	15-17	2-3	3-5
Grape hyacinth	14-15	2-3	3-5
Hyacinth	10-12(pre-cooled) 11-14(not pre-cooled)	2-3	3
Paperwhite *(Narcissus tazetta)*	none	3-5	5-7
Tulip	14-20	2-3	5

Bulb Forcing Guide

Container
* Plant bulbs in clay pots that are twice as tall as the bulbs. Use 1 inch spacing for bulbs and neck of the bulb should rest just below the pot rim. Any container will work that provides good drainage. Leave tops of bulbs uncovered on tulips and Narcissus.

Soil mix
*Use potting mix that is equal parts peat moss, soil, and vermiculite or perlite. Never use garden soil.

Water
*Water to moisten potting mix. Keep potting mix slightly moist for duration of cold storage. Don't forget to check on them.

Cold storage
*Store in a cool, dry, dark area for the 8 to 15 weeks of recommended cold storage. Store at 40 to 45 degrees, a refrigerator works best and is more consistent with temperature.
*Start checking for new growth after 8 weeks.

Post storage
*When foliage appears or cold requirement time has been met, remove pots from the dark and move them toward light gradually over a week.

Move from cool indirect light to warm direct light. Room temperatures around 60 to 65 degrees work best.

Water culture – Paperwhites and hyacinths can be planted in gravel or marbles and water; keeping water just below bulbs to avoid rot. Every two weeks plant additional bulbs for continuous bloom throughout the winter. Bulbs forced in water are best discarded after bloom instead of transplanting in the garden.

Bulb Forcing Tips

* New bulbs that are prepared to perform will bloom regardless of your green thumb. The second year will be iffy and then they grow more reliably.
* Choose early-blooming and short cultivars when buying bulbs to force.
* Warm temperatures will encourage flowers to open faster.
* Cool temperatures will help flowers last longer.
* Keep stored and flowering bulbs away from all fruit, which emit a hormone called ethylene gas that ages flowers and leafy vegetables; bad chemistry.
* Discard forced tulips and all bulbs forced in water.

 Roses

Gather ye rosebuds while ye may
Old time is still a-flying
And this same flower that smiles today
Tomorrow will be dying.
　　　　　-Robert Herrick (1591-1674)

* To allow plants to harden before winter apply granular fertilizer for the last feed of the season around Labor Day. Use a fertilizer such as 10-10-10 with an application of 1/4 cup per bush. This last fertilization should be applied about 6 weeks before the first expected frost. Frost usually occurs mid-October in Tennessee.
* Deadheading roses should be discontinued around Labor Day to allow roses to prepare for winter.
* Remove leaves infected with black spot or mildew and discard.
* Secure climbers with twine. Allow for movement in the wind and for stem diameter increase. In other words, don't tie them too tight.
* Try propagating roses by taking cuttings from stems. Use pieces that are about 8 inches long with all but the top set of leaflets removed. Each cutting should have two eyes under the soil. Refer to page 122 for instructions.
* Try layering a rose to form a new bush for next fall. Look for layering instructions in Chapter Four, Trees and Shrubs.

The rose looks fair, but fairer it we deem for
that sweet odour which doth in it live.
　　　William Shakespeare (1564-1616)

Herbs

Herbs are the friend of the physician and the pride of cooks.
-Charlemagne (c. 742-814)

* Dig and divide perennial herbs.
  Bee balm (*Monarda didyma*)
  Betony (*Stachys officinalis*)
  Clary sage(*Salvia sclarea*)
  Comfrey (*Symphytum officinale*)
  Feverfew (*Tanacetum parthenium*)
  Germander (*Teucrium chamaedrys*)
  Goldenrod (*Solidago spp.*)
  Horsetail *(Equisetum spp.)*
  Hyssop (*Hyssopus officinalis*)
  Lady's bedstraw (*Galium verum*)
  Lemon balm *(Melissa officinalis)*
  Marjoram (*Origanum majorana*)
  Marsh mallow (*Althaea officinalis*)
  Mint *(Mentha spp.)*
  Mugwort (*Artemisia vulgaris*)
  Pennyroyal, English (*Mentha pulegium*)
  Rue *(Ruta graveolens)*
  Sage *(Salvia officinalis)*
  Savory, winter (*Satureja montana*)
  Soapwort (*Saponaria officinalis*)
  Sorrel *(Rumex spp.)*
  Southernwood (*Artemisia abrotanum*)
  Sweet cicely (*Myrrhis odorata*)
  Sweet woodruff *(Galium odoratum)*
  Tansy (*Tanacetum vulgare*)

* Remove old mint and save new growth. Mint is very invasive, you may want to pot it in a plastic container and plant the whole unit into the ground to help control spreading.
* Remove flower stalks from basil, parsley, sage, borage, and mint to increase production.

Annuals
  Chervil *(Anthriscus cerefolium)*
  Coriander *(Coriandrum sativum)*
  Dill *(Anethum graveolens)*
  Mustard *(Brassica spp.)*

Biennials
  Caraway *(Carum carvi)*

* Pot herbs for winter seasonings. These herbs need maximum light (south-facing window) for good health. Don't over-water.
  Basil (*Ocimum basilicum*)
  Chives (*Allium schoenoprasum*)
  Oregano or marjoram (*Origanum vulgare or O. majorana*)

Parsley (*Petroselinum crispum*)
Rosemary (*Rosmarinius officinalis*)
Tarragon *(Artemisia dracunculus)*
Thyme (*Thymus vulgaris*)

* Add horseradish to your herb garden. One plant is enough.
* Try making homemade herb vinegar to give as gifts for the holidays.
    1. Harvest herb and rinse well. (Use just one herb or try a combination)
    2. Pat leaves dry and allow all moisture to evaporate.
    3. Put 1-cup fresh herb into clean jar and fill jar with heated red wine vinegar or cider vinegar. Use several layers of plastic wrap over jar before replacing metal lid.
    4. Place jar in the sun for 2 weeks or just store in a cool, dry place for 3 weeks.
    5. Strain vinegar of herbs by using a coffee filter and plastic colander. Pour vinegar into another clean jar and store in a dark place.
    6. Mix with salad dressing mix as needed or give as a gift.
    7. If giving vinegar as gifts, pour into decorative bottles and add a fresh sprig of herb for looks.

> *How could such sweet and wholesome hours*
> *Be reckoned but with herbs and flowers?*
> *-Andrew Marvel (1621-1678)*

 Seeds   *Bad seed is a robbery of the worst kind; for your pocket book not only suffers by it, but your preparations are lost and a season passes away unimproved.*
-George Washington (1732-1799)

* Sow biennial seeds in cold frame or directly to the garden.
    Canterbury bells (*Campanula medium*)
    Foxglove (*Digitalis*)
    Hollyhock (*Alcea*)
    Honesty, money plant (*Lunaria annua*)
    Sweet William *(Dianthus barbatus)*
    Wallflower (*Cheiranthus cheiri*)

* Harvest mature seeds; save for next spring or give them away. Don't forget to reorder your favorites this winter to make sure you get the best quality seeds to sow.
    Cosmos
    Hollyhock (*Alcea rosea*)
    Mexican sunflower (*Tithonia rotundifolia*)
    Nicotiana
    Spider flower (*Cleome hasslerana*)
    Zinnia

Garden Lore

• *Upon removing all but twenty kernels of corn, hang a corncob over your doorway. The first single man to enter will become your husband.*

• *Tomatoes in the windowsill protect a house.*

• *A red ear of corn brings good luck.*

• *Hang a corn stalk over your mirror for good luck.*

Truths are first clouds; then rain, then harvest and food.
  Henry Ward Beecher (1813-1887)

Up from the meadows rich with corn,
Clear is the cool September morn.
  -John Greenleaf Whittier (1807-1982)

* Sow cool-weather seeds directly to the garden. These early seedlings will supply the garden with early flowers next spring.

Cornflower or bachelor's button (*Centaurea cyanus*)
Forget-me-not (*Myosotis sylvatica*)
Johnny-jump-up (*Viola tricolor*)
Larkspur (*Consolida ambiqua*)
Love-in-a-mist (*Nigella damascena*)
Poppy; corn, Flanders, or Shirley (*Papaver rhoeas*)
Poppy, Iceland (*Papaver nudicaule*)
Pot marigold (*Calendula officinalis*)
Sweet Alyssum (*Lobularia maritima*)

Vegetables

Through sunny days and yellow weeks,
With clouds that melt in tears,
The glory of the harvest speaks
In all the silken ears.
  -J. Hazard Hartzell (1830-1890)

* Sow cover crops or "green manure" where land is fallow. The use of cover crops will prevent soil erosion, soil compaction, and return nutrients to depleted soil in the form of humus. Cover crops also discourage weeds from occupying empty gardens. If you do not want to sow cover crop, incorporate compost, manure, rotted straw, and mulched leaves into empty garden plots. Suggested cover crops:

Crimson and white clover
Hairy vetch
Ryegrass, annual
Winter wheat

* Control weeds before they set seed and multiply.
* Remove spent foliage and over-ripe vegetables and apply to compost pile.
* Avoid planting chrysanthemums to close to lettuce; bad chemistry.
* By the first week of September it is time to plant cool-weather vegetables.

Seeds:	Transplants:
Carrots	Broccoli
Lettuce, bibb, leaf	Brussels sprouts
Kale, collards	Cabbage
Mustard	Cauliflower
Radish	Garlic cloves
Spinach	Kale, collards
	Kohlrabi
	Turnip
	Winter onions

* Plant garlic to deter Japanese beetles, caterpillars, aphids, root maggots, and snails from your garden.
* Harvest winter squash when spot touching the ground turns creamy gold.

Fruit

*Live each season as it passes; breathe the air,
drink the drink, taste the fruit,
and resign yourself to the influences of each.*
-Henry David Thoreau (1817-1862)

* Spray fruit trees as needed to control insects and disease.
* Spray peach & cherry trees for the last time this season to control borers.
* Finish planting strawberries, blueberries, and brambles, which include blackberries, raspberries, dewberries, loganberries, and boysenberries.
* Prune plum trees after harvest for an increased harvest next year.
* Propagate currants and gooseberries by taking hardwood cuttings from this year's wood. Refer to page 159 for instructions.
* Keep an eye out for the Tennessee state wild animal, the raccoon. They will leave their cozy hollow tree to pick all the grapes on your vine.

Trees and Shrubs

*Solitude is a silent storm that breaks down all our dead branches;
Yet it sends our living roots deeper into the living heart of the living earth.*
-Kahlil Gibran (1883-1931)

* It's too late to prune. Pruning now will trigger new growth that will be susceptible to winter kill.
* Prune dead, diseased, and out-of-bounds limbs only on trees and shrubs.
* Do not prune tree peonies *(Peony suffruticosa)*. They do not die like the herbaceous peony.
* Wait to transplant deciduous trees and shrubs when leaves start to change colors.
* Wait until next spring to plant bare-root stock. Container and burlapped plants can be planted until the ground freezes.
* Plant landscape plants now that temperatures are cool. Keep in mind how delicate roots are. The more soil you transfer along with the root ball the less stress that plant will have.
* Plant and transplant needle-leafed (conifers) and broad-leafed evergreens before mid-October. They will require more water due to the evergreen foliage. There is still time to establish new roots before a hard frost. These evergreens help provide interest in every season.
* Avoid planting walnut, butternut, hickory, and pecans trees near other plantings; Leaves and roots of these trees release juglone which is toxic to many plants.
* It is a natural occurrence for pine trees, yews, arborvitae, and junipers to drop needles this time of year.
* When deciduous trees and shrubs begin to lose their leaves fertilizer can be used to build strong root systems.
* Remove unwanted tree seedlings in the landscape before they get harder to pull.

Garden Lore

September blow soft until the apples be in the loft.

*Kind hearts are the garden,
Kind thoughts are the roots
Kind words are the blossoms,
Kind deeds are the fruit.*
John Ruskin (1819-1900)

Garden Lore

*Try layering these plants for new plants in the spring or next fall: Look for layering instructions in Chapter Two; Trees and Shrubs.

Bayberry (*Myrica pensylvanica*)
Carolina allspice (*Calycanthus floridus*)
Cotoneaster
Forsythia
Fothergilla
Juniper (*Juniperus*)
Mountain Laurel (*Kalmia latifolia*)
Red-barked dogwood (*Cornus alba*)
Rose daphne, garland flower (*Daphne cneorum*)
Spike winter hazel (*Corylopsis spicata*)
Viburnum

Lawn Care

There is not a sprig of grass that shoots uninteresting to me.
-Thomas Jefferson (1743-1826)

* Autumn is the best time to pamper your lawn. The soil is warm, air temperatures are cooling; moisture is retained in the soil longer to obtain a lush lawn.

Maintenance

* Cool-season lawns such as Kentucky bluegrass, perennial ryegrass, and fescues are entering their growing stage after a hot summer. They thrive best when night time temperatures are in the 50s and 60s and day time temperatures are 70 to 80 degrees.
* Seed early this month to allow grass to establish before the onset of winter.
* Try sowing Kentucky bluegrass under the walnut tree. Kentucky bluegrass is more tolerant of this toxic tree than other grasses.
* On established lawns it's time to dethatch if thatch is more than 1/3 inch thick.
* Aerate the lawn as needed to discourage compact soil. This works best if the soil is not hard and dry.
* Continue to mow until lawn goes dormant. Some years this may be as late as Thanksgiving.
* Edging will keep lawns and landscape looking manicured.
* Layered leaves will suffocate underlying grass; remove fallen leaves before they accumulate.

Fertilization

* It is best to cancel fertilizing the lawn until mid-October. If your lawn is stressed, fertilizer compounds the problem.
* When you do apply the first application, it is important to space applications every 6 to 8 weeks. You may choose to make one fall application of lawn fertilizer if you prefer a low maintenance situation.

Seeding

* Getting a soil test will ensure proper soil amendments and fertilizer prior to seeding.
* Seeding can take place now through mid-October. This time of year cool-season grasses will establish if they are watered daily.

>   Fescue
>   Kentucky bluegrass
>   Perennial ryegrass

* You should water newly seeded areas 30-60 minutes daily for the first 2 to 3 weeks or until the lawn is established and growing well enough to require mowing.

Insect and Weed Control

* Do not apply weed control to areas to be seeded for 4 weeks prior to planting.
* Rosettes of thistles should be removed as they appear in the fall. Try to dig the entire perennial root and discard to prevent their growth into spring with flower and seed head.

A garden is never as good as it will be next year.
    -Thomas Cooper (1759-1839)

* Start a compost pile in a well-drained area. Start with a layer of soil and leaves in the base of a bin or pile and just start adding ingredients. Sprinkle layers with manure, 10-10-10 and lime; alternating application.
* *Choose a site that is:*

>   Not soggy
>   Well-draining
>   Light shade

* Sprinkle the ground surrounding pile with limestone.
* 2 to 3 inch pile is all that is needed to heat up.
* Create your pile with a mix of "green" and "brown" material. "Green" material is usually wet and high in nitrogen. "Brown" material is usually dry and high in carbon.
* Shred debris into 2 inch pieces for faster decomposing.
* Shred leaves before applying to compost pile for faster decomposing.
* Water compost pile during dry periods to keep it active.
* Turn compost pile once a month to increase oxygen to center of pile.
* If temperatures are above 70 degrees compost may be ready in 3 months. Over winter, compost is ready in 8 to 10 months.
* 160 degrees is optimum temperature for a compost pile.
* *Problem solving:*

>   Stinky pile? – Turn compost and increase air.
>   No heat? – Needs more nitrogen. Pile-on "green" plant material.
>   Too wet? – Add dry material "brown".
>   Too dry? – Add water.

Do not put in your compost pile:

Woody garden debris
Invasive vines and grasses
Diseased or insect infested
  plants
Any plant treated with a
  chemical
Food
Dairy products
Bread
Animal fats
Meat products
Pet manure
Coal ashes or charcoal ash
Oils
Waxes

Weeds that have bloomed
  and set seed
Harmful weeds
Poisonous plants *"Leaflets
  three let it be, Leaflets five
  let it thrive."*
Leaves, magnolia,
  eucalyptus, black walnut
Red cedar trees
Corncobs
Grapefruit and orange
  peelings
Paper with ink
Plastic

Pile it on!

Shredded leaves
Lawn clippings
Shredded woody material
Manure (from cows, horses,
  sheep, pigs, and chickens)
  not pets
Soil
Plant debris
Hay/straw
Tea from tea bag
Coffee grounds
Dust from vacuum bags
Dead rats
Bone meal
Pine needles
Spoiled cereals
Jelly
Fruit scraps
Weeds-young
Plants
Hair

Sawdust
Rock powders (rock phos-
  phate, and granite dust)
Seaweed
Fish scraps, must bury in
  pile!! *P.U.*
Vegetables scraps, (no
  corncobs)
Eggshells, clean
Faded blooms
Pet fur
Shredded newspaper
Wood ashes
Dried blood
Hoof and horn meal
Discarded bulbs
Pond scum
Alfalfa meal
Cottonseed meal
Soybean meal

Loam wasn't built in a day!
-Unknown

Water Ponds

* Remove debris from pond.
* Remove dead and dying foliage by cutting foliage to 1 inch above water surface.
* Feed fish high-protein feed to build reserves before winter. When temperatures drop below 50 degrees stop feeding fish. Goldfish and koi cannot digest food at cold temperatures.

* Dig and divide water plants.
* Stop fertilizing water plants at the beginning of the month to prepare for winter.

September Indoor Gardening

Look deep, deep into nature, and then you will understand everything better.
-Albert Einstein (1879-1955)

* All tropical plants should be indoors before temperatures drop into the 40s. Place them in a south-facing window for the best sunlight. West and east-facing windows will allow sufficient light to overwinter tropical plants. See that houseplants get at least four hours of sunlight a day and if you want blooms throughout winter supplemental lighting will be needed.
* Sudden leaf drop on houseplants usually means that they were exposed to cool nighttime temperatures and should have been brought indoors earlier. Decrease in light will also cause leaf drop.
* As fall approaches and daylight decreases, houseplants will require less fertilizing. Growth will slow during this season.
* Blooming houseplants such as amaryllis, African violets, orchids, bromeliads, and holiday cactus will benefit from diluted fertilizer while they are in bloom.
* Switch phalaenopsis or moth orchids to a bloom-booster fertilizer, this application along with cool-nights will induce flower buds. Keep orchids in east-facing window, with temperatures in the 70 to 80's. As with most plants, do not let them sit in water.
* Withhold water from Christmas cactus and allow cactus to stay in 55 degree temperatures during the night to allow flower buds to set. An application of 0-10-10 liquid fertilizer this month and next will help develop flower buds. 10 hours of sunlight and 14 hours of darkness will create optimum flowering. You can go to the trouble and force your cactus to bloom or just let it bloom when it's ready. The blooms will be enjoyed no matter the time of year.
* If you have saved a poinsettia, move it into the house to a room that is cool and gets no light at night (including television light, street lights or porch lights). 10 hours of sun light and 14 hours of darkness will create optimum flowering. During daylight hours give poinsettia a lot of sunlight (south-facing window). An application of 0-10-10 liquid fertilizer this month and next will help develop flower buds. Keep room temperature around 65 to 70 degrees.
* Store gloxinias in the basement and withhold water until April.
* Propagate African violets by taking stem cuttings; Refer to to page 122 for instructions.

October Garden Chore List

In the Garden:
- ❑ Tidy gardens by removing dead and diseased foliage.
- ❑ Gather and store garden stakes.
- ❑ Remove weeds before seeds mature.
- ❑ Clean, repair, and sharpen garden tools.
- ❑ Move terra-cotta pots to a shed, garage or basement to protect from winter damage.

Flowers and Herbs:
- ❑ Last chance to move perennials to their new location.
- ❑ Trim spent perennials to 2 inches above the ground.
- ❑ Remove warm-weather annuals.
- ❑ Plant cool-weather annuals.
- ❑ Plant spring-flowering bulbs.
- ❑ Dig tender summer bulbs, corms, and tubers; and store.
- ❑ Stop cutting spent blooms on roses to prepare plants for winter.
- ❑ Remove fallen and diseased leaves and canes around roses.
- ❑ Pot herbs for winter seasonings.

Vegetables and Fruits:
- ❑ Harvest summer and fall vegetables.
- ❑ Plant for spring harvest.
- ❑ Prune grape vines.

Trees and Shrubs:
- ❑ Plant and transplant deciduous trees and shrubs after leaves have fallen.
- ❑ Give established deciduous trees and shrubs a light application of 10-10-10 after their leaves begin to fall.
- ❑ Take hardwood or mature cuttings from stems of trees and shrubs for propagating.

Lawn Care:
- ❑ Keep leaves off the lawn.
- ❑ After the last rake of leaves mow the lawn at 2 to 2.5 inches.
- ❑ Apply a complete fertilizer such as 10-10-10.
- ❑ Apply a pre-emergent herbicide to target winter annual weeds.
- ❑ Apply a post-emergent broadleaf herbicide.

Composting:
- ❑ Add leaves and spent annuals to compost pile.
- ❑ Avoid diseased foliage when adding debris to compost pile.

Water Ponds:
- ❑ Remove dead or dying debris.
- ❑ Dig and divide water plants.
- ❑ Lift tropical water plants and store for the winter.
- ❑ Cover pond with a fine-mesh.

Indoors Plants:
- ❑ Hold off repotting houseplants until spring.
- ❑ Place open containers filled with water or a humidifier among your indoor plants.

Chapter 8
October Garden

Bright yellow, red and orange,
The leaves come down in hosts;
The trees are Indian princes,
But soon they'll turn to ghosts.
-William Allingham (1824-1889)

This month the cool winds of autumn blow in a stunning display of color. Sunny days and cool nights bring a spectacular color show as nature prepares for change. Once again russet and gold dominate the color scheme as the season changes. Free falling leaves add color to the breeze and just as spring amazed us, fall surprises us with its color. The crisp breeze blows in cold rain and the first autumn frost. Country drives take the monotony away as nature paints a different picture every day. As October exits it will take most color with it; but evergreens will shine long after leaves fall.

Chrysanthemums reign and fodder displays decorate the harvest season.

The pumpkin patch glows orange as goldenrod waves yellow in the breeze. As the brief Indian summer passes, the rustle of leaves will calm and the autumn air will comfort.

General cleaning is priority this month. Finalize the digging and dividing chores and planting bulbs for the spring landscape. By the end of this month the garden will be a memory and you can relax by the fire and sip your favorite tea. For many of us, hay fever season is ending and that is relief by itself. Take time to reflect on this past season's successes and failures and learn from them. You will be rewarded in just the next season.

In-The-Garden Maintenance

Just after the death of flowers,
And before they are buried in snow,
There comes a festival season
When nature is all-aglow.
　　　　　　-Author unknown

* Tidy gardens by removing dead and diseased foliage. Gather and store garden stakes and prepare for winter. Removing debris from the garden will be your best defense against next year's insects and disease.
* Continue to remove weeds before seeds mature.
* Clean, repair, and sharpen garden tools. Cleaning is important to reduce a transfer of diseases to your new plantings. Tools should be scoured with steel wool to remove rust and cleaned with hot soapy water. Soak tools in a solution of 10% bleach or wipe with rubbing alcohol to reduce diseases. Towel-dry tools and spray with a metal protectant to reduce rust. Lightly sand handles and wipe with linseed oil; if needed.
* Do not allow fallen leaves to accumulate in thick layers over the garden. A mat of leaves will trap moisture and rot the plants beneath. Plants may benefit from some leaves to help reduce freezing/thawing stresses in the soil and moderate temperatures.
* If frost comes early cover tender plants with burlap, sheets, or boxes. Do not use plastic because it will not retain warmth. Uncover plant material as soon as temperatures rise.
* Take time to make notes about this year's garden and what you would like to do next year. Mark the location of plants that will require your attention.
* Prepare empty cold frame by amending soil with peat moss, sand, compost, and aged manure. A south-facing cold frame will perform best.

The tints of autumn
a mighty flower garden blossoming
under the spell of the enchanter,
Frost.
　　　-John Greenleaf Whittier (1807-1892)

Create a New Garden

Fall is a great time to create and prepare a new garden. Before deciding on a new garden take a good look at your landscape, pay attention to the sun and how it shines in your yard and decide where a shade garden should be installed and where would a sun garden do best. Ask yourself does the water drain well or does the water just sits on top and flood every time it rains. After some observation you can create a garden to meet your needs.

Here is a guide to help you decide which direction will best suit your garden. To create a full-sun bed let the bed lie east to west with small plants up front and tall plants in the back.

South-facing garden:

Warms quickly in spring
Perennials bloom quicker
More susceptible to frost kill
Hot in summer- choose heat-loving plants
  (especially against a white house)
Flowers drop quicker
Soil dries faster
Mulch extra
Thaw/freeze problems

North-facing garden:

Warm slow in spring
Last to keep snow
Cool in summer
Longer bloom time
Less prone to frost heave
Plants must be shade loving and tolerate moist soil

The easiest way to install a garden is to eliminate the grass entirely by using an herbicide weed killer or covering grass with black plastic. If the soil is dry, you may want to water the new site the night before to soften the ground before. It is recommended to loosen the soil about 10 inches deep. Tilling the soil is not meant to turn your soil to flour. Garden soil should be made up of various sizes of soil particles to enhance drainage.

If you want to raise the garden 4 to 6 inches this will benefit most plants. A raised garden will let water drain easier around the roots and will not sit in water causing rot. A raised bed has better air circulation. If your garden is large enough you can create rows of raised earth and grow seeds in the trenches.

Soil is the most important subject in gardening. It is recommended taking a soil sample to your county extension office to get the closest amendment guide for you new garden. It takes a few weeks to get the soil test results and then you will be ready to amend the soil. If you have a compost pile you will have access to a great soil amendment. Until the debris decomposes you can buy peat moss, compost, and manure by the bag or bulk to work into your new garden.

When you receive the results of the soil test, if you are instructed to add sulfur, you will create a more acidic garden. If you are instructed to add lime, your soil is to acidic and lime will raise pH, making it more alkaline.

A complete fertilizer such as 10-10-10 can be added prior to spring planting. When spring arrives if ordinary soil needs more organic matter add 2 inches of peat moss and if the soil is heavy clay or sandy add up to 4 inches of peat moss.

> *It would be worthwile having a cultivated garden*
> *if only to see what Autumn does to it.*
> *Alfred Austin (1835-1913)*

*He who works with his hands
    is a labourer.
He who works with his hands
    and head is a craftsman.
He who works with his hands,
    his head and his heart is an
    artist.*
    -St. Francis of Assisi (c.1181-1226)

*Where there is hatred, let me
sow love…*
    -St. Francis of Assisi

*Take a moment on October 4th
to appreciate animals and the
environment. This is the feast
day of St. Francis of Assisi*

*Plan a getaway around mid-
October to see the colors of the
countryside and hope that
"St. Luke's Little Summer"
(warm spell) cooperates.*

Container Gardening

*I must own that I would do almost
anything, and grow almost anything,
for the sake of fragrance.*
    -Reginald Farrer (1880-1920)

* Move terra-cotta pots to a shed, garage or basement to protect from winter damage.
* Store potted lilies in a cool, dry place withholding water and removing stalks as they yellow. Repot in spring using fresh compost.
* Mandevillas or dipladenias need to be cut to several feet tall and brought inside. Treat as a houseplant using a bright window.
* Overwinter confederate jasmine (*Trachelospermum jasminoides*) indoors until May.

Perennials and Biennials

*Our task must be to free ourselves by widen-
ing our circle of compassion to embrace
all living creatures and the whole of nature
in its beauty.*
    -Unknown

* Last chance to move perennials to their new location. Dig and divide plants, add compost and water well.
* Trim spent perennials to 2 inches above the ground.
* Dispose of dead hollyhock (*Alcea*) and peony foliage to avoid the spread of disease. Do not add to compost pile.
* Leave some foliage untrimmed for winter texture:
    Astilbe
    Black-eyed Susan (*Rudbeckia fulgida*)
    Chinese lantern (*Physalis alkekengi*)
    Honesty, money plant (*Lunaria annua*)
    Ornamental and native grasses
    Russian sage (*Perovskia atriplicifolia*)
    Showy stonecrop (*Sedum spectabile*)
    Spiky sea holly (*Eryngium*)

* Top-dress peonies with manure.
* If planting or transplanting peonies, keep the red eyes 1 to 1 ½ inches below the soil. Add bone meal when replanting to aid in root development.
* Chrysanthemums are not reliable perennials. To aid in their winter survival, leave spent foliage on the plant to protect as mulch or dig-up and overwinter in a greenhouse or cold frame.
* Wisteria can be pruned to leave at least 3 buds for next year's flowers to grow.

*Warm October,
    cold February.*

Down in the Hallowtide Garden of Dreams,
Nothing is shallow nor hard, as it seems;
I built a rare bower of all the fair flowers,
For keeping us warm in the evening hours;
A Columbine cellar and Violet sills,
Dormers of Absinthe and Daffodils;
Cornflower tables and Lavender halls,
Doorways of Lotus in Quatrefoil walls;
Trefoil gables and Rose windowpanes,
Fleur-de-Lys thatching to catch all the rains;
A Sunflower chimney uncharred in its seams,
Down in the Hallowtide Garden of Dreams.
                    -Chant of Archangel Uriel "Flame of God"

Annuals

The sun's away
And the bird estranged;
The wind has dropped,
And the sky's deranged;
Summer has stopped!
        -Robert Browning (1812-1889)

* Cut remaining warm-weather annuals for an indoor arrangement before they are frost bitten.

* Remove warm-weather annuals that are at the end of their life cycle and put in the compost pile or discard.

* For flowers next spring, plant cool-weather annuals before night temperatures drop below 40 degrees. Plant annuals with 10-10-10 for food and blood meal to deter animals.

* Pansies & snapdragons are heavy feeders and since they are annuals they will benefit from 20-20-20 liquid fertilizer every two weeks.

* Pot fuchsias and bring indoors for the winter. If not stored in a greenhouse or sunny window, reduce water, trim to 6 inches and store in a cool spot (50 degrees) with low light for the winter. Be cautious of white flies.

* Refer to September Annuals on page 136 on how to overwinter geraniums (*Pelargonium*).

Garden Lore

• *Every fog in October will bring a snow come winter.*

• *If October brings much frost and wind, then January and February will be mild.*

• *If the woolly worm has more black than brown fuzz, winter will be bad.*

• *If ducks do slide at Hallowtide,*
At Christmas they will swim;
If ducks do swim at Hallowtide,
At Christmas they will slide.

Garden Lore

• *Deter witches by hanging mistletoe from the eaves of your home.*

• *If a man gathers 10 ivy leaves on Halloween and places one leaf under his pillow, he will dream of his future bride.*

• *When a woman gathers ivy leaves she should recite:*
"Ivy, ivy, I love you,
in my bosom I put you,
the first young man who speaks to me,
my future husband he shall be."

• *In October, dung your field and all your land its wealth will yield.*

Bulbs, Corms, Rhizomes, and Tubers

*And 'tis my faith, that every flower enjoys
the air it breathes.*
-William Wordsworth (1770-1850)

* Continue to plant spring-flowering bulbs until the ground freezes.
* Plant bulbs to force for indoor winter bloom. Refer to forcing bulbs in Chapter Seven.
* Do not cut flower stalks on true lilies (*Lilium*) until they turn brown.
* Dig tender summer bulbs, corms, and tubers; and store. They can be replanted next spring.

> Banana Trees (*Musa*)
> Basket flower, Peruvian daffodil (*Hymenocallis narcissiflora*)
> Calla Lily (*Zantedeschia aethiopica*)
> Canna (hardy in USDA zone 7 if mulched)
> Dahlia (hardy in USDA zone 7 if mulched)
> Elephant ears (*Caladium esculenta*)
> Gladiolus (hardy in USDA zone 7 if mulched)

* Tuberous begonias and gladiolus should be dug before first frost due to cold intolerance. Remove foliage when it turns brown and store in moist peat moss to 45 to 50 degrees until March.
* As caladiums and elephant ears lose their leaves due to cold weather, dig and store them in an area that is above 60 degrees dark and dry.

Guide to storing tender bulbs and tubers

* Dig carefully after frost has blackened foliage.
* Remove excess dirt.
* Cut brown foliage 1 inch above tuber or bulb.
* Spread bulbs to dry (cure) in a shaded area for a few days to one week.
* Dust with a fungicide powder or sulfur to prevent rot.
* Layer dried bulbs in well-vented baskets, trays or mesh bags with dry peat moss padding (dahlias should be stored in a paper bag so they don't dry excessively.)
* Store in a cool, dry place. Temperature should be no cooler than 45 to 50 degrees (caladiums should be stored at around 70 degrees.)
* If bulbs show signs of rot over winter, discard them. If they start to shrivel, give them a light mist of water.
* It is best to separate and divide tender bulbs, tubers, and corms in the spring when there will be less damage to bulbs or tubers.

General planting guide for spring bulbs, corms, rhizomes, and tubers:

Spring planting bulbs need to be planted in the fall.

	Planting Depth*	Spacing*
Allium	5 to 8	5 to 10
Arum *(Arum Italicum)*	5	12
Crocus	5	1
Crown Imperial *(Fritillaria imperialis)*	8	12
Daffodil, Jonquil *(Narcissus)*	5 to 8	3 to 5
Glory-of-the-snow *(Chionodoxa)*	5	2 to 3
Hyacinth, grape *(Muscari)*	5	1 to 3
Hyacinth *(Hyacinthus orientalis)*	6	4
Iris, Dutch *(Iris x hollandica)*	5	4
Snowdrop *(Galanthus nivalis)*	5	2
Spanish bluebells *(Hyacinthoides hispanica)*	5	3 to 6
Spring snowflake *(Leucojum vernum)*	5	3
Tulip *(Tulipa)*	8 to 12	2 to 4
Windflower *(Anemone blanda)*	5	2
Winter aconite *(Eranthis)*	3 to 4	3

* = inches

* If in doubt, plant bulbs at a depth 3 times the thickness of the bulb itself.
* When planting bulbs, remember to plant daffodils first. They need several weeks of temperatures above freezing to develop a good root system. Tulips develop roots quickly allowing them to be planted later in the fall.
* When planting bulbs, stay away from wet sites. If you are concerned, pour water in the holes you dig; water should move through soil quickly if the planting site is optimum.
* Plant pansies when you plant bulbs; this will create late winter color and lots of spring color.
* Mice are less likely to eat bulbs if they are planted deep and if you mix gravel into soil.
* Remember, if you are planting bulbs under deciduous trees, they will have full sun until trees leaf-out.
* Do not put foliage from iris, peony, or dahlia into compost pile due to possible insect and disease problems.

> *No spring nor summer beauty hath such grace as*
> *I have seen in one autumnal face*
> -John Donne (1572-1631)

More exquisite than any other is the autumn rose.
-Theodore Agrippa d'Aubigne
(1552-1630)

 Roses

'Tis the last rose of summer,
Left blooming alone;
All her lovely companions
Are faded and gone.
-Thomas Moore (1779-1852)

* Stop cutting spent blooms to prepare plants for winter. Leaving seed pods (rose hips) on canes to die will add winter interest and animal food in the landscape.
* Remove fallen and diseased leaves and canes.
* Discontinue spray program after a good frost, which is usually mid-October.
* This is a great month to plan and prepare for a new rose garden.

When I converted to Catholicism I chose Therese as my confirmation name. St. Therese, also called "the little flower", said, "I will spend my heaven doing good on Earth. I will let fall a shower of roses". Buy a bouquet on her feast day, which is October 1, since she is the patron saint of florists and flower growers.

 Herbs

If you have a garden and a library, you have everything you need.
-Marcus Tullius Cicero (106-43 B.C.)

* Continue to dig and divide herbs as needed.
* Pot herbs for winter seasonings. These herbs need maximum light for good health.

  Basil (*Ocimum basilicum*)
  Chives (*Allium schoenoprasum*)
  Oregano or marjoram (*Origanum vulgare or O. marjoram*)
  Parsley (*Petroselinum crispum*)
  Rosemary (*Rosmarinius officinalis*)
  Tarragon (*Artemisia dracunculus*)
  Thyme (*Thymus vulgaris*)

* Protect parsley with cloches or bushel baskets.

And the fruit thereof shall be for meat, and the leaf thereof for medicine.
Ezekiel 47.12

Garden Lore

• *Ward off evil spirits by hanging St. John's wort (Hypericum calycinum) in your doorway.*
• *Nab a witch by hanging a mixed bundle of ivy, agrimony, broomstraw, and rue.*
• *Carry angelica to repel witches.*

Garden Lore
• *Deter vampires with onions or garlic.*

Vegetables

My love is like a cabbage
Divided into two,
The leaves I give to others
But the heart I give to you!
-Traditional

* Harvest summer and fall vegetables.
* Harvest sweet potatoes when the vines begin to yellow. Leave them outside to dry for a few hours and then move them to a warm humid room to cure for two weeks. Try using a black plastic bag in front of a sunny window.
* Harvest Brussels sprouts from the bottom first before leaves diminish.
* Pick gourds when they are matured with a hard exterior or when frost arrives. Leave a 6-inch stem on gourd and store to dry. It may take 6 months to completely dry.
* Harvest frost-sweetened carrots, kale, Brussels sprouts, cabbage, and endive.
* Thin lettuce and spinach that was sown last month.
* Tomatoes can be ripened in a cool, dark area if frost comes too early. Select tomatoes that are without bruises and bugs. Hang tomatoes plants by the roots inside until tomatoes ripen.
* Harvest pumpkins and winter squash with the stems attached to prevent early rotting.
* Dig and divide overcrowded clumps of rhubarb.

*Time to plant for spring harvest.

Seed	**Transplants**
Beets	Brussels sprouts
Carrots	Cabbage
Garlic	Cauliflower
Shallots	Chard
Turnips	Kale
	Leeks
	Onions

* Harvest turnips when they are 3 inch in diameter.
* It's an American tradition to plant garlic "toes" on Columbus Day.
* Use cloches, horticulture fleece, or heavy layer of straw to protect vegetables from frost.

We've laughed round the corn heap
With hearts all in tune,
Our chair a broad pumpkin-
Our lantern the moon.
Telling tales of the fairy who traveled like steam
In a pumpkin shell coach
With two rats for her team.
-John Greenleaf Whittier (1807-1892)

Harvest-home. Harvest-home.
We have ploughed, we have
sowed,
We have reaped, we have
mowed,
We have brought home every
load,
Hip, Hip, Hip,
Harvest home!
-Tradional

Garden Lore

• *A tough apple skin means a hard winter.*

Fruit

And when the silver habit of the clouds
Comes down upon the autumn sun, and with
As sobered gladness the old year take up
His bright inheritance of golden fruits,
A pomp and pageant fill the splendid scene.
    -Henry Wadsworth Longfellow (1807-1882)

* Prune grape vines this month.
* Take hardwood cuttings for new plants. Refer to page 159 for instructions.

The grim frost is at hand, when apples will fall thick,
almost thunderous, on the hardened earth.
    - David Hubert Lawrence (1885-1930)

Deer Control

Controlling deer is always a challenge. Unless you build a ten-foot fence around your garden you will need to know what plants attract and repel deer. Knowing that plants with sticky, rough or fuzzy texture and fragrant leaves will often repel deer will aid in defending your garden.

Trees and shrubs that repel deer

Hackberry	Red-leaf or Japanese barberry
Hawthorn	Rhododendron
Holly	Spicebush
Honeysuckle bush	Spruce, blue
Juniper	Sweet gum
Maple	Walnut
Oak	Wild lilac

Plant material that repel deer

Ageratum, flossflower	Dusty Miller	Naked lady lily
Anemone	English ivy	Oriental poppy
Bells of Ireland	Foxglove	Pearly everlasting
Black-eyed Susan	Gaillardia, blanket	Red-hot poker
Bleeding heart	flower	Rhubarb
Calla lily	Goldenrod	Salvia
Canterbury bell	Hyacinth, Grape	Santolina
Carpet bugle	Iceland poppy	Showy stonecrop
Chives	Iris	Snow-on-the-mountain
Chrysanthemum	Lady fern	Thyme
Clematis	Lavender	Yarrow
Coneflower	Marjoram	Yucca
Coreopsis	Milkweed	Zinnia
Creeper, Virginia	Mint	
Daffodil	Narcissus	

If you enjoy deer in your garden here are a few plants they love

Cardinal flower   Hosta   Phlox
Cranebill geranium   Impatiens   Rose
Crocus   Iris   Sunflower
Daylily   Pansy   Tulip
Hollyhocks   Peony   Wood hyacinth

Trees and Shrubs

Come said the wind to the leaves one day,
come o'er the meadows and we will play.
put on your dresses scarlet and gold,
for summer is gone and the days grow cold.
-A children's song of the 1880's

* It is optimum time to plant and transplant deciduous trees and shrubs after leaves have fallen. Planting while temperatures are cool will allow roots to establish before spring. A root stimulator used when planting will encourage quick root development.
* Deciduous trees that may have a difficult time adjusting if planted prior to winter are dogwood, beech, Japanese maple, magnolia, and birch. Wait until spring to plant these trees because their thin bark may crack more easily during winter.
* Do not fertilize with high nitrogen for the first year after planting trees and shrubs. A "starter" fertilizer with high phosphorus can be used to trigger root growth.
* Give established deciduous trees and shrubs a light application of 10-10-10 after their leaves begin to fall.
* Don't shear hedges; it's too late, wait until spring. New growth may be susceptible to winter kill.
* Take hardwood or mature cuttings from stems of trees and shrubs for propagating. After leaves fall, trees are dormant making this a great time for propagating. No leaf means less water is required from plant. Hardwood cutting are easier to propagate because they require less care than softwood cuttings taken from new growth.

> Butterfly bush (*Buddleia davidii*)
> Camellia (USDA zone 7)
> Cherry *(Prunus)*
> Conifers (spruce, pines, junipers, hemlocks)
> Forsythia
> Holly *(Ilex)*
> Japanese kerria *(Kerria japonica)*
> Lilac *(Syringa)*

Propagation by Hardwood Cuttings
• Use a sharp knife instead of pruning equipment.
• Cuttings should not be larger than 1 inch in diameter and about one foot long.
• Do not take cuttings from stem or branches that show signs of insect and disease.

*Now autumn's fire burns
slowly along the woods.*
 -William Allingham (1824-1889)

• Choose branches with nodes spaced close together.
• Label each cutting.
• Store cuttings between 65 and 70 degrees for 5 weeks.
• Store cuttings until planting time in an area closer to 40 degrees.
• Put cuttings in boxes and store in an unheated basement or garage. Lay cuttings in moist sand in a box until planting or bury cuttings in the garden until spring.
• Keep cuttings moist.
• Plant cuttings in the spring.

*Again rejoicing nature sees
Her robe assume its vernal hues
Her leafy locks wave in the breeze,
all freshly steep'd in morning dews.*
 –Robert Burns (1759-1796)

* Take note of trees and shrubs with great fall color and put them on your shopping list.

Trees	*Shrubs*
Buckeye *(Aesculus)*	Barberry *(Berberis)*
Dogwood *(Cornus)*	Beautyberry *(Callicarpa bodinieri)*
Flowering pear *(Pyrus)*	Burning bush (*Euonymous alata*)
Ginkgo biloba	Camellia (USDA zone 7)
Ironwood *(Ostrya virginiana)*	Dwarf Fothergilla *(Fothergilla gardenii)*
Red maple *(Acer rubrum)*	
Red oak *(Quercus rubra)*	European cranberry bush *(Viburnum opulus)*
River birch *(Betula nigra)*	
Serviceberry *(Amelanchier)*	Heavenly bamboo *(Nandina domestica)*
Sour gum, black gum *(Nyssa sylvatica)*	Oak leaf hydrangea *(Hydrangea quercifolia)*
Sourwood *(Oxydendron arboreum)*	Pyracantha
Sugar maple *(Acer saccarum)*	Red-barked dogwood *(Cornus alba)*
Sumac *(Rhus glabra)*	Red chokeberry *(Aronia arbutifolia)*
Sweet gum *(Liquidambar styraciflua)*	Viburnum
	Virginia sweetspire *(Itea virginica)*

* Extend the fall beauty by preserving branches of colorful leaves. Peel bark off the base of each branch. Boil mixture of 1 part glycerin and 2 parts water to dissolve glycerin. When water is luke warm add branches. Keep exposed ends completely immersed for one week to preserve the fall color.
* To preserve leaves, try dripping a thin film of melted beeswax on top.
* Make room for one of Tennessee's state insects, the ladybeetle, ladybird or ladybug. Dedicated to the Virgin Mary, this "Beetle of Our Lady" often finds winter homes in tree trunks or they just move in with local residents. In years past, many believed this beetle could cure measles and colic.

October gave a party;
The leaves by hundreds came-
The Chestnuts, Oaks, Maples,
And leaves of every name.
The sunshine spread a carpet,
And everything was grand,
Miss Weather led the dancing,
Professor Wind the band.
-George Copper (1792-1830)

A thing of beauty is a job forever.
-John Keats (1795-1821)

Maintenance

* Keep leaves off the lawn. If you have a compost pile, mow leaves before adding to pile.
* After the last rake of leaves mow the lawn at 2 to 2.5 inches. Don't scalp the lawn but shorter grass is less likely to smother when snow and ice arrive this winter. The lower cut allows more energy to be directed toward root development.
* For the last mow, add enough oil/gas mix to finish the job for the winter and store lawnmower empty of fluids.

Fertilization

* Cool-season lawns are entering their growing season (Kentucky bluegrass, tall fescue, red fescue, ryegrass), Energy will be focused on root growth rather than stem growth. Apply a complete fertilizer such as 10-10-10.
* Refer to most recent soil test before applying fertilizer to lawn.

Seeding

* You have until mid-October to seed or over-seed the lawn before the first frost. Be sure to cultivate the area so that new seed is in contact with soil for good germination.
* Now through mid-November is a great time to sod.

Insect and Weed Control

* In early October apply a pre-emergent herbicide to target winter annual weeds. When night temperatures drop into the 50's these seeds will germinate. This pre-emergent herbicide kills the weeds as they germinate, thus halting their invasive growth during winter months. Don't mow for 3 to 4 days following the application.
    Common chickweed *(Stellaria media)*
    Crabgrass *(Digitaria)*
    Henbit *(Lamium amplexicaule)*
    Speedwell *(Veronica spp.)*

Garden Lore

• *The Welsh created the lore of the Wood Spirit, also called "Jack o' the Green", "Green Man" or "Green George" of the forest. He is the keeper of the forest and all who lives there. If you actually see the Wood Spirit, he brings you good fortune and health.*
• *The best wood for a witches broom is willow.*

If you could paint one autumn leaf you could paint the world.
-John Ruskin (1819-1900)

*Apply a post-emergent herbicide to control broadleaf perennial weeds. Apply to wet grass or use a water hose attachment. Use product as directed on label.

      Chickweed (*Stellaria media*)
      Dandelion (*Taraxacum officinale*)
      Plantain (*Plantago major*)
      Poison hemlock (*Conium maculatum*)
      Wild carrot, Queen-Anne's-lace (*Daucus carota*)

* Don't apply a pre-emergent herbicide this month if you are seeding the lawn.

Composting

> *Behold this compost!*
> *Behold it well!*
>   -Walt Whitman (1819-1892)

* Continue to add leaves and spent annuals to compost pile.
* Run the lawn mower over lawn leaves before adding to compost pile. Smaller debris will breakdown much quicker.
* Avoid diseased foliage when adding debris to compost pile.
* After Halloween, cut Jack-o-lanterns into small pieces and add to compost pile.
* If you don't have a compost pile or bin, now is a great time to start. Refer to September Composting for ingredients.

Water Ponds

> *Love the earth and embrace*
> *it's wonder.*
>   -unknown

* Continue to remove dead or dying debris; cut foliage to 1 inch above water surface.
* Dig and divide water plants.
* Lift tropical water plants and store for the winter. Store tender plants in damp peat moss in an unheated garage (55 degrees) or basement or keep in water and subject them to bright light.
* Hardy water plants that are in baskets should be lowered to the deepest section of the pond (preferable 12 to 18 inches) to avoid freezing.
* Cover pond with a fine-mesh net to catch leaves and debris over winter.

October Indoor Gardening

> *Flower in the crannied wall,*
> *I pluck you out of the crannies,*
> *I hold you here, root and all, in my hand,*
> *Little flower--but if I could understand*
> *What you are, root and all, all in all,*
> *I should know what God and man is.*
>   Lord Alfred Tennyson (1809-1892),
>   "Flower in the Crannied Wall"

*Hold off repotting houseplants until spring. This time of year roots do not develop as quickly as they do in the spring. Repotting this time of year may lead to root rot.

* Place plants that require high light near a south-facing window.
* Place open containers filled with water or a humidifier among your indoor plants. Most houseplants like to have 50% or higher of relative humidity.
* Decrease water to Christmas cactus this month; continue regular watering in November.

Come, ye thankful people come,
Raise the song of harvest-
home!
All is safely gathered in,
Ere the winter storms begin.
  Henry Alford (1810-1871)

OCTOBER'S BRIGHT BLUE WEATHER
by Helen Hunt Jackson (1830-1885)

O suns and skies and clouds of June,
And flowers of June together,
Ye cannot rival for one hour
October's bright blue weather;

When loud the bumble-bee makes haste,
Belated, thriftless vagrant,
And Golden-Rod is dying fast,
And lanes with grapes are fragrant;

When Gentians roll their fringes tight
To save them for the morning,
And chestnuts fall from satin burrs
Without a sound of warning;

When on the ground red apples lie
In piles like jewels shining,
And redder still on old stone walls
Are leaves of woodbine twining;

When all the lovely wayside things
Their white-winged seeds are sowing,
And in the fields, still green and fair,
Late aftermaths are growing;

When springs run low, and on the brooks,
In idle golden freighting,
Bright leaves sink noiseless in the hush
Of woods, for winter waiting;

When comrades seek sweet country haunts,
By twos and twos together,
And count like misers, hour by hour,
October's bright blue weather.

O suns and skies and flowers of June,
Count all your boasts together,
Love loveth best of all the year
October's bright blue weather.

November Garden Chore List

In the Garden:
- ❑ Drain garden hoses and store for the winter.
- ❑ Secure all vines and climbers.
- ❑ Feed established bulbs with 10-10-10 fertilizer.
- ❑ Continue to plant bulbs.

Vegetables and Fruits:
- ❑ Cut asparagus foliage and cover stubs with mulch.
- ❑ Continue to harvest collards, such as kale, that has been sweetened by the cold weather.
- ❑ Cut canes of raspberries, with exception to ever-bearing, and other brambles to the ground.
- ❑ Plant bare-root fruit trees and bushes.
- ❑ Mulch strawberries with weed free wheat straw.

Trees and Shrubs:
- ❑ Plant and transplant deciduous trees and shrubs.
- ❑ Remove sucker growth.
- ❑ Established evergreens may benefit from light fertilization this month.

Lawn Care:
- ❑ Cut lawn short enough to hold snow without bending.
- ❑ Mow leaves, leaving nutrients on the lawn.

Composting:
- ❑ Give the compost pile a turn and add more chopped leaves.

Water Ponds:
- ❑ Leaves should be removed from ponds that have fish.
- ❑ Float a ball on your fishpond to avoid a totally frozen pond.

Indoors Plants:
- ❑ Check plants weekly for insects or disease.
- ❑ Don't over water!

Chapter 9

November Garden

The festival of color fades before us and evergreens once again become noticed and appreciated. The daylight fades as quickly as turning leaves. November offers up serene afternoons, when it's not raining. These days are glorious when "Indian Summer" arrives and these glorious days are autumns last call for outdoor activities and chores before settling in for a restful winter. The sun is intense as it shines deep in our windows. The November air is calm and peaceful, it teases us for a few days and then cold winds revisit and send us running inside. The spring garden will be resting while we rest and before you know it the foliage will emerge again.

We go through "withdrawal" as summer becomes a memory and winter approaches. The days fade so quickly in November making it hard to finish a project outside. Take the pleasant days as they come and work toward winterizing and preparing the garden for spring planting by amending the soil.

With many indoor hours ahead, indoor activities and chores will be tackled over winter. Make the most of these last days to prepare for winter and spring. Write down those new plants you would like to try next season. Read books to pass the time and learn more about gardening and your favorite plants.

General Maintenance

Garden Lore

• *Rain before seven, clear before eleven.*

• *If the first snowfall lands on unfrozen ground, the winter will be mild.*

• *If All Saint's Day will bring out winter, St. Martin's Day will bring out Indian summer.*

• *Around mid-November "St. Martin's summer" or "Indian Summer" brings us the last blast of warm weather.*

• *If Martinmas ice will bear a duck then look for a winter of slush and muck.*

• *If the geese on St. Martin's Day stand on ice, they will walk in mud at Christmas.*

• *If sheep feed facing downhill, prepare for a snowstorm.*

• *Flowers in bloom in November foretell a harsh winter.*

• *Thunder in the fall foretells a cold winter.*

Water

Water is the best of all things.
-Pindar (c. 522-438 B.C.)

* Moisture is very important this time of year as plants prepare for dormancy. Keep newly planted plant material watered well throughout any dry periods.
* Slow, deep soakings are best when watering most plants. This method will reduce water run-off and encourage roots to grow deeply.
* As temperatures cool, the soil will retain moisture more easily. Although water is very important, you can over water especially where soils are heavy.
* Conifers and broadleafed evergreens need extra moisture to withstand the winter. During winter, evergreens continue to lose moisture through their broadleaf leaves and needles. Watering boxwood and holly shrubs now could reduce brown tips acquired through the winter. Just as skin dries in winter, plant material also suffers.
* Don't forget to water plants that are planted under larger evergreens and eaves of the house.

In-The-Garden Maintenance

No shade, no shine,
no butterflies, no bees.
No fruit, no flowers,
no leaves, no birds!
No-vember!
-Thomas Hood (1799-1845)

* Take advantage of the remaining nice days by cleaning the garden.
* Warm-season weeds are killed by a good hard frost while cool-season weeds are encouraged to grow. By November, most have germinated making this a good month to greatly reduce weed problems through next spring.
* Drain garden hoses and store for the winter.
* Clean and store clay pots inside to reduce winter damage.
* Gather remaining garden stakes and store.
* To reduce ice on sidewalks and driveways use sand, sawdust or non-clumping cat litter. Avoid rock salt; which will harm plants. Read label to learn ingredients of product before you apply.
* Secure all vines and climbers.
* Plan for next season's garden by taking a walk and deciding successes and failures in the landscape.
* Open cold frame on warm sunny days to ventilate plants; be sure to close before the sun goes down to help trap warm air in for the evening. Keep soil moist inside cold frame.
* Clean and repair gutters to avoid damaging overflows of water onto foundation plants.

Container Gardening

There is enough in a single flower for the ornament of a score of cathedrals.
-John Ruskin (1819-1900)

* There is plenty of plant material to be gathered for indoor and outdoor arrangements. Choose from evergreens branches, bittersweet, holly berries, boxwood trimmings, magnolia leaves, branches with crabapples, rose hips, pinecones, red-twig dogwood, pyracantha, dried wheat, teasels, red seed heads from the sumac tree, and ornamental and native grasses.
* Continue to water container plants, especially prior to a hard freeze, to help them survive the winter. Apply mulch around top of containers for added protection.
* Containers can be buried in a trench in the ground to provide insulation so roots do not freeze. When spring arrives remove pots and rinse.

Perennials and Biennials

The scarlet of maples can shake me
Like a cry
Of bugles going by.
And my lonely spirit thrills
To see the frosty asters like smoke
Upon the hills.
-William Bliss Carman (1861-1929)

* Success of a spring garden depends on fall planting.
* Check to see that all climbing vines are secure for winter.
* Take the time to trim perennials that have not been trimmed.
Clear gardens of debris; good sanitation in the garden will decrease insect and disease problems for future gardens.
* If you have a wildflower meadow, it's time to mow it down.

Bulbs, Corms, Rhizomes, and Tubers

Between two moments, bliss is ripe.
Think in the morning, Act in the noon,
Eat in the evening, Sleep in the night.
In seed time learn, in harvest teach,
in winter enjoy.
-William Blake (1757-1827)

* Feed established bulbs with 10-10-10 fertilizer.
* Continue to plant bulbs through November, before the ground freezes, for spring color.

Garden Lore

• *Create a necklace out of rose hips to bring love your way.*

Roses

What's in a name? That which we call a rose by any other name would smell as sweet.
-William Shakespeare (1564-1616)

* If you want to transplant a rose, cut bush to 24 inches for easy handling. Transplant before the ground freezes and water well.
* Remove lower leaves on rose bush up to 12 inches and leaf litter from around roses to decrease insects and diseases.
* Secure climbers to protect from winter winds. Some may need to be wrapped in burlap for extra winter protection.
* Old garden roses and shrub roses are hardy and do not need extra winter protection. On the other hand, many of the modern roses such as hybrid teas, floribundas, and grandifloras will need extra winter protection. After two hard freezes mulch with loose material such as pine straw or well shredded leaves or mulch; preferably 12 to 18 inches high around each bush.

Herbs

Nothing is more the child of art than a garden.
-Sir Walter Scott (1771-1832)

* Harvest remaining chives and freeze them for winter use.

Seeds

Remember that what you believe will depend very much on what you are.
Noah Porter (1811-1892)

• *On the first of November if weather is clear, an end to the sowing you do for the year.*
• *If the first snow sticks to the trees, it foretells a bountiful harvest.*

* If you choose to save seeds from your garden, store seeds in the refrigerator or a cool room in an airtight container. Use a moisture-absorbing product such as silica gel packets, nonfat dry milk, rice, corn starch or corn meal.

Vegetables

O, it sets my heart a clickin' like the tickin' of a clock.
When the first frost is on the punkin and the fodders in the shock.
-James Whitcomb Riley (1849-1916)

Time to Plant:
Asparagus crowns
Garlic cloves

* Cut asparagus foliage and cover stubs with mulch or compost for the winter.
* Continue to harvest collards, such as kale, that has been sweetened by the cold weather. Harvest bottom leaves first to encourage plant to keep growing.

Garden Lore

• *The early Americans had to ration their food supply to survive the winters in the new world. During Thanksgiving it became tradition to remind them of harder times by placing 5 kernels of corn on each plate:*

One kernel to remind us of the autumn beauty around us.
One kernel to remind us of our love for each other.
One kernel to remind us of God's love and care for us.
One kernel to remind us of our friends; especially our Indian brothers.
One kernel to remind us we are free people.

-Unknown

Dry leaves upon the wall,
Which flap like rustling wings and seek escape,
A single frosted cluster on the grape
Still hangs, -and that is all.

-Sarah Chauncey Woosley (c. 1845-1905)

* Cut canes of raspberries, with exception to ever-bearing, and other brambles to the ground. Thin sections that have overgrown to discourage disease. Mulch area to retain moisture.
* Plant bare-root fruit trees and bushes.
* Use chicken wire around base of fruit trees to deter rodents.
* Mulch strawberries with straw or row cover if temperatures fall below 20 degrees. If possible buy weed free wheat straw to avoid a weed problem.
* Dormant spraying, if needed to control overwintering insects, can be applied after leaves have fallen and daytime temperatures are above 40 degrees.

Here we go round the bramble-bush,
The bramble-bush, the bramble-bush;
Here we go round the bramble-bush
On a cold frosty morning!

Here we round the mulberry-bush,
The mulberry-bush, the mulberry-bush;
Here we go round the mulberry-bush
On a sunshiny morning.

-Mother Goose

Garden Lore

• If berries and nuts are plentiful, prepare for a harsh winter.

• The job of Spirit Fairies is to change the color of the leaves in the fall. You will often find them wearing acorn hats.

• If the tops of trees are bare while the sides are full of leaves, winter will be mild.

• If the leaves fall first from the sides, the winter will be severe.

• If the first snow falls on unfrozen ground, expect a mid winter.

• It will be a bad winter if trees keep their leaves until late in the fall.

• Do not choose elder (God's stinking tree) to burn in your fireplace or the devil will sit on top of the chimney; will he come down?

When the leaves are on the ground,
Instead of on the trees,
I like to make a great big pile of them
Way up to my knees.
I like to run and jump in them
And kick them all around.
I like the prickly feel of them
and the crickly, crackly sound.

Trees and Shrubs

November's sky is chill and drear,
November's leaf is red and sear.
-Sir Walter Scott (1771-1832)

* This is a great time to plant and transplant deciduous trees and shrubs, keep them watered. Root systems still have time to establish roots before winter.

* Drying winds and cold soil make it difficult for conifers to establish roots. If you can wait, spring is the preferred planting season.

* Wait to plant bare-root stock next spring. Container and burlapped plants can be planted throughout fall until the ground freezes.

* Use protective tree wrap to protect trees from mice and rabbits if they are a big problem in your neighborhood. Remove all screening and wraps early next spring. In most situations, wrapping trees is not a recommended practice.

* You may choose to do some minor pruning in November, i.e. water sprouts, suckers, damaged limbs, and excessive shoots on multi-stemmed shrubs. Do not prune plant material that will have a spring bloom. Some tender shrubs, such as boxwood, prefer to be trimmed in their growing season due to their cold sensitivity. Major pruning is best left as a spring job.

* Remove sucker growth from:

> Crab apple *(Malus)*
> Crape myrtle *(Lagerstroemia indica)*
> Forsythia
> Lilac *(Syringa)*
> Pyracantha
> Red-barked dogwood *(Cornus alba)*
> Virginia sweetspire *(Itea virginica)*

* Established evergreens may benefit from light fertilization this month. Apply 10-10-10 prior to rain.

* Remove weeds and grass from around tree trunks. Do not use a weed eater. Always avoid tree bark injury to promote healthy trees.

* Collect disease free pine needles from the yard to use as mulch on azaleas, rhododendrons, and other acid-loving plants.

* Watch for slight blooming on forsythia bushes if weather has been warm.

Fall, leaves, fall; die, flowers, away;
Lengthen night and shorten day;
Every leaf speaks bliss to me,
Fluttering from the autumn tree.
I shall smile when the rose should grow;
I shall sing when night's decay
Ushers in a drearier day.
-Emily Brontë (1818-1848)

Out of the bosom of the air,
Out of the cloudfolds of her garment shaken,
Over the woodlands, brown and bare
Over the harvest-fields forsaken,
Silent, and soft, and slow
Descends the snow.
-Henry Wadsworth Longfellow (1807-1882)

The creation of a thousand forests is in one acorn.
-Ralph Waldo Emerson (1803-1882)

Lawn care

Nothing is more pleasant to the eye than green grass kept finely shorn.
-Sir Francis Bacon (1561-1626)

Maintenance

* Continue to mow the lawn if needed. Cut lawn short enough to hold snow without bending.
* Raking the leaves is a must unless you have a bag on your mower. Use shredded leaves in your garden as light mulch.
* Mow leaves, leaving nutrients on the lawn.
* Sod can be laid for an instant lawn as long as the ground is not frozen.

Composting

The poetry of the earth is never dead.
-John Keats (1795-1821)

* Give the compost pile a turn and add more chopped leaves. Keep pile moist to speed decomposition.
* Run the lawn mower over lawn leaves before adding to compost pile. Smaller debris will breakdown much quicker.

Water Ponds

This we know, the earth does not belong to man, man belongs to the earth
-Chief Seattle (1786-1866)

* If you are not using a net, leaves should be removed from ponds that have fish. The leaves will decompose and emit methane gas that is harmful to fish.
* When temperatures drop into the 40's replace pump with a low-voltage pond heater if you have fish.
* Float a ball on your fishpond to avoid a totally frozen pond.
* Continue to feed fish with a high-protein food until water temperature drops below 70 degrees. Mix feed with an easier-to-digest formula until water temperatures drop to 60 degrees; then switch totally to easy-to-digest food. During winter fish will eat little or no food.

Tonight the winds began to rise
And roar from yonder dropping day;
The last red leaf is whirled away,
The rooks are blown about the skies.
        -Lord Alfred Tennyson (1809-1892)

November Indoor Gardening

Every season hath its pleasures;
Spring may boast her flowery prime,
Yet the vineyard's ruby treasures
Brighten Autumn's soberer time.
        -Thomas Moore (1478-1535)

* Now that your indoor plants are all snug and warm, take time to check them weekly for insects or disease. If insects are suspected, separate from the other plants and apply insecticidal soap until the insects are gone.
* Don't over water! When soil is dry 1 inch below surface it's time to water. (Just use your finger to test soil moisture.)
* Your Christmas cactus should set buds soon due to short days and cool nights. Reduce water until cactus blooms. You can go to the trouble and force your cactus to bloom or just let it bloom when it's ready. The blooms will be enjoyed no matter the time of year.
* Keep an eye on amaryllis bulbs for new growth. After 2 to 3 month rest period or when new growth emerges, pot bulbs and lightly water until new growth appears. Move to higher light as bulbs grow. Don't be disappointed if your bulb doesn't bloom in the next cycle, be patient, it's worth the wait.
* If you have a collection of amaryllis, over the years they will produce babies. Remove baby and make sure to get plenty of roots. Repot to a small pot.

Planting a new amaryllis:
* Prior to planting new bulbs, soak roots for 10 to 12 hours.
* Amaryllis roots love to be root bound, choose a clay pot that is about 1 inch larger than the diameter of the bulb. Plant bulb with the top ½ of the bulb uncovered while only using 1 to 2 inches of soil under bulb.
* Water lightly until bulb blooms, and then increase water. Excessive moisture may cause rot.
* Rotate pots daily to keep stalk from bending toward the light. Use a stake to support bloom.
* Amaryllis bulbs love warmth. They require heat for good root and stem development. Keep away from drafty areas and use bottom heat by placing over or near a heat source.
* Place bulbs in a south-facing window. Higher light will strengthen stems while low light will increase bending or breaking of stalk.
* When bloom opens move bulb to lower light to prolong bloom time. Room temperatures around 65 to 70 degrees are best for amaryllis.
* Remove spent flower stalk on amaryllis 2 inches above the bulb and hope for a second stalk. Cutting after bloom fades will prevent seed formation and wasted energy.
* For extended blooming, pinch yellow anthers as soon as bloom opens. This will keep the energy directed toward the bloom and away from seed production.

When chill November's surly blasts
Made fields and forests bare.
-Robert Burns (1759-1796)

Oh, Adam was a gardener, and God who made him sees
That half a proper gardener's work is done upon his knees,
So when your work is finished, you can wash your hands and pray
For the Glory of the Garden, that it may not pass away!
And the Glory of the Garden it shall never pass away!
Rudyard Kipling (1865-1936)

December Garden Chore List

In the Garden:
- ❑ When night temperatures are below 50 degrees consistently, add 2 to 3 inches of mulch to gardens.
- ❑ Bulbs can be planted as long as the soil is not frozen.
- ❑ Purchase a new amaryllis bulb to add to the collection.

Vegetables and Fruits:
- ❑ Sift 2 inches of compost over asparagus and rhubarb beds.
- ❑ Dig carrots and other root crops before the ground freezes.

Trees and Shrubs:
- ❑ If the ground is not frozen most deciduous trees and shrubs can be planted or transplanted.
- ❑ Harvest mistletoe to ensure lots of kisses.

Lawn Care:
- ❑ Don't walk or drive on frozen lawn to avoid damage.

Composting:
- ❑ Turn compost pile once this month for even decomposition.

Water Ponds:
- ❑ Replace pump with a low voltage pond heater if you have fish.

Indoors Plants:
- ❑ Due to the decrease in sunlight, routine fertilizing is not recommended.
- ❑ Increase humidity around houseplants.
- ❑ Shop for festive plants such as Christmas cactus, cyclamen, amaryllis or poinsettia.

Chapter 10

December Garden

That's no December sky!
Surely 'tis June
Holds now her state on high
Queen of the noon.
Only the tree-tops bare
Crowning the hill,
Clear-cut in perfect air,
Warn us that still.
Winter, the aged chief,
Mighty in power,
Exiles the tender leaf,
Exiles the flower.
  - Robert Fuller Murray (1863-1894)
    "A December Day"

The festive season of giving is so hectic; it just makes sense that there is little on our garden chore list. Time to relax and have hot cocoa by the fire and review the stack of seed catalogues that are piling up by your favorite chair. Work on your spring plant list and review notes from the past season. Catalogues can be a great source of ideas, reference, and education. These catalogues will fill the voids of winter with exciting possibilities for the upcoming season.

As you travel along the way take note of plants that add interest to the landscape such as ornamental and native grasses and berry producing trees and shrubs. Now that the leaves have fallen and perennials are underground, it is a great time to evaluate the design of your landscape. Evergreens are scene savers thanks to their forever-green foliage. Dare to dream how next winter can look and get inspired by what you see now and take note. When spring arrives these notes will be handy while shopping for new plant material.

As long as the weather permits there will still be chores outside. If you have been a busy gardener this fall it is time to take a break, spend time with family and friends, and enjoy the winter break.

In-The-Garden Maintenance

The hills look gaunt in russet garb:
Against the sky the leafless woods
Are dark, and in their solitudes
The chill wind pierces like a barb.
-Clinton Scollard (1860-1932)

Whether we wake or sleep.
Whether we carol or weep,
The Sun with his Planets in
chime,
Marketh the going of Time.
-Edward Fitzgerald (1809-1883)

* Continue to clean spent herbaceous flowerbeds as needed.
* When night temperatures are below 50 degrees consistently, add 2 to 3 inches of mulch to gardens. Keep mulch away from trunks and stems to minimize insect, disease, and animal damage. Applying mulch before the ground freezes will protect soil from excessive frost heave due to freezing and thawing. Mulch truly helps moderate soil temperature.
* Don't neglect your cold frame. Prop it open on warm sunny days above freezing to ventilate and prevent over-warming of plant material; be sure to close before the sun goes down to help trap warm air in for the evening. Keep soil moist inside cold frame. In severe cold weather pile blankets on for added protection from freezing or install incandescent light bulb turned on at night. Install a thermometer inside the cold frame to monitor temperature.

Container Gardening

Do what you can, with what
you have, where you are.
-Theodore Roosevelt (1858-1919)

* Jot down ideas for next year's container plants and window boxes.
* Add an obelisk to containers and string with lights for the holidays.

Perennials and Biennials

Heaven is under our feet as
well as over our heads.
-Henry David Thoreau (1817-1862)

* Add compost to peonies for nutrients. Be sure not to add more than 2 inches of compost.
* Protect hardy chrysanthemums with mulch or straw to aid in the overwintering process. Do not cut dead foliage until spring.

Annuals

Flowers in a city are like lipstick on a woman
it just makes you look better to have a little color.
-Lady Bird Johnson (b.1912)

* Don't forget to water annuals that you are overwintering indoors.

Bulbs, Corms, Rhizomes, and Tubers

Shed no tear-
O, shed no tear!
The flower will bloom another year.
Weep no more-
O, weep no more!
Young buds sleep in the root's white core.
-John Keats (1795-1821)

* Bulbs can be planted as long as the soil is not frozen.
* Purchase a new amaryllis bulb to add to the collection. When it blooms remove yellow anthers and place out of direct sunlight to prolong bloom time.
* After paperwhites fade, trim foliage blunt at the top and use as a foliage arrangement until it dies back. Greenery is always nice during the winter. If you place paperwhites in a hurricane glass container, the glass will hold the tall foliage upright.

Roses

God gave us memories, that we might have
June roses in the December of our lives.
-Sir James Matthew Barrie (1860-1937)

* Mulch roses with 12 to 18 inches of mulch if you neglected to do so at Thanksgiving.
* After about 2 weeks of a hard freeze (consistently cold) rose bushes are dormant. Dormancy for roses in USDA zone 6 is usually induced around mid-December.
* Cut modern (not climbers, antique or once-flowering roses) to 18 to 36 inches to help reduce wind damage.
* Remove fallen leaves from around rose bushes to prevent spread of disease.
* Spray canes with dormant oil to reduce overwintering insects.

Seeds

How deeply seated in the human heart is
the liking for gardens and gardening.
-Alexander Smith (1860-1867)

* Order or plan to shop locally for the upcoming season. Make sure you are buying new seeds and not last years seeds.

Vegetables

Cabbage:
A familiar garden vegetable about
as large and wise as a man's head.
Ambrose Bierce (1842-1914)

* Sift 2 inches of compost over asparagus and rhubarb beds.
* Dig carrots and other root crops before the ground freezes. Parsnips will sweeten if they are subjected to near freezing temperatures for about one month.

A green December 25th means a heavy harvest.

Garden Lore

• Grow ivy on the outside of your home to protect all who dwell there from bad luck.

A man of words and not of deeds,
is like a garden full of weeds;…
Mother Goose

With holly and ivy,
So green and so gay,
We deck up our houses
As fresh as the day,
With bays, and rosemary,
And laurel complete;
And every one now
Is a king in conceit.
-Poor Robin's Almanac (1695)

Garden Lore

• *If holly has few berries this year the winter may be milder than if the holly has many berries.*

• *If there's thunder during Christmas week,*
The Winter will be anything but meek.

• *The nearer the New Moon to Christmas Day, the harder the winter.*

• *If Christmas day be bright and clear there'll be two winters in the year.*

• *Thunder in December presages fine weather.*

• *Like in December like all the yearlong.*

• *Take the family out to gather wood from the apple or oak tree. This wood will protect those who gather it from harm in the New Year. This Yule log brings light into the dark days of winter.*

Christmas tide comes in like a bride with holly and ivy clad.
-Old English Carol

Fruit

Orchards are even more personal in their charms than gardens,
as they are more nearly human creations.
-Amos Bronson Alcott (1799-1888)

* Wait to cut fall-bearing fruit canes in February or March.
* Mulch strawberries with 3 inches of straw to avoid winter injury.
* Coating fruit with aloe gel will allow it to stay fresher five times longer.

Trees and Shrubs

Trees are the best monuments that a man can erect to his own memory.
They speak his praises without flattery, and they are blessings to children yet unborn.
-Lord Orrery (1707-1762)

* If the ground is not frozen most deciduous trees and shrubs can be planted or transplanted. Keep newly planted trees and shrubs watered.
* If you trim foliage for your holiday decoration be sure to prune properly so that the shrub will not be out of shape come spring.
* It is normal for azaleas to have leaves that turn yellow. The older leaves will fall only to be replaced by new leaves in the spring.
* Winter injury can be harsh on the landscape. The snow and ice along with drying winds and the sun can do damage to all plants not to mention road salt if you are an urban gardener. When temperatures drop below freezing, winter injury can occur. To avoid unwanted damage choose plants for your landscape that are appropriate for your zone. Winter injury is more common in evergreen plants. Their foliage is susceptible to the drying wind and sun. Moisture is lost and hard to replace if soil is frozen.
* If you have a problem with snow deforming your favorite evergreen shrub you may want to pre-tie it to protect from heavy snow. Use a broom to gently remove the heavy load of snow to keep the top from deforming.

Seasonal Interest

It is in society as in nature-
not the useful, but the ornamental,
that strikes the imagination.
Sir Humphrey Davy (1778-1829)

Christmas Trees

* If you buy a cut live tree you may want to give the trunk a fresh cut. This will allow the trunk to uptake water more easily, promoting a longer life for your tree. Replenish warm water daily to ensure freshness of your tree. The tree may drink up to one gallon of water on the first day. Use the limbs of discarded trees to protect perennial flowerbeds from severe weather. Choose from these cut live trees for great smell and needle retention.

Balsam fir (*Abies balsamea*)
Canaan fir (*Abies balsamea var. phanerolepis*)
Colorado blue spruce (*Picea pungens*)

Fraser fir (*Abies fraseri*)
Noble fir (*Abies procera*)
White pine (*Pinus strobus*)

* Harvest mistletoe, "thief of the tree", to ensure lots of kisses during the holidays.
* Prior to hanging, mist live garland, roping, and wreaths with water and let dry.
* Keep live plant material away from heat vents, ceiling fans, dehumidifiers, and full-sun windows.
* If you want a live tree and want to plant it in your yard after Christmas, pre-dig a hole now before the ground freezes. The hole should be 1 ½ times the size of the root ball. Keep soil from digging in a bucket and store in the garage to keep from freezing; use this dirt at planting time. Blue spruce, hemlock or firs are great choices for live trees in Tennessee. A suitable-sized waterproof tub with handles will facilitate your moving the ball-and-burlaped tree to its indoor location, and finally to the pre-dug planting hole. Keep the burlap moist during the tree's short time inside. Gradually move a live tree indoors. Start by putting the tree in the garage or basement to acclimate to the house temperatures, and then move the tree to its final destination for decorating. A live tree should stay in the house no longer than 5 days until the gradual move outdoors should start. Remove all wires and tags, but the burlap stays on the root-ball; it will rot and the roots will grow through it. After planting outdoors, mulch thoroughly and water regularly.

The holly and the ivy,
When they are both full grown,
Of all the trees that are in the wood
The holly bears the crown.
-Old English Christmas Carol, 1800's

Holiday Greenery

At Christmas, play and make good cheer,
For Christmas comes but once a year.
-Thomas Tusser (1515-1580)

* Choose from pine, holly, boxwood, yew, ivy, rhododendron and juniper to make garland, swags, wreaths, and arrangements. Also gather berries, grasses, pinecones, and interesting seedpods for a natural look.

Lawn Care

To me a lush carpet of pine needles or spongy grass is more welcome to me than the most luxurious Persian rug.
-Helen Keller (1880-1968)

Maintenance

* Don't walk or drive on frozen lawn to avoid damage.
* Continue to mow as needed and remove leaves and debris that have settled on the lawn and in the shrubs.
* A soil test is recommended for proper application of nutrients for lawn. Refer to most recent soil test for needed amendments.

O Christmas tree, O Christmas tree,
How are thy leaves so verdant!
O Christmas tree, O Christmas tree,
Much pleasure doth thou bring me!
Christmas Carol

Garden Lore

• *If you bring home a tree for Christmas and find a bird's nest, it brings a year of good health and happiness.*
• *The Christmas tree legend comes from England and a monk named Wilford. Wilford knocked-down a huge oak tree and it split into four pieces. From the center emerged a fir tree. This fir tree symbolizes peace and endless life due to its evergreen needles. As it points to God the Christmas tree is now the tree of the Christ child and we cut it and bring it in our homes to celebrate. Gifts should circle the tree as a symbol of love and kindness.*

Garden Lore

• *Holly is a great protector of lightning, thunder, poison, witches, and evil spirits.*

• *A sprig of holly on your bedpost brings sweet dreams.*

• *In Ireland holly decorations are saved and burned while cooking pancakes on Shrove Tuesday.*

• *In England, holly bundles are placed in stables on Christmas Eve to bring good luck.*

• *The pointed leaves of the holly leaf represent the crown of thorns wore by Jesus; the berries represent his drops of blood.*

• *It is bad luck to leave the holly décor in the house past the Twelfth Night (January 5th).*

• *Bring evergreen boughs into your home to give warmth and remove evil spirits.*

• *Juniper berries sprinkled at the door discourages thieves.*

• *Mature juniper berries can be strung and hung in the house to attract love.*

• *Mistletoe hung over the entrance to protect the home from lightning; and keeps the witches out.*

• *Magic wands are best made from the almond tree or oak branches and mistletoe.*

• *When kissing under the mistletoe, the man must pick one berry when he kisses. When berries are gone; no more kissing!*

• *A common medieval belief held that mistletoe was the wood used to make the crucifix. No longer welcomed, it was doomed to live as a parasite growing on trees.*

• *No matter how long the winter, spring is sure to follow.*

• *If the sun shines through the limbs of the apple tree on Christmas Day, expect a good crop.*

Composting

Oh, the incredible profit by digging of ground.
-Thomas Fuller (1608-1661)

* Turn compost pile once this month for even decomposition. Continue to add ingredients listed on page 145.

Water Ponds

At Christmas I no more desire a rose than wish a snow in May's newfangled mirth; but like each thing that in season grows.
-William Shakespeare (1564-1616)

* Replace pump with a low voltage pond heater if you have fish. This heater will keep part of the surface ice-free. Some bare water surface is necessary to vent decomposition gases. If completely iced over, set a hot water kettle on the ice to melt an opening. Don't chop or hammer ice, as it will damage the hearing ability of the fish and the shock waves may kill them.

December Indoor Gardening

Autumn to winter, winter into spring,
Spring into summer, summer into fall,
So rolls the changing year, and so we change;
Motion so swift, we know not that we move.
-Dinah Mulock Craik (1826-1887)

* Keep an eye on houseplants and remove any dead or dying leaves. Also look for signs of insects. If you spot aphids, spray them with a solution of rubbing alcohol, a drop of dish soap, and water.
* Don't be afraid to touch the soil; this is an effective way of determining moisture in soil. Allow soil to dry between watering.
* Due to the decrease in sunlight, routine fertilizing is not recommended until spring.
* Increase humidity around houseplants by placing containers of water or a humidifier around plants.
* Cactuses should be kept in a cool spot around 50 degrees. Until they are out of dormancy in the spring; withhold water.

Seasonal Indoor Plants

I heard the bells of Christmas Day,
Their old familiar carols play.
And wild and sweet the words repeat
Of peace on earth, good will to men.
-Henry Wadsworth Longfellow (1807-1882)

*Shop for festive plants such as Christmas cactus, cyclamen, amaryllis or poinsettia (flower of the Holy Night). Always remove the pretty foil wrap to avoid rot due to wrapping holding water. Protect plants from the cold temperatures by wrapping with a paper bag when carrying to the car and into the house. Keep plants away from hot or cold drafts. Keep them in a sunny spot, evenly moist and not soggy.

* Reduce water to Christmas cactus to prolong bloom time.

* After amaryllis bloom fades remove spent flower and stalk 2 inches from the base. Leave foliage to feed the bulb for the next bloom.

January Garden Chore List

In the Garden:
- ❑ Cool-weather weeds are thriving. Pull weeds if weather permits.
- ❑ Leave snow on the garden as an added protective blanket.

Flowers and Herbs:
- ❑ Reset plants that have been lifted from freezing and thawing.
- ❑ Check on stored summer bulbs.
- ❑ When potted bulbs have met their cold storage requirement and are well rooted, start bringing them out of cold storage gradually into the sunlight.
- ❑ It is time to buy seeds, containers, heating pads, and seed-starting mix.

Vegetables and Fruits:
- ❑ Plan vegetable gardens and crop rotation for the upcoming season.

Trees and Shrubs:
- ❑ If rain is scarce water evergreen trees and shrubs.
- ❑ As long as the soil is not frozen you can plant and transplant trees and shrubs.
- ❑ Consider trees and shrubs that have winter interest for your landscape.
- ❑ Try forcing cornelian cherry, forsythia, witch hazel, and branches from the pear tree.

Composting:
- ❑ Turn compost pile at least once this month.

Water Ponds:
- ❑ Continue to remove leaves and debris if you did not cover pond.

Indoors Plants:
- ❑ Take leaf cuttings from African violets.
- ❑ Keep plants away from drafty areas.
- ❑ More houseplants are killed from over-watering rather than not enough water.
- ❑ Increase humidity around houseplants.

Chapter 11
January Garden

O Winter! Frozen pulse and heart of fire,
What loss is theirs who from thy kingdom turn
Dismayed, and think thy snow a sculptured urn
Of death! Far sooner in midsummer tire
The streams than under ice. June could not hire
Her roses to forego the strength they learn
In sleeping on thy breast.
— Helen Hunt Jackson (1830-1885)

As Mother Nature tucks us in for a long winter's nap and blankets our landscape with snow, the contrast brightens and beautifies our homes and our lives. There is no doubt these days bring the blues, but gardening can lift our spirits by dreaming and creating the next garden. With the nights longer there are more hours to dream. A passion for gardening is here regardless of the time of year.

January is a dormant month for most plant material, but it can be a very productive month for gardeners. This is the time to plot and plan for the upcoming season. Now is the time for mental changes and these changes work best if you jot them down in a journal or note pad. It's good to review last season's notes and make changes and improvements on paper. Maybe you would like to create a new garden or improve the one you have. The great thing about landscaping is you can do anything you want and if it doesn't work you can change it.

Take time this month to make a list of all the annuals and perennials that you will need for the upcoming season. When spring arrives you will be more than ready to plant or transplant in those problem and new areas. When "January Thaw" arrives (a warm spell) take a walk and look at the landscape and take note. As soon as the garden centers open with their vast array of plant material, plans are forgotten and a new plan takes over. It is still a good idea to have a partial plan. Along with winter comes plant and seed catalogues. We are showered with these wonderful sources throughout the year. When ordering, choose seed companies that have reputable names to ensure that your seeds and supplies are of good quality and true to cultivar name. It is also nice to help out the local businesses that have a great selection of seeds. Growing your own plants can be very rewarding Starting plants from seeds and cuttings is always a nice challenge for gardeners.

In-The-Garden Maintenance

When smiling lawns and tasteful cottages begin to embellish a country, we know that order and culture are established.
Andrew Jackson Downing (1815-1852)

January brings the snow,
Makes our feet and fingers glow.

February brings the rain,
Thaws the frozen lake again.

March brings breezes loud and shrill,
Stirs the dancing daffodil.

April brings the primrose sweet,
Scatters daisies at our feet.

May brings flocks of pretty lams,
Skipping by their fleecy dams.

June brings tulips, lilies, roses,
Fills the children's hands with posies.

Hot July brings cooling showers,
Apricots and gillyflowers.

August brings the sheaves of corn,
Then the harvest home is borne.

Warm September brings the fruit,
Sportsmen then begin to shot.

Fresh October brings the pheasant,
Then to gather nuts is pleasant.

Dull November brings the blast,
Then the leaves are whirling fast.

Chill December brings the sleet,
Blazing fire and Christmas treat.

Mother Goose,
"January brings the snow"

* Cool-weather weeds are thriving. Pull weeds if weather permits and soil is not too wet. Cool-weather weeds include:

> Carolina geranium (*Geranium carolinianum*)
> Common chickweed (*Stellaria media*)
> Henbit (*Laminum amplexicaule*)
> Purple dead nettle (*Lamium purpureum*)
> Shepherd's purse (*Capsella bursa-pastoris*)
> Wild garlic, wild onion (*Allium spp.*)
> Wild hemlock and other members of the carrot family

* Cool-weather annual weeds germinated last fall and will flourish in your lawn and garden until spring and summer when they drop seeds again for fall germination.

* Leaving dead foliage in the garden to insulate through the winter is okay if you are not concerned about residual disease and insects.

* Leave snow on the garden as an added protective blanket against icy winds.

* If there is a break in the weather it is never too late to remove spent plants and clean the garden. Avoid working in the garden if the soil is too wet; you don't want to compact the soil.

* Open cold frame on warm sunny days to ventilate plants; be sure to close before the sun goes down to help trap warm air in for the evening. Keep soil moist inside cold frame.

* Check garden for plants that have been lifted or heaved from the ground due to freezing and thawing. Reset the plant by pressing or tucking.

* If you had a live cut indoor Christmas tree, cut some large branches and lay across your garden for added winter protection.

* Are you bored? Shop your local garden centers for post-Christmas items. This is the best time to find bargains on containers, tools, and yard art.

Mulching

Mulching can be done most any time of year. It is almost a necessity in the landscape not only for maintenance but also for looks. It is recommended to wait until the ground has frozen to lock in moisture. If applied too early your plants will be fooled into thinking the temperatures are not as cold as they really are and this makes it hard for them to prepare for winter. There is a technique for mulching. Mulch should be kept 1" away from the foliage, stems, and trunks. Mulching too close may encourage root rot, insect, and rodent damage. Mulch should be applied 2 to 3 inches high; when the mulch breaks down, reapply a layer of 1 to 2 inches. All you have to do is look around; most mulch jobs are applied incorrectly. Small diameter circles of mulch piled at the base of a tree to

6 to12 inches will cause long-term damage to tree trunks and root. As with good soil requirements, plants need good quality mulch bought from a reputable distributor. Color is the best guideline; a dark rich brown is preferred. Many items/dyes are added to mulch; it is best to know what has been added.

Container Gardening

Nature speaks in symbols and signs.
John Greenleaf Whittier (1807-1892)

* Remove holiday decorations and replace with more greenery for the winter.
* Gather magnolia leaves, branches with crabapples, rose hips, holly sprigs, pinecones, red-twig dogwood, ornamental and native grasses, broadleafed and needled evergreens, and other greenery for winter containers. Use proper pruning skills to avoid a malformed shrub or tree. Soak cuttings in water for at least two hours prior to arranging.
* Continue to water outdoor containers with woody and other perennial plants during dry spells, especially prior to a hard freeze.

Annuals

We are what we repeatedly do.
Excellence, then, is not an act, but a habit.
-Aristotle (384-322 B.C.)

* If you planted cool-weather annuals last fall, they may need to be pressed into the soil. After the soil freezes and thaws, roots may be lifted from the soil. Lightly step on the soil around plants to replace them to their original position. It is recommended not to compact the soil if it is too wet, so you may want to pat them down with your hands. While you are re-anchoring your pansies, go ahead and deadhead blooms and leggy growth.

Seasonal Interest

* Before you decide to keep that beautiful poinsettia as a houseplant, remember it was forced into bloom for you to buy and its energy was used early in its life. Save yourself room and energy and throw it out. If you decide you want the challenge of getting it into bloom for next Christmas, keep the plant in the full sun and water when the soil dries. When the color begins to fade cut plant by half. Keep indoors until after the last frost in May; then move it outdoors so it can receive maximum light for photosynthesis and regrowth.

Garden Lore

• *When the snow falls dry, it means to lie; but flakes light and soft bring rain oft.*
• *If in January, the sun much appear March and April pay full dear.*
• *English customs tell us to burn mistletoe on the Twelfth Night or January 5th to ensure that all who kissed under it would marry.*
• *Plough Monday is the Monday following the Twelfth Night. It is the unofficial day to get to work and plough for spring crops. Some even celebrate the plough itself in hopes of that good spirits will watch over the crops.*
• *Human-like characters that live in gardens are called Gnomes. They are usually less than 2 feet tall. While they are very mischievous, they are kind to anyone who helps them protect Mother Nature.*

Bulbs, Corms, Rhizomes, and Tubers

Anyone who has a bulb has spring.
                    -Anonymous

* Fluctuating temperatures can cause foliage to emerge on spring bulbs. Don't worry, the tips of the foliage may turn brown but the flower will be fine. Do not mulch foliage at this time or you will create more insulation for the bulb promoting more growth during intermittent high temperature sunny days that warm the soil considerably.
* If you stored summer bulbs over winter you should check on them. Discard the ones that have rotted and lightly mist those that have shriveled. Bulbs may start new growth if subjected to heat. Keep storage area dry, and 45 degrees F. for optimum results.
* When potted bulbs have met their cold storage requirement and are well rooted, start bringing them out of cold storage gradually into the sunlight. Leave some pots in storage for the weeks to come, so there will be flowers inside all winter. Stagger crocus, tulips, and daffodils weekly. Keep pots in a cool area, such as an unused room where you have closed the vents, until plant begins to grow. Forcing bulbs slowly in bright light will ensure a good bloom. This may mean you'll need to wash some windows to maximize the availability of winter sunlight. Refer to page 138 for cold requirements.
* Sow grass seed in forced bulb container for a bed of grass.
* Plan now for placement of summer bulbs. Summer bulbs include lilies, caladiums, cannas, gladiolus, and dahlias. With exception of lilies and cannas (USDA Zone 7), summer bulbs are usually not hardy in Tennessee and will need to be lifted and stored every winter.
* If you do not have late-winter blooming bulbs; find a place. These sweet hardy little bulbs can brighten winter when they break through the snow and ice. You will want to make note of this in your journal for fall planting. Choose from snowdrops, winter aconite, and glory-of-the-snow.

Seeds

Aside from the garden of Eden, mans great temptation took place when he first received his seed catalogue.
-Henry Wadsworth Longfellow (1807-1882)

* It is time to buy seeds, containers, heating pads, and seed-starting mix for those who attempt to grow their own plants. If you choose to order from catalogues, it is recommended to choose seeds for plants that are suggested for your zone for best results. In fact, if you live in zone 6, and a plant's maximum hardiness is listed as zone 6 ("hardy in zone 6-8") this plant will not survive many winters in your area. Choose plants listed as "hardy in zones 4-6" to play it safe.

There is a great pleasure in working in the soil, apart from the ownership of it.
The man who has planted a garden feels that he has done something for the good of the world.
-Charles Dudley Warner (1829-1900)

* Work the soil if it crumbles when squeezed in the hand.
* Plan vegetable gardens and crop rotation for the upcoming season.

He that plants trees loves others besides himself.
Thomas Fuller (1608-1661)

* Plan to purchase fruit trees for spring planting.
* Spray fruit trees with dormant oil spray to decrease insects and disease. Follow directions on all pesticide or fungicide.

Garden Lore

• On the 5th of January (Twelfth Night), English custom brings us wassailing of the orchard. Farmers would toast the trees and throw their cider over the trunk of the largest tree. This is a celebration of good health and good fruit. They would give thanks to the wood spirits and the spirits that protected the orchard.

Wassaile the trees that they may beare
You many a plum and many a peare;
For more or less fruits they will bring
As you so give them wassailing.
-Robert Herrick (1591-1674)

Here's to thee, old apple-tree,
Whence thou mayst bud,
Whence thou mayst blow,
Whence thou mayst bear apples enow!
Hats-full! caps-full!
Bushel, bushel, sacks-full!
And my pockets full, too! Hurra!

Stand fast, root! bear well, top!
Pray God send us a good howling crop:
Every twig, apples big;
Every bow, apples enow!

Garden Lore

• Pixies are mischievous tiny spirits that live on the farm to help farmers and gardeners with crop and flower production. Unless you want total chaos in the garden I wouldn't place a Gnome where a Pixie might live.
• The Celtic people chose Lugh as their Sun God and God of good harvest.
• The Welsh created Amaethon as their God of agriculture.
• The Italians chose Ceres to be their Goddess of agriculture, grain, and good harvest. Fana was the goddess of the Earth and her consort Faunus was the god of the forest.
• Before Venus was the Roman Goddess of Love, she was also the protector of gardens and vineyards.
• Demeter was the Goddess of Earth, agriculture, grain, harvest, and fertility in Greece.
• Persephone was the Greek Goddess of fertility and the revival of nature in spring.
• The Greeks also chose Antheia, an attendant of Aphrodite, to be the Goddess of vegetation, gardens, blossoms, the budding earth, and love.
• Year of snow, crops will grow.
• Eat 12 grapes on New Year's Day and have money all year.

Trees and Shrubs

I think that I shall never see,
A poem as lovely as a tree.
-Joyce Kilmer (1886-1918)

* As long as the soil is not frozen you can plant and transplant. If the ground is frozen, put off planting until temperatures warm.
* You should consider trees and shrubs that have winter interest for your landscape. Many trees and shrubs have unique branch structure, interesting fruit and seed heads, as well as shiny and exfoliating bark. These varieties can be very rewarding in the gray of winter. Place your selection close to the house, near a window or walkway so you can enjoy their show.

* *Plants with shiny, colored, unusual or exfoliating bark:*
> American beech (*Fagus grandifolia*)
> Amur cork tree (*Phellodendron amurense*)
> Barberry, female (*Berberis*)
> Chinese elm (*Ulmus parvifolia*)
> Coralbark maple (*Acer palmatum*)
> Crape myrtle (*Lagerstroemia indica*)
> Ginko (*Ginko biloba*)
> Golden weeping willow (*Salix 'Chrysocoma*)
> Harry Lauder's walking stick, contorted hazel (*Corylus avellana 'contorta*)
> Japanese red pine (*Pinus densifolia*)
> Lacebark pine (*Pinus bungeana*)
> Moosewood, striped maple (*Acer pensylvanicum*)
> Paperbark maple (*Acer griseum*)
> Quacking or American aspen (*Populus tremuloides*)
> Red-twig dogwood (*Cornus stolonifera*)
> River birch (*Betula nigra*)
> Sassafras
> Serviceberry (*Amelanchier*)
> Shagbark hickory (*Carya ovata*)
> Sweet cherry (*Prunus avium*)
> Sycamore (*Acer pseudoplatanus*)
> Trident maple (*Acer buergeranum*)

* *Plants with fruit, berries, or seed heads:*
American cranberrybush (*Viburnum trilobum*)
American holly (*Ilex opaca*)
Chinese holly (*Ilex cornuta*)
Common quacking grass (*Briza media*))
Cranberry cotoneaster (*Cotoneaster apiculatus*)
Heavenly bamboo (*Nandina*)
Hummingbird summer sweet (*Clethra alnifolia*)
Possumhaw (*Ilex decidua*)
Sumac (*Rhus*)
Tea viburnum (*Viburnum setigerum*)

Winter King hawthorne *(Crataegus viridis)*
Winterberry *(Ilex verticillata)*

Plants with winter bloom, fragrance or foliage:
Juniper *(Juniperus)*
Winter honeysuckle *(Lonicera fragrantissima)*
Witch hazel *(Hamamelis)*
Wood spurge *(Euphorbia amygdaloides)*

* Keep new plant material well watered throughout the winter. Lack of water can be fatal for plant material by placing added stress of drought to already stressful low temperatures. Evergreen plants may even need a anti-desiccant to help hold moisture in the leaves and needles and reduce "scorch" due to dry winter wind. More plants die from desiccation than extreme cold.
* Reduce the effects of frost by protecting sensitive plant material with burlap, horticulture fleece, straw or cut Christmas tree branches.
* Carefully remove heavy snow from evergreens with a broom. This will decrease breakage and malformation of your landscape. Wrap conifers with twine to hold branches together during winter. If ice is present do not remove, let it thaw naturally. When ice bends branches all the way to the ground often-permanent damage results. When assessing winter damage, remember that trees and shrubs have great reserves. After a lousy winter (extremely low temperatures, heavy snow/ice loads) the next 2 to 3 years, the woody plant may look fine. But often, in year 3 – 4 after a harsh winter, these plants will show signs of stress and decline. The decline should be blamed on events 3 – 4 years earlier.
* Check young trees for injuries due to rodents. Use protective collars or wire mesh to avoid injuries. Remove mulch that has been applied too close to the trunk.
* Try forcing cornelian cherry, forsythia, witch hazel, and branches from the pear tree this month. Other spring-bloomers need a few more weeks of dormancy to be forced successfully. The cornelian cherry, after cutting, will take about two weeks to bloom yellow blossoms indoors. The forsythia, which is the easiest to force, will bloom yellow in about one to three weeks. Witch hazel will bloom yellow and fragrant in about one week. The pear takes about four to five weeks to bloom white fragrant flowers.

Forcing Branches

* Bring the outdoors in and brighten any home or office with an arrangement of spring blossoms. Nothing delivers the feeling of spring more than forced branches. Most branches can be forced one to two months before their natural bloom outdoors. These trees and shrubs must be spring-flowering woody plants whose flower buds were created last fall.
Apple *(Malus spp.)*
Apricot, Japanese *(Prunus mume)*
Azalea *(Rhododendron)*
Cherry *(Prunus serrulata)*
Cornelian cherry *(Cornus mas)*
Dogwood *(Cornus)*

Garden Lore

• *Female spirits, called dryads, live within the forest and protect the woodland plants. They are thought to punish those who harm their home among the trees.*
• *Always expect a thaw in January.*
• *Fog in January brings a wet spring.*

Forsythia
Hawthorn (*Crataegus*)
Honeysuckle (*Lonicera*)
Horse chestnut (*Aesculus*)
Lilac (*Syringa*)
Magnolia
Magnolia, star (*Magnolia stellata*)
Maple, red (*Acer rubrum*)
Mock orange (*Philadelphus coronaries*)
Peach (*Prunus spp.*)
Pussy willow (*Salix discolor*)
Quince (*Chaenomeles speciosa*)
Redbud (*Cercis canadensis*)
Shadblow serviceberry (*Amelanchier canadensis*)
Spicebush (*Lindera benzoin*)
Spiraea
Wisteria

* If branches are cut too early they will be impossible to force. The closer the branches are to their natural bloom time the easier it will be to force them. Many varieties need 8 weeks of temperatures above 40 degrees to set buds, which means after mid-January.
* Shrubs prove to be easier to force than trees so try forcing shrubs first for encouragement. Collect branches on a day when temperatures are above freezing. Cut branches that are 2 feet long for nice arranging length. Use good pruning practices while cutting branches for forcing. Cut limbs first that cross, inward growing branches and misplaced branches. This should fulfill your need for your arrangement while improving the shrub or tree's structure.
* Choose branches with many flower buds that are usually larger and fatter than leaf buds. Wait until buds swell and gather a bundle of branches. Cut branches at an angle to keep stem from sitting flush in containers and impeding water uptake. Soak branches overnight in a warm bath (100 degrees) to stimulate bud development.
* Remove and re-cut branches from bath. Make 2-inch slits in the stems and place in a vase with warm water. Amend water with lemon-lime soda and bleach (½ Tbs. per quart) or a floral preservative to decrease bacterial growth and increase bloom time. Change water every few days. To encourage bloom time, increase humidity by covering branches with a plastic bag and place in temperatures 60 to 65 degrees.
* When buds open, move to a location with maximum sun and cool temperature. Re-cut branches every week to encourage more water uptake and longer lasting blooms. Bloom time should vary between 10 to 14 days. After branches are in full bloom work into any arrangement. Remember more branches give a greater effect while a few sprigs look puny.

To exist as a nation, to prosper as a state, and to live as a people, we must have trees.
    -*Theodore Roosevelt (1858-1919)*

Nothing great in the world has ever been accomplished without passion.
        -*George Wilhelm Hagel (1770-1831)*

If you are planning for a year, sow rice;
if you are planning for a decade, plant trees;
if you are planning for a lifetime, educate people.
Chinese Proverb

Nature never breaks
her own laws.
-Leonardo da Vinci
(1452-1519)

Lawn Care

Well done is better than well said.
Benjamin Franklin (1706-1790)

Maintenance

* Don't walk or drive on frozen lawn to avoid damage.
* If the winter has been mild and soil is not too wet, sod can be laid in early winter.
* Plan for February seeding of trouble spots in your lawn where last fall's seeding was unsuccessful. Dormant seeding can be preformed in January but germination will not occur until the end of March due to soil temperatures. Cold temperatures will not hurt grass seed but birds, erosion, and wind will.

Composting

Announced by all the trumpets of the sky;
Arrives the snow.
-Ralph Waldo Emersom (1803-1882)

* If you have a compost pile you will need to turn it at least once this month.

Water Ponds

The grand old poem called winter.
-Henry David Thoreau (1817-1862)

* Continue to remove leaves and debris if you did not cover pond.
* Bog or marginal plants are plants that love the edges of the pond.
* Floater plants love to lie on the surface of the pond. They help shade the water.
*Oxygenating plants, while not exciting, these plants play an important role in cleaning the water.

Garden Lore
• *A mild January, a chilly May.*

January Indoor Gardening

Those who labor in the earth are the chosen people of God.
-Thomas Jefferson (1743-1826)

* Check the soil level of houseplants and add fresh potting soil if needed.

* Take leaf cuttings from African violets; place in a north or northeast-facing window. Refer to page 122 for instructions.

* Keep all plants away from drafty areas. Room temperature of 65 degrees is better for indoor plants than 72 to 75 degrees. At least at night, lower your thermometer to benefit plants.

* If plants are growing leggy they are not getting enough sun.

* Maintain poinsettias at 55 to 70 degrees and keep out of drafty areas. They need 6 hours a day of bright indirect light. Don't allow wilting or becoming too wet. When color starts to fade, cut plant by half and treat like a houseplant.

* More houseplants are killed from over-watering rather than not enough water. With the shorter days, less water will be needed unless plants are situated close to heated air. Never allow plants to sit in a saucer full of water.

* Water houseplants with room temperature water. Let water sit for 24 hours before using.

* If you have free time, research your houseplants and try to position them in the house that is similar to their original environment.

I believe it is no wrong Observation,
that Persons of Genius,
and those who are most capable of Art,
are always most fond of Nature,
as such are chiefly sensible,
that all Art consists in the Imitation and Study of Nature.
Alexander Pope, "The Guardian" (1688-1744)

The beginning is the most important part of the work.
-Plato (c. 428-347 bc)

February Garden Chore List

In the Garden:
- ❑ Open cold frame on warm sunny days to ventilate plants.
- ❑ Repair garden accessories, furniture, arbors, and trellises.
- ❑ Soil is ready to be worked when soil crumbles between your fingers.
- ❑ Add organic matter to improve soil quality.

Flowers and Herbs:
- ❑ Keep forced bulbs that are in bloom away from heat.
- ❑ Apply bone meal and 10-10-10 to emerging bulbs.
- ❑ Transplant rose bushes when weather permits.
- ❑ Review fertilizer and spray program (fungicide) for the season.

Seeds:
- ❑ Buy seeds and seedlings from a reputable company to ensure good quality.

Vegetables and Fruits:
- ❑ Till cover crop or "green manure" when weather permits.
- ❑ Sow early crops under glass, cloche or in a cold frame.
- ❑ Don't forget to rotate your crops.
- ❑ Plant fruit trees, shrubs, and vines if the ground is not frozen.
- ❑ Fertilizer fruit trees with 10-10-10.
- ❑ Prune grape vines.
- ❑ Cut side branches on black raspberries to one foot.
- ❑ Prune fruit trees before buds begin to swell.
- ❑ Plant strawberries.

Trees and Shrubs:
- ❑ Prune deciduous trees and shrubs.
- ❑ Force branches from Japanese quince, cherry, plum, flowering almond, forsythia, and pussy willow this month.
- ❑ Plant and transplant dormant deciduous and evergreen trees and shrubs.
- ❑ Fertilize established trees and shrubs with 10-10-10.
- ❑ Use an acid-type fertilizer (sulfur) to feed evergreens that enjoy acidic soil.

Lawn Care:
- ❑ Service lawnmower for the up-coming season.
- ❑ Rake the lawn of winter debris; fill low spots with topsoil.
- ❑ 3rd best time to seed the lawn is mid-February until late March.
- ❑ Mow lawn at a higher setting for early spring mowing.
- ❑ On established cool-weather lawns, fertilize with 10-10-10.

Composting:
- ❑ Add 10-10-10 to compost pile and turn it.

Water Ponds:
- ❑ Continue to remove leaves and debris if you did not cover pond.

Indoors Plants:
- ❑ Repot houseplants.
- ❑ Treat faded amaryllis as a houseplant.
- ❑ Clean houseplants.

Chapter 12

February Garden

Out of the bosom of the Air,
Out of the cloud-folds of her garments shaken,
Over the woodlands brown and bare,
Over the harvest-fields forsaken,
Silent, and soft, and slow
Descends the snow.
- Henry Wadsworth Longfellow (1807-1882)

Our landscape continues to be mulched with snow, which proves to be a great protectant from winter's wrath. As the days grow longer, we long for springtime. The dormancy will soon be over and greenery will prevail. As the snow thaws, under gray skies, there are still sites to behold. The February scene is full of pleasantries such as fields dotted with hay rolls and the orange hew of perennial broom sedge unmowed in the fields. We can't forget the white bark of the sycamores that line the Tennessee River, "Hogoheegee" or "Big River" as the Cherokee called it. Even the fencerows that are full of dried Queen-Anne's-lace and prairie grasses give us something to see as we travel along. The unusual red seed head of the sumac tree gives winter interest as well as the glowing red new growth on trees and shrubs. Witch hazel will bring spring to your back door as the perfume of the winter honeysuckle sweetens the breeze.

February teases our spirits with warm days filled with bright sunlight only to be followed by a cold blizzard. Soon the cold blanket will liquefy and offer a drink to nature as dormancy breaks. Nature seems to come to life as a result of melting snow.

Spend this month finalizing your new season plans and gear up for the busy months approaching. Plan now, because when the weather warms there will be less time for journal entries. If you are ahead of the upcoming season take this time to read anything that interests you, maybe topiaries or window boxes. The list is endless.

If you are a romantic at heart, this is your month. February and Hallmark bring us Valentine's Day. Flowers should be sent anytime of year for any reason; nothing lifts the spirits more than flowers. Send a message with your gift of flowers in the form of bouquets, nosegays, or "tussy-mussys". Refer to page 91 for Florigraphy.

In-The-Garden Maintenance

The February sunshine steeps your boughs
And tints the buds and swell the leaves within.
-William Cullen Bryant (1794-1878)

Garden Lore

• *If Candlemas Day is fair and bright,*
Winter will take another flight;
If Candlemas Day brings storm and rain,
Then winter will not come again.

• *If February brings no rain,*
'tis neither good for grass nor grain.
• *If February gives much snow,*
A fine summer it doth foreshow.
• *A February spring is worth nothing.*

* Open cold frame on warm sunny days to ventilate plants; be sure to close before the sun goes down to help trap warm air in for the evening. Keep soil moist inside cold frame.
* Use this time to repair garden accessories, furniture, arbors, and trellises.
* Press plant material into soil that may have been lifted or heaved from the ground due to soil freezing and thawing.
* Working the soil can be tough this time of year but if the soil is not too wet it can be done. Soil is ready to be worked when soil crumbles between your fingers.
* Add organic matter, to improve soil quality, such as well-rotted compost, pine straw, and sphagnum peat moss. If you have heavy clay soil, add sharp sand or granite meal. Add dried leaves that have been chopped by the lawn mower. Whole leaves will take longer to break down and if the layer is thick it may repel water, depriving roots of water. You can add a small application of nitrogen to speed decomposition. The leaves will decompose into compost by spring. Does the soil need lime? Probably not; check your latest soil test.
* Working the soil will bring bugs to the surface for the birds to devour or winter to take care of. You will want to turn the soil again in early spring.

Perennials and Biennials

There is a time for everything,
and a season for every activity under heaven:
a time to be born, and a time to die,
a time to plant and a time to uproot,....
-Ecclesiastes, 3:1-2

* If perennials have been lifted from the ground due to freezing and thawing, gently press or tuck them into the ground.

Annuals

Winter is in my head, but
spring is in my heart.
Victor Hugo (1802-1885)

* If cool-weather annuals have been lifted from the ground due to freezing and thawing, gently press or tuck them into the ground.
* Plant cool-weather annuals as they become available.
* Buy a bouquet of flowers on February 6th; this is the feast day for St. Dorothy of Caesarea. Dorothy is the patron saint of florists, fruit and nut growers, and gardeners.

Bulbs, Corms, Rhizomes, and Tubers

As is the garden such is the gardener.
A man's nature runs either to herbs or
weeds.
-Sir Frances Bacon (1561-1626)

Garden Lore
• *It is bad luck to bring snowdrops*
into a home if someone is ill.

* Keep forced bulbs that are in bloom away from heat to encourage a longer bloom period. An unused cool bedroom or unheated sun porch is a good place to keep them provided there is ample light available.
*Bring potted bulbs in to be forced to continue a succession of indoor blooms.
* Wait until daffodils are in the bud stage with a hint of color before cutting to bring indoors.
* Don't mix cut daffodils with other cut flowers. Their chemistry will reduce the life of the other flowers in the vase.
* Apply bone meal and 10-10-10 to emerging bulbs.

Roses

A garden must be looked unto and dressed, as the body.
-George Herbert (1593-1633)

* Amend soil with organic matter. Gather materials for planting your new roses such as coarse sand, peat moss, and compost. Sharpen shovel for the new season.
* Transplant rose bushes when weather permits.
* Review fertilizer and spray program (fungicide) for the season. If you do not want to spray to have beautiful rose choose an antique variety or try Rosa rugosa. Modern roses require more care and spraying.
* Make sure sprayer is clean and in good working order.

Seeds

Spade! …Thou art a tool of honor in my hands;
I press thee, through a yielding soil, with pride.
-William Wordsworth (1770-1850)

* Buy flower and vegetable seeds and seedlings from a reputable company to ensure good quality. Buy soon to get the selections you want before they sell out.
* If you have old seeds, test 10 seeds from each pack for 48 hours at room temperature in a moist paper towel. If a majority germinates then use the old seeds. Discard if a majority of seeds do not germinate.
* Clean and prepare seed trays for indoor seed sowing.
* When calculating dates for sowing seeds, remember seedlings need up to ten days to harden-off before planting in the garden.

Deep down within the frozen brook
I hear a murmur faint and sweet,
and lo! The ice breaks as I look,
and living waters touch my feet.
-Jane Goodwin Austin (1831-1894)

Sowing Seeds

I have great faith in a seed.
Convince me that you have a seed there,
and I am prepared to expect wonders.
--Henry David Thoreau (1817-1916)

One of the greatest joys for gardeners is to watch the growth of a seed sprout into a beautiful plant. Annuals are the best choice of seeds due to their easy germination. Most seeds will germinate and grow in just about any container as long as it drains. I have fond memories of my grandmother's windowsills lined with soup cans and cut milk cartons. However you choose to sow seeds, remember, life is obtained by supplying the appropriate warmth, light, air, and moisture. There are many advantages to growing your own transplants, such as getting a head start on the season, more cultivar selections, and it's less expensive. The disadvantage is you must exert some effort.

Seed Selection:
* It is best to buy new seeds every season, although some seeds can be saved for years.
* Some seeds will need light to germinate. Some seeds need complete darkness to germinate. In the latter case the seed container needs to be covered with a newspaper until seeds have sprouted.
* Determine planting date by counting 6 weeks before your zone's last frost date. Seedlings will be spindly if they are kept indoors too long. Each selection will vary when it comes to planting dates. It is better to have sturdy plants that are planted late then to have spindly plants that have to stay indoors too long.
* Before planting, place seeds in water; the good seeds will sink, the nonviable seeds will float.

Potting Mix:
* Sterile, potting mix is the key ingredient for seed germination. This media should be loose for proper oxygen exchange. Never use topsoil or used potting soil as this almost always ends with damping-off disease. (Damping-off is a fungus disease caused by poor draining soil and over-watering. Seedlings will shrivel, turn brown and fall over.)
* Potting mix should be dampened prior to sowing. Use warm water for quick absorption.
* Warm water will speed germination and cold water will slow germination.

Container:
*Select growing containers that are 2 to 3 inches deep with drainage holes. Choose peat pots, peat pellets, or flats. Peat pots and peat pellets are easiest to transplant. If you choose not to purchase new pots you will need to clean old pots with a solution of 10% bleach.

Sowing seeds:
*The size of the seed determines its planting depth. Small seeds should be sown on the surface to 1/8 inch deep. Large seeds should be sown 1/4

inch deep and covered by a thin layer of potting mix or just vermiculite. Always read seed packet for sowing directions.

* Always plant 2 or 3 seeds in each container to ensure successful germination of at least one plant. If more than one sprouts, select the best seedling and snip the remaining seedlings.

* Lightly sprinkle milled sphagnum moss, a natural fungicide, over seeds to protect against damping-off. When planting small seeds you may just want to drop the tiny seed onto the sphagnum moss covering to increase the light germination they require.

*You can use heating cables to speed germination. These cables should be placed under the flats. Most seeds like their soil temperatures to be around 70 to 80 degrees.

*Label all seed containers.

Humidity:

*To get 100% humidity until germination use a plastic covering. Do not place in direct sunlight and no additional water is needed until plastic has been removed; remove plastic if too much moisture accumulates.

*Remove plastic covering when 1st seed germinates.

Water:

*Soil should be kept moist at all times. If the soil dries, germination growth may be terminated.

Light and temperature:

* Place seedlings in a south-facing window for optimum production or use fluorescent lighting located 3 to 4 inches above the container while seeds are germinating.

* Plants need maximum light, 60 to 75 degree day temperatures and 50 to 65 degree night temperatures.

Indoors lighting:

* If you are using fluorescent bulbs they need to be kept 4 inches above the seedlings and kept on 16 to 18 hours a day. Two 40-watt bulbs are usually recommended. Use automatic timers to control the light. Note: Regular fluorescent lamps are almost as effective as growth lamps.

Fertilization:

* When first leaves are formed feed with a liquid fertilizer such as 20-20-20; feed every 4th watering.

Petting:

* When seedlings are 3 inches tall lightly touch several times day with your hand or a stick to encourage sturdy stems. A fan will do the same.

Transplanting:

*Transplant when plants are 1 ½ inches tall with 2 or 3 true leaves. They will need to be transplanted to 4-inch pots with a potting mix that contains compost. Lift seedlings out of soil mix with a pencil for easy thinning and transplanting. Gently hold seedlings by their leaves and roots to avoid breaking their fragile stem.

To see the world in a grain of sand
And heaven in a wildflower,
Hold infinity in the palm of your hand
And eternity in an hour.
    -William Blake (1757-1827)

Hardening-off or acclimating:
* Slow growth of plants by watering less, no fertilizer, and give them cool temperatures (45-50 degrees). Set plants outdoors with protection from the sun and wind. Increase outdoor exposure everyday for two weeks before transplanting after the last frost.
* Do not mulch around plants until the soil has had time to warm or the plants will get a slower start.

Stratification:
* Perennials are more challenging to grow from seed because they require some exposure to cold and moist conditions in order to germinate. This cold treatment is called stratification. Place seeds between paper towels and surround them with moist potting mix inside a plastic bag. Chill the seeds in the refrigerator for 4 to 12 weeks. The seeds are then ready to be sown in moist potting mix and placed in a warm location for germination.

Scarification:
* If seeds have extremely hard coats the surface can be nicked with a file or immersed in hot (170-212 degrees) water. Place these seeds in a cup and pour the hot water on them. Allow water to cool 12 to 24 hours and then remove seeds and plant into growing medium as described for annual plant production.

Hoe your ground, set out cabbages and convey water to them in conduits.
    Saint Jerome (c. 340-420 A.D.)

* Before the vegetable season gets going, here is a review of temperature tolerance. Tender vegetables are damaged by a light frost, they include:

Beans	Pepper
Corn	Pumpkin
Cucumbers	Squash
Eggplant	Sweet potato
Muskmelon	Tomato
Okra	Watermelon

* Semi-hardy vegetables can tolerate light frost but not hard frost.

Beets	Endive
Carrot	Lettuce
Cauliflower	Parsnip
Celery	Potato
Chard	

* Hardy vegetables can tolerate a hard frost.

Broccoli	Onion
Brussels sprouts	Peas
Cabbage	Radish
Kale	Spinach
Kohlrabi	Turnip
Mustard greens	

* Till cover crop or "green manure" when weather permits.
* Amend garden with well-rotted manure, peat moss, and compost.
* Select disease-resistant varieties when choosing seeds.

*Sow directly to garden:
> Kale
> Mustard
> Onion sets
> Peas- snow or Chinese, snap, and
> > shelling or English (dust with inoculate
> > nitrogen fixing bacteria that increases crop)
> Radish
> Shallot sets
> Spinach

*Sow early crops under glass, cloche, or in a cold frame. Don't forget to ventilate on sunny days.
> Broccoli
> Cabbage
> Cauliflower
> Lettuce
> Radish

*Plant directly to the garden:
> Asparagus
> Horseradish
> Rhubarb

* Cover rhubarb to accelerate spring crops.
* Don't forget to rotate your crops. Rotating vegetables will reduce insect and disease to this year's crop.

 *Fruits*

How wonderful it is that nobody need wait a single moment before starting to improve the world.
-Anne Frank (1929-1945)

* If you plant your orchard on a northeast slope, the morning sun will dry the morning dew and reduce chance of disease. Also the cool temperatures of the north slope will retard full flower development too early in the spring.
* Plant fruit trees, shrubs, and vines if the ground is not frozen. Choose dwarf varieties to make harvest easier.
* Plant and transplant grapes.
* Apply a general fertilizer around the drip line and beyond of fruit trees such as 10-10-10.
* Prune grape vines while they are dormant. Prune this year's lateral stems to one strong bud.
* Cut side branches on black raspberries to one foot.
* With exception to ever-bearers, raspberries, and blackberries should have all canes that produced fruit last season removed.
* Prune fruit trees before buds begin to swell. Prune dead, diseased,

Garden Lore
• *If Candlemas Day be fine and clear, corn and fruits will then be dear.*
• *On Candlemas Day sow beans in the clay.*
• *A good farmer should have on Candlemas Day, half his turnips, and half his hay.*
• *When the sun is shining on Shrovetide Day (fat Tuesday), it is meant well for rye and peas.*

Garden Phenology
• *Plant peas, spinach, and lettuce when daffodils begin to bloom.*

Garden Lore

- *Thunder on Shrovetide Day foretelleth wind, store of fruit, and plenty.*
- *So much as the sun shineth on Pancake Tuesday, the like will shine every day in Lent.*
- *Dry Lent, fertile year.*

damaged, and crossing branches. Do not prune plums, cherries, gages or peaches, which are best pruned as new growth appears. There is no need to paint or seal fresh cuts. Remember, fruit grow on horizontal limbs not vertical. Thin canopy to increase air circulation that aids in reducing fungal diseases. Remove all sucker growth.
* Add wood ashes to fruit trees and berries. Wood ashes contain potash that may raise the pH slightly.
* Plant strawberries as soon as they become available.
* Apply a post-emergent weed killer to winter weeds under fruit trees.

Trees and Shrubs

Oh, what a goodly and glorious show!
The stately trees have decked themselves with white,
And stand transfigured in a robe of light;
Wearing for each lost leaf a flake of snow.
  -Richard Wilton, Old Farmer's Almanac (1903)

* Force branches from Japanese quince, cherry, plum, flowering almond, daphne, forsythia, and pussy willow this month.
* Plant and transplant dormant deciduous and evergreen trees and shrubs. Complete this chore before buds begin to swell to decrease stress on the plant. Remove metal wires, roping, and nonbiodegradable burlap on new plants.
* Fertilize established trees and shrubs with 10-10-10 fertilizer. Apply all fertilizers to the drip line and beyond. Feeder roots extend great distances from the trunk, sometimes estimated at 2-3 times the diameter of the drip line branches.
* Add wood ashes to soil around lilac to increase alkalinity and potassium to enhance blooms.
*Use an acid-type fertilizer (sulfur) to feed evergreens that enjoy acidic soil.

> Conifers (pines, spruces, firs, and junipers)
> Broadleafed evergreens (rhododendron, azaleas, and camellias)

* Inspect for insect and disease damage while pruning. Always follow directions before applying pesticides.
* Winter freeze damage is evident by bronzing golden tips on evergreen shrubs. If you have noticed this symptom, delay pruning until late spring when you can be sure how much tissue is damaged.
* Keep all newly planted material well watered throughout the winter.

Pruning

Pruning is a necessary part of landscaping. The quicker pruning is learned and accepted the better your landscape will be. Trees need routine, correct pruning to control size and shape as well as reap maximum benefit of improved photosynthesis potential. If you have fruit trees, pruning optimizes fruit size and color. The right selection of tree or shrub that obtains a desirable shape by itself will avoid stress that results from pruning.

If a tree dies, plant another in its place.
  -Carl Linnaeus (1707-1778)

What to prune:

* Pruning should be done to remove damaged, diseased, or dead branches. Branches that cross each other will rub together creating entry points for insects and disease. One of these branches should be removed. Choose the weaker of the two or you may want to remove both branches if wounds have been created. You can also remove misplaced and troublesome branches.
* On young trees, if the branches grow at a tight angle they will be more likely to split and break in high winds than branches that have a larger trunk to branch angle. The Bradford pear has a very tight trunk to branch angle and this will almost always result in breakage and thus a malformed tree that once was breathtakingly beautiful.
* There should be 12 to 18 inches between scaffold branches. If you want to control growth of your tree, remove no more than 1/3 of its new growth. To get the correct shape cut at an angle 1/4 inch above an outward facing bud. Thin interior branches as well to allow light into center of tree.
* Remove suckers – spindly shoots that grow from the base of the trunk. Also remove water sprouts that are similar to suckers except they grow on the branches. These shoots drain precious energy and can be unsightly.

How to prune:

* The key to successful pruning is to use sharp tools of good quality. If the branch is smaller than 1-1/2 inches in diameter use lopping shears or hand pruners, always cutting at an angle. If the branch is larger than 1-1/2 inches, use a pruning saw to make an undercut away from the trunk about 6 to 8 inches. Then come back with an over-cut and allow the branch to fall. This will decrease splitting if branch is too heavy. Repeat with an undercut and a final over-cut at the branch collar, but not flush with the trunk.
* Cutting too close to the trunk will not allow the wound to heal properly and opens the tree to disease and insects. It is not recommended to paint freshly cut wounds. The branch collar, which is the raised or swollen area at the base of branch, will callous over into a circular shape to protect the tree from infection.
* It is not good practice to top trees. This ruins the natural beauty of the tree and encourages weak sprouts. Older trees cannot recover from such harsh pruning. Pruning top terminal branches will produce a low spreading tree. Pruning lateral and side branches will promote upward growth and less bushy form. When pruning hedges it is recommended to leave the base wider than the top to allow light to reach lower branches.

When to prune:

* Avoid pruning in the spring when trees and shrubs are budding. Avoid pruning deciduous plants in the fall. This may encourage new growth during warm wet weather that will be damaged by the low temperatures of winter.

Pruning guide:

* Trees that flower before end of May – prune immediately after flower.
* Trees that flower after the end of May – prune in spring before new growth begins.
* Shade trees /deciduous plants – prune in late-winter during dormancy before they leaf out, late February to early April.
* Conifers – Prune in May when new growth or "candles" are produced. Prune candle tips to force new shoots below cuts.
* Fruit trees can be pruned in late winter along with the deciduous trees. The harder you prune, the more vigorous the re-growth.

Coppicing

* Coppicing or stumping has been a long-time practice of European gardeners. This drastic cut on shrubs can be used on many woody plants. Coppicing creates bold foliage, intense variegation, and prolific flowers and fruit. Before using this pruning practice, make sure you know the growth habit of the tree or shrub you are about to cut down. This pruning method works best on shrubs that produce fruit and flowers on new wood rather than last year's growth. Coppicing should not be practiced on grafted plants. Coppicing is simple to do, but timing is important. On shrubs simply cut entire plant back 3 to 5 inches from the ground. This technique should not be used on woody plants less than one year old. Coppicing can be practiced around late winter and early spring, usually about one month before new growth emerges.

Good plants for coppicing:
>   Abelia
>   Bluebeard *(Caryopteris x clandonensis)*
>   Bodinier beautyberry *(Callicarpa bodinieri)*
>   Butterfly bush *(Buddleia davidii)*
>   Forsythia
>   Hydrangea, oak-leaf *(Hydrangea quercifolia)*
>   Hydrangea, 'Peegee', 'Grandiflora', 'Tardiva' *(Hydrangea paniculata)*
>   Lilac (Syringa)
>   Privets *(Liqustrum)*
>   Red-twig dogwood *(Cornus alba)*
>   Rose of Sharon *(Hibiscus syriacus)*
>   Spiraea

May I a small house and large garden have;
And a few friends, and many books,
both true, both wise, and both delightful too!
-Abraham Cowley (1618-1667)

Garden Lore

• *It was once thought that drinking common chickweed tea would decrease the chances of becoming obese.*

Maintenance

* Service lawnmower for the up-coming season; change spark plug, check the oil, replace the filter, and have blades sharpened.
* If the weather is mild and dry the lawn can be mowed. Pay attention to winter weeds and as soon as temperatures permit you can spray them with a post-emergent herbicide.
* Rake the lawn of winter debris; fill low spots with topsoil.
* Seeding the lawn is optimal in mid-August through late-September. The second best time to seed is September through October; 3rd best time mid-February until late March. If you can wait to seed in August, you will experience more success. For lawn seeding instructions review page 127.
* Mow lawn at a higher setting for early spring mowing.

Fertilization

* In the spring, cool-weather lawns will do well with just one application of fertilizer such as 10-10-10. It is recommended to apply fertilizer when rain is predicted to avoid burning of lawn.

Insect & Weed Control

* Don't use crabgrass control until your April fertilizer application. If applied now it will leach before crabgrass has germinated.
* When the daytime temperatures are 50 degrees consistently you can apply a post-emergence herbicide on annual weeds. For now, all you can do is use the hand pulling method, which proves to be much safer for everyone. These annual weeds germinated last fall and will flourish in your lawn until spring and summer when they drop seeds again for fall germination. Keep an eye out for:

>   Carolina geranium (*Geranium carolinianum*)
>   Common chickweed (*Stellaria media*)
>   Henbit (*Laminum amplexicaule*)
>   Shepherd's purse (*Capsella bursa-pastoris*)

* Avoid using weed killer on newly seeded areas.

Composting

That grand old poem called winter.
-Henry David Thoreau (1817-1862)

* Add 10-10-10 to compost pile and turn it.
* When temperatures reach above 45 degrees consistently, decay will begin.

Water Ponds

In all things of nature there is something of the marvelous.
-Aristotle (384-322 B.C.)

* Continue to remove leaves and debris if you did not cover pond.
* Before you decide to build a pond, it is wise to check into your community regulations for water ponds. Your pond will be a hugh hit for children and they need to be protected.

February Indoor Gardening

Adopt the pace of nature; her secret is patience.
-Ralph Waldo Emerson (1803-1882)

* This is a great time to repot houseplants. Remove plant, soil and all, and if the roots look crowded it's time to pot-up to the next size container. Use a potting mix and include a slow-release fertilizer such as 10-10-10; water well. If it's not time to re-pot, just remove the spent top layer of soil without interfering with roots and add fresh potting mix.
* Pinch leggy plants back such as umbrella tree or schefflera, polka dot plant, ivies, aluminum plant, and wandering Jew. This will promote bushy plants and you can use the trimming to create more plant for summer containers.
* Treat faded amaryllis as a houseplant and set outside in May to live until its time for cold storage in the fall. Give it lots of sunlight and moist soil.
* Remove dust from houseplants with a damp sponge or warm shower.
* Clean houseplants by sponging glossy-leafed plants and lightly brushing plants that have fuzzy or textured foliage with a soft brush.
* Repot orchids when roots climb out of the container.

Earth, my dearest, I will. Oh believe me, you no longer
need your springtimes to win me over - one of them,
ah, even one, is already too much for my blood.
Unspeakably, I have belonged to you, from the first.
- Rainer Maria Rilke, Duino Elegies, 9th, 1923

In the end,
there is really nothing more important
than taking care of the earth
and letting it take care of you.
Charles Scott (1733-1813)

GARDEN TIMETABLE

Growing Time ◇◇◇◇◇◇◇◇◇◇◇
Harvest Time ▬▬▬▬▬▬▬

When & What to Plant	March	April	May	June	July	August	Sept.	Oct.	Nov.	Dec.	Jan.
Spinach	Growing	Growing	Harvest								
Peas	Growing	Growing	Growing	Harvest							
Lettuce	Growing	Growing	Harvest	Harvest							
Onion Sets	Growing	Harvest	Harvest								
Radish	Growing	Harvest									
Cabbage	Growing	Growing	Growing	Harvest	Harvest						
Potatoes		Growing	Growing	Growing	Harvest	Harvest					
Kale		Growing	Growing/Harvest	Harvest	Harvest						
Onion Seed		Growing	Growing	Growing	Harvest	Harvest					
Cauliflower		Growing	Growing	Harvest	Harvest	Harvest					
Broccoli		Growing	Growing	Harvest	Harvest	Harvest					
Kohlrabi		Growing	Growing/Harvest	Harvest	Harvest						
Beets		Growing	Growing/Harvest	Harvest							
Lettuce		Growing	Growing/Harvest	Harvest							
Carrots		Growing	Growing/Harvest	Harvest	Harvest						
Beans		Growing	Growing	Harvest							
Corn		Growing	Growing	Growing	Harvest						
Corn			Growing	Growing	Harvest	Harvest					
Cucumbers			Growing	Growing	Harvest	Harvest					
Beans			Growing	Growing	Harvest						
Tomato			Growing	Growing	Growing	Harvest	Harvest	Harvest	Harvest		
Peppers			Growing	Growing	Growing	Harvest	Harvest	Harvest			
Eggplant			Growing	Growing	Growing	Harvest	Harvest				
Summer Squash			Growing	Harvest	Harvest						
Muskmelon			Growing	Growing	Growing	Harvest	Harvest				
Watermelon			Growing	Growing	Growing	Harvest	Harvest				
Okra			Growing	Growing	Growing	Harvest	Harvest				
Sweet Potato			Growing	Growing	Growing	Growing	Harvest	Harvest			
Beets			Growing	Growing	Harvest						
Carrots			Growing	Growing	Growing	Harvest					
Corn				Growing	Growing	Harvest	Harvest				
Beets				Growing	Harvest	Harvest					
Summer Squash				Growing	Harvest	Harvest					
Okra				Growing	Growing	Harvest	Harvest				
Pumpkin				Growing	Growing	Growing	Growing	Harvest	Harvest		
Beets				Growing	Growing	Harvest	Harvest				
Carrots				Growing	Growing	Harvest	Harvest	Harvest			
Carrots					Growing	Growing	Harvest	Harvest	Harvest		
Beets					Growing	Growing	Harvest	Harvest			
Cabbage					Growing	Growing	Harvest	Harvest			
Beans					Growing	Harvest	Harvest				
Parsnips					Growing	Growing	Growing				
Summer Squash					Growing	Harvest	Harvest	Harvest	Harvest	Harvest	Harvest
Corn (70 day)					Growing	Growing	Harvest	Harvest			
Cabbage						Growing	Growing	Harvest			
Beans						Growing	Harvest				
Beets						Growing	Growing	Harvest	Harvest	Harvest	
Carrots						Growing	Growing	Harvest	Harvest		
Broccoli						Growing	Growing	Harvest	Harvest	Harvest	
Kohlrabi						Growing	Harvest	Harvest	Harvest		
Cauliflower						Growing	Growing	Harvest	Harvest	Harvest	
Snow Peas						Growing	Growing	Harvest	Harvest		
Kale						Growing	Growing	Harvest	Harvest	Harvest	
Spinach						Growing	Growing	Harvest	Harvest		
Radish							Growing	Harvest	Harvest		
Spinach							Growing	Growing	Harvest	Harvest	Harvest
Turnips							Growing	Growing	Harvest	Harvest	
Lettuce							Growing	Growing	Harvest	Harvest	

Bibliography

The Old Farmer's Almanac <u>www.almanac.com</u>, Thank you for permission to use lore and poetry.

US Department of Agriculture, transparency of USDA hardiness zones

Book Sources:

Gardener's Latin, by Bill Neal, Algonquin Books of Chapel Hill, NC, 1992

Rodale Books, series; Weldon Russell Pty Ltd,1995

The American Horticulture Society Encyclopedia of Garden Plants, Macmillan Publishing Co. NY 1989

The Way of Flowers, by Tovah Martin, The Hearst Corporation, 1994

The Complete Mother Goose, by dilithium Press, Ltd. 1987

The Helen Oxenbury Nursery Rhyme Book, by Brian Anderson,William Morrow and Company, Inc./New York, 1974

Saints, by Elizabeth Hallam, Tessa Clark, and Celcilia Walters, Edison Saad Editions, 1994

The Complete Pond Builder, by Helen Nash, Sterling Publishing Company Inc., New York1996

The Pruner's Handbook, by John Malins, A David & Charles Book, 1992

The Cultivated Gardener, by Cathy Wilkinson Barash & Jim Wilson, Simon & Schuster, Judd Publishing, NewYork 1996

Internet Sources:

Anglian Gardener, by Paul Ward, 2000-2004

Ashlynn's Grove; pagen Information Resources, 1996-2004, by Ashlynn Ward and pagenism .com

Celtic Attic, 2003

The Origins and Traditions of Mayday, by Eugene W. Plawiuk, 1996.

<u>folkloremagicandsuperstions @ groups.msn.com</u>

More Sayings VII, <u>Suite101.com,</u> 1996-2003, Creative Marketeam Canada Ltd.

<u>Enchanted Learning.com</u>

INDEX